HISTORICAL DICTIONARIES OF RELIGIONS, PHILOSOPHIES, AND MOVEMENTS

Jon Woronoff, Series Editor

1. *Buddhism*, by Charles S. Prebish, 1993. *Out of print.*
2. *Mormonism*, by Davis Bitton, 1994. *Out of print. See no. 32.*
3. *Ecumenical Christianity*, by Ans Joachim van der Bent, 1994
4. *Terrorism*, by Sean Anderson and Stephen Sloan, 1995. *Out of print.*
5. *Sikhism*, by W. H. McLeod, 1995. *Out of print. See no. 59.*
6. *Feminism*, by Janet K. Boles and Diane Long Hoeveler, 1995. *Out of print. See no. 52.*
7. *Olympic Movement*, by Ian Buchanan and Bill Mallon, 1995. *Out of print. See no. 39.*
8. *Methodism*, by Charles Yrigoyen Jr. and Susan E. Warrick, 1996. *Out of print. See no. 57.*
9. *Orthodox Church*, by Michael Prokurat, Alexander Golitzin, and Michael D. Peterson, 1996
10. *Organized Labor*, by James C. Docherty, 1996. *Out of print. See no. 50.*
11. *Civil Rights Movement*, by Ralph E. Luker, 1997
12. *Catholicism*, by William J. Collinge, 1997
13. *Hinduism*, by Bruce M. Sullivan, 1997
14. *North American Environmentalism*, by Edward R. Wells and Alan M. Schwartz, 1997
15. *Welfare State*, by Bent Greve, 1998. *Out of print. See no. 63.*
16. *Socialism*, by James C. Docherty, 1997. *Out of print. See no. 73.*
17. *Bahá'í Faith*, by Hugh C. Adamson and Philip Hainsworth, 1998. *Out of print. See no. 71.*
18. *Taoism*, by Julian F. Pas in cooperation with Man Kam Leung, 1998
19. *Judaism*, by Norman Solomon, 1998. *Out of print. See no. 69.*
20. *Green Movement*, by Elim Papadakis, 1998. *Out of print. See no. 80.*
21. *Nietzscheanism*, by Carol Diethe, 1999. *Out of print. See no. 75.*
22. *Gay Liberation Movement*, by Ronald J. Hunt, 1999

23. *Islamic Fundamentalist Movements in the Arab World, Iran, and Turkey*, by Ahmad S. Moussalli, 1999
24. *Reformed Churches*, by Robert Benedetto, Darrell L. Guder, and Donald K. McKim, 1999. *Out of print. See no. 99.*
25. *Baptists*, by William H. Brackney, 1999. *Out of print. See no. 94.*
26. *Cooperative Movement*, by Jack Shaffer, 1999
27. *Reformation and Counter-Reformation*, by Hans J. Hillerbrand, 2000. *Out of print. See no. 100.*
28. *Shakers*, by Holley Gene Duffield, 2000
29. *United States Political Parties*, by Harold F. Bass Jr., 2000. *Out of print.*
30. *Heidegger's Philosophy*, by Alfred Denker, 2000. *Out of print. See no. 101.*
31. *Zionism*, by Rafael Medoff and Chaim I. Waxman, 2000. *Out of print. See no. 83.*
32. *Mormonism*, 2nd ed., by Davis Bitton, 2000. *Out of print. See no. 89.*
33. *Kierkegaard's Philosophy*, by Julia Watkin, 2001
34. *Hegelian Philosophy*, by John W. Burbidge, 2001. *Out of print. See no. 90.*
35. *Lutheranism*, by Günther Gassmann in cooperation with Duane H. Larson and Mark W. Oldenburg, 2001
36. *Holiness Movement*, by William Kostlevy, 2001. *Out of print. See no. 98.*
37. *Islam*, by Ludwig W. Adamec, 2001. *Out of print. See no. 95.*
38. *Shinto*, by Stuart D. B. Picken, 2002
39. *Olympic Movement*, 2nd ed., by Ian Buchanan and Bill Mallon, 2001. *Out of print. See no. 61.*
40. *Slavery and Abolition*, by Martin A. Klein, 2002
41. *Terrorism*, 2nd ed., by Sean Anderson and Stephen Sloan, 2002. *Out of print. See no. 38 in the War, Revolution, and Civil Unrest series.*
42. *New Religious Movements*, by George D. Chryssides, 2001
43. *Prophets in Islam and Judaism*, by Scott B. Noegel and Brannon M. Wheeler, 2002
44. *The Friends (Quakers)*, by Margery Post Abbott, Mary Ellen Chijioke, Pink Dandelion, and John William Oliver Jr., 2003
45. *Lesbian Liberation Movement: Still the Rage*, by JoAnne Myers, 2003

46. *Descartes and Cartesian Philosophy*, by Roger Ariew, Dennis Des Chene, Douglas M. Jesseph, Tad M. Schmaltz, and Theo Verbeek, 2003
47. *Witchcraft*, by Michael D. Bailey, 2003
48. *Unitarian Universalism*, by Mark W. Harris, 2004
49. *New Age Movements*, by Michael York, 2004
50. *Organized Labor*, 2nd ed., by James C. Docherty, 2004
51. *Utopianism*, by James M. Morris and Andrea L. Kross, 2004
52. *Feminism*, 2nd ed., by Janet K. Boles and Diane Long Hoeveler, 2004
53. *Jainism*, by Kristi L. Wiley, 2004
54. *Wittgenstein's Philosophy*, by Duncan Richter, 2004
55. *Schopenhauer's Philosophy*, by David E. Cartwright, 2005
56. *Seventh-day Adventists*, by Gary Land, 2005
57. *Methodism*, 2nd ed., by Charles Yrigoyen Jr. and Susan Warrick, 2005
58. *Sufism*, by John Renard, 2005
59. *Sikhism*, 2nd ed., by W. H. McLeod, 2005
60. *Kant and Kantianism*, by Helmut Holzhey and Vilem Mudroch, 2005
61. *Olympic Movement*, 3rd ed., by Bill Mallon with Ian Buchanan, 2006
62. *Anglicanism*, by Colin Buchanan, 2006
63. *Welfare State*, 2nd ed., by Bent Greve, 2006
64. *Feminist Philosophy*, by Catherine Villanueva Gardner, 2006
65. *Logic*, by Harry J. Gensler, 2006
66. *Leibniz's Philosophy*, by Stuart Brown and Nicholas J. Fox, 2006
67. *Non-Aligned Movement and Third World*, by Guy Arnold, 2006
68. *Salvation Army*, by Major John G. Merritt, 2006
69. *Judaism*, 2nd ed., by Norman Solomon, 2006
70. *Epistemology*, by Ralph Baergen, 2006
71. *Bahá'í Faith*, 2nd ed., by Hugh C. Adamson, 2006
72. *Aesthetics*, by Dabney Townsend, 2006
73. *Socialism*, 2nd ed., by Peter Lamb and James C. Docherty, 2007
74. *Marxism*, by David M. Walker and Daniel Gray, 2007
75. *Nietzscheanism*, 2nd ed., by Carol Diethe, 2007
76. *Medieval Philosophy and Theology*, by Stephen F. Brown and Juan Carlos Flores, 2007

Historical Dictionary of Jesus

Daniel J. Harrington, S.J.

Historical Dictionaries of Religions,
Philosophies, and Movements, No. 102

The Scarecrow Press, Inc.
Lanham • Toronto • Plymouth, UK
2010

Published by Scarecrow Press, Inc.
A wholly owned subsidiary of The Rowman & Littlefield Publishing Group, Inc.
4501 Forbes Boulevard, Suite 200, Lanham, Maryland 20706
http://www.scarecrowpress.com

Estover Road, Plymouth PL6 7PY, United Kingdom

British Library Cataloguing in Publication Information Available

Library of Congress Cataloging-in-Publication Data

Harrington, Daniel J.
    Historical dictionary of Jesus / Daniel J. Harrington.
        p. cm. — (Historical dictionaries of religions, philosophies, and movements ;
    no. 102)
    Includes bibliographical references (p.   ).
    ISBN 978-0-8108-7667-5 (cloth : alk. paper) — ISBN 978-0-8108-7668-2
    (ebook)
        1. Jesus Christ—Dictionaries. I. Title.
    BT199.5.H37 2010
    232.03—dc22   2010010564

Printed in the United States of America

Contents

Preface

Jesus of Nazareth is arguably the most famous and influential human being who has ever lived on Earth. Only the most skeptical observers have denied his existence as a historical figure. According to the Christian tradition, Jesus was born, lived, and died in the land of Israel/ Palestine some two thousand years ago. Yet even after his shameful death on a cross, he remains the center of the world's largest religion. And many people today all over the world guide their lives by asking: What would Jesus do?

Intended as neither a devotional work nor an apologetic–theological treatise, this historical treatment of Jesus covers the ancient literary sources about him, modern methods of approaching them, the major events in his life, persons and places associated with him, the form and content of his teachings, what can be said about his death and the claims about his resurrection, and the contributions of major modern scholars to the quest for the historical Jesus.

This volume consists of three major parts: (1) an introduction to the major topics pertaining to Jesus as a historical figure, providing a road map for what appears in the main part; (2) the historical dictionary, containing over four hundred entries. Within the individual entries some words appear in **boldface** type, which indicates that important related information can be found in those other entries; and (3) the bibliography, listing some of the most important books related to Jesus and the world in which he lived and worked. For biblical quotations and for the spellings of names and places in this volume, I have generally followed the New Revised Standard Version (NRSV) of the Bible.

In the historical dictionary, I have included entries on some modern scholars whose works on Jesus have become classics (Albert Schweitzer, C. H. Dodd, Joachim Jeremias, and others) and some who in recent years have made important and original contributions (such as E. P.

Sanders, John P. Meier, N. T. Wright). If I were to include many more such entries, there would be no end and the figure of Jesus might be overwhelmed by his modern interpreters. For those who wish to pursue in even greater detail developments in modern Jesus scholarship from the mid-1950s to the present, I suggest consulting the back issues of *New Testament Abstracts*, with which I have been associated for many years.

I have also included articles on the major parables of Jesus. Many scholars contend that these short narratives allow us best to hear the voice of Jesus on what was undoubtedly the central theme of his teaching and activity, the kingdom of God. The Gospel parables are not merely clever stories or timeless fables; rather, they make essential contributions to our historical understanding of Jesus in his role as the prophet of God's kingdom. For those in search of further enlightenment on various topics, the many books listed in the bibliography provide ample resources. They have been chosen because they are representative of what I regard as especially significant developments in modern research on Jesus as a historical figure.

Since Jesus was a religious teacher, the dictionary necessarily deals with some theological topics. But in my presentation here I have made every effort to be concise and objective, leaving the decision to accept, admire, doubt, or reject the person and teachings of Jesus up to the reader. Indeed, I frequently point out the historical difficulties involved in various matters pertaining to him.

For persons of faith, of course, the witness of the four Gospels is more important than the historian's Jesus. Nevertheless, I believe that the application of historical methods can help everyone to better understand the nature of the tradition about Jesus and encounter Jesus as the personality behind the Gospels and their traditions. If anyone wishes to see how I put this material together for a general audience from my own Christian faith perspective, please consult my books *Jesus: A Historical Portrait* (2007) and *Jesus, the Revelation of the Father's Love: What the New Testament Teaches Us* (2010).

About ten years ago, Jon Woronoff contacted me about the possibility of my writing the *Historical Dictionary of Jesus* for Scarecrow Press. After giving his invitation much thought, I felt I had to decline because of several other commitments I had at that time. But I always regretted passing up such a wonderful opportunity. Indeed, I often consulted the website to see if someone else had taken up the project. In the fall of 2009, I had a visit from Sarah Stanton of Rowman & Littlefield about another project and mentioned this to her. She put me in contact with her colleague Ed Kurdyla of Scarecrow Press. I am very grateful to all concerned for giving me both the idea and the opportunity to rectify a past mistake and to carry out a labor of love. I also thank Blair Andrews for his editorial suggestions and his work on my manuscript.

Abbreviations of Biblical Books

OT	Old Testament
Gen	Genesis
Exod	Exodus
Lev	Leviticus
Num	Numbers
Deut	Deuteronomy
Josh	Joshua
Judg	Judges
1–2 Sam	1–2 Samuel
1–2 Kgs	1–2 Kings
Isa	Isaiah
Jer	Jeremiah
Ezek	Ezekiel
Hos	Hosea
Joel	Joel
Amos	Amos
Obad	Obadiah
Jonah	Jonah
Mic	Micah
Nah	Nahum
Hab	Habakkuk
Zeph	Zephaniah
Hag	Haggai
Zech	Zechariah
Mal	Malachi
Ps	Psalms
Job	Job
Prov	Proverbs
Ruth	Ruth

Cant	Canticles
Eccl	Ecclesiastes
Lam	Lamentations
Esth	Esther
Dan	Daniel
Ezra	Ezra
Neh	Nehemiah
1–2 Chr	1–2 Chronicles
1–2 Macc	1–2 Maccabees
Sir	Sirach
Tob	Tobit
Wis	Wisdom

NT	**New Testament**
Matt	Matthew
Mark	Mark
Luke	Luke
John	John
Acts	Acts
Rom	Romans
1–2 Cor	1–2 Corinthians
Gal	Galatians
Eph	Ephesians
Phil	Philippians
Col	Colossians
1–2 Thess	1–2 Thessalonians
1–2 Tim	1–2 Timothy
Titus	Titus
Phlm	Philemon
Heb	Hebrews
Jas	James
1–2 Pet	1–2 Peter
1–2–3 John	1–2–3 John
Jude	Jude
Rev	Revelation

Introduction

The topics covered in this introduction include the major ancient sources about Jesus, the challenge of getting back to the historical Jesus, the problems and efforts at reconstructing Jesus' life and teachings, the quest for the historical Jesus, the world in which Jesus lived and worked, the kingdom of God as his major theme, his roles as a teacher and a miracle worker, his attitudes toward women and sexuality, his views on social and political issues, his condemnation and death, and his resurrection.

SOURCES

The four canonical Gospels—Matthew, Mark, Luke, and John—are the major sources for what we know about Jesus. However, they do not allow us to write a full biography about him. The Evangelists were more interested in exploring Jesus' religious significance and his impact as a moral teacher than in providing a chronicle of events in Jesus' life. They wrote their Gospels in light of the early Christians' convictions about Jesus' resurrection and his continued existence with the one whom he called "Father." The claims that these authors made about him ("Jesus is Lord") go beyond what is said about even the greatest human heroes.

The first three Gospels are often called the Synoptic Gospels, because they share a common outline and present a common vision of Jesus. Mark's Gospel, written around 70 CE, perhaps in Rome, tells of Jesus' public ministry in Galilee, his journey with his disciples to Jerusalem, and his short ministry there as well as his passion, death, and resurrection. While portraying Jesus as a wise teacher and powerful miracle worker, Mark gave special attention to Jesus as the suffering Messiah and to the mystery of the cross.

Around 85–90 CE, Matthew and Luke seem to have independently produced their own revised and expanded versions of Mark's Gospel. They added a large amount of teaching material from the Sayings Source Q and other traditions. Matthew emphasized the Jewishness of Jesus and his fulfillment of Israel's Scriptures, the books that Christians call the Old Testament (OT). Luke stressed Jesus' significance not only for Israel but also (especially in his second volume, the Acts of the Apostles) for all the peoples of the world.

Although John's Gospel has much in common with the Synoptic Gospels and contains many pieces of solid historical information, it spreads Jesus' public ministry over three years instead of one, introduces many different characters, and focuses more on Jesus himself as the revealer and the revelation of God rather than on his message about the kingdom of God. Because of their wide use in the churches, orthodox theological context, and association with the apostles, these four Gospels became part of the church's list of approved books (the canon of Scripture).

The only substantial ancient description of Jesus apart from early Christian sources appears in *Jewish Antiquities* 18.63–64 by the Jewish historian Flavius Josephus in the late first century CE. However, the explicit statements about Jesus' identity as the Messiah and about his resurrection suggest that Christian scribes may have inserted some of their own convictions about Jesus in the passage.

The Gospels attributed to Thomas, Peter, Mary Magdalene, Philip, James, and others did not become part of the church's New Testament canon. This was due in part to their lack of wide usage in the churches, sometimes unorthodox theological teaching, and relatively late dates of composition. They may contain some early authentic traditions about Jesus, though it is very difficult to isolate them from their less credible contents. Likewise, there are stray sayings that are "not written" (*agrapha*) in the four Gospels but are attributed to Jesus in other early Christian writings; it is almost impossible to prove definitively which (if any) of these sayings originated with Jesus.

GETTING BACK TO JESUS

Jesus died around the year 30 CE. The first complete Gospel, Mark, appeared some 40 years later. The early Christians were clearly more interested in experiencing the risen Jesus and the Holy Spirit than in writing books about Jesus. In the intervening four decades, there was a lively process in which traditions from and about Jesus, whether in oral or written form, circulated among Christians. These traditions were often shaped and reshaped in response to the pastoral needs of their communities. Understanding the Gospels requires that we keep in mind three phases: the work of the Evangelists (70–95 CE), the transmission and development of oral and written traditions from and about Jesus (30–70 CE), and the time of Jesus' public activity (around 30 CE).

How can we get back to Jesus? Biblical scholars have developed several instruments to isolate materials in the Gospels that very likely go back to Jesus himself. If a teaching is unlike anything in Jewish and early Christian tradition, then it probably can be assigned directly to Jesus. Two examples of this criterion of "double dissimilarity" are Jesus' prohibitions against taking oaths (Matt 5:34) and against divorce (Luke 16:18). Other such criteria include multiple attestation (when a tradition appears in several different traditions, such as the Lord's Supper), local Palestinian coloring (Aramaic words, regional farming methods), embarrassment at what might reflect badly on Jesus (for example, his receiving John's "baptism of repentance for the forgiveness of sins"), what led to Jesus' death (the "cleansing" of the temple), and coherence (what fits well with what can be established by the other criteria). These historical methods do not tell us everything we might like to know about Jesus nor do they necessarily establish what was most important about him—but they can and do tell us some significant things about Jesus.

RECONSTRUCTING JESUS' LIFE AND TEACHING

Study of the Gospels and application of these historical criteria make it possible to develop a rough outline of Jesus' public career and teachings. Having been raised in Nazareth in Galilee, Jesus accepted baptism from John and may have been a member of John's movement up to the latter's arrest and execution. When Jesus went out on his own when he was "about thirty years old" (Luke 3:23) to continue and adapt John's mission, he gathered disciples near the Sea of Galilee at Capernaum, including some of John's followers. He spent much of his public ministry preaching about the kingdom of God and how to prepare for it.

He also healed the sick as a sign of the presence of God's kingdom. Before Passover, in the spring of 30 CE, Jesus and his followers made a long journey from northern Galilee to Jerusalem, during which Jesus continued to teach his disciples and others. At Jerusalem he continued to teach but ran into intense opposition from some other Jews and from the Roman authorities. Under the Roman governor or prefect Pontius Pilate, Jesus was executed by crucifixion as a rebel/insurgent and a religious troublemaker. He was said to have appeared alive again to some of his followers.

Careful study of the Gospels also allows us to reconstruct the major themes in Jesus' teaching. At the center was the kingdom or reign of God in both its present and its future dimensions. Jesus' relationship to God was so close that he addressed God as "Father" and invited his followers to do the same. He proclaimed the possibility of the forgiveness of sins and of reconciliation with God. He challenged his followers to love their enemies and told them how to act in anticipation of the coming kingdom of God. He showed special concern for marginal persons—the poor, the lame, "sinners and tax collectors," prostitutes, and so on—and manifested a free attitude toward traditions associated with the Jewish law and the Jerusalem temple. Most of these themes appear in the Lord's Prayer/Our Father (Matt 6:9–13/Luke 11:2–4), which most scholars regard as conveying the voice of Jesus.

THE QUEST FOR THE HISTORICAL JESUS

The Jesus whom modern historians seek to recover and investigate by using the tools of historical research is sometimes called "the historical Jesus." A more accurate term would be "the historian's Jesus." This Jesus is not the whole person of Jesus, nor is he the traditional object of Christian faith. The Jesus whom Christians worship is not only the earthly Jesus who lived 2,000 years ago but also and especially the risen Jesus whom they believe lives on and will come again in glory. Christians assume that there is a close continuity between the earthly Jesus and the Christ of faith, and that the two cannot be totally separated.

The quest for the historical Jesus, however, refers to the project of trying to separate the earthly or historical Jesus from the Christ of faith. It began among some very liberal German Protestants in the late eighteenth century in an effort to peel away the wrappings given to Jesus in church tradition and to recover the simple and "real" figure of the historical Jesus. Many of the early questers discarded the miracles of Jesus and rejected his virginal conception and resurrection as "unhistorical." Their major interests were his "ethical" teaching and moral significance.

One important development in the late nineteenth century was the recognition of the kingdom of God as the focus of Jesus' teaching activity and its roots in Jewish hopes about God's future action on behalf of his people in Israel (sometimes called eschatology or apocalyptic). In the twentieth century, the quest focused on the parables of Jesus as a way of recovering the "voice" of Jesus about the kingdom, developing criteria for identifying material from Jesus, and situating Jesus within Judaism. Recent presentations of the historical Jesus have depicted him as a prophet of God's kingdom, a wisdom teacher, a nonviolent but political insurgent, a practical philosopher, and a poet skilled in using images and stories.

THE WORLD OF JESUS

The birth, life, and death of Jesus took place about 2,000 years ago in Palestine, also known as the Land of Israel and as the Holy Land. It lies between Lebanon/Syria to the north and Egypt to the south. The Mediterranean Sea provides the western border. The northern area, with the Sea of Galilee and the Jordan River at its eastern border, is called Galilee. This was Jesus' home for most of his life. The central portion is Samaria, and the southern section is Judea. The capital of Judea and the center of Jewish religious practice in Jesus' time was Jerusalem, where Jesus was put to death.

According to Matt 2:1, Jesus was born in Bethlehem of Judea (see also Luke 2:4) "in the time of King Herod." This presumably refers to Herod the Great, a client king of the Romans who died in 4 BCE. According to Matt 2:23 and Luke 2:39, Jesus was raised by Mary and Joseph in Nazareth of Galilee. During Jesus' adult life, Galilee was ruled by Herod Antipas, one of the sons of Herod the Great. Judea was overseen directly by the Roman prefect or governor, Pontius Pilate, from 26 to 36 CE. From the mid-second century BCE on, the Romans had served as allies and protectors of the Judeans. However, by the first century CE they had integrated Palestine into their empire and taken direct control of Judea.

Jews in Jesus' time were united by three great institutions: the Temple of Jerusalem, the Land of Israel, and the Law of Moses ("the Law"). However, within that general framework there were several different ways of being a Jew. The Pharisees were a progressive lay movement that sought to extend the temple purity rules to all Israel and emphasized common meals featuring religious discussion. The Sadducees were a more conservative group that, by Jesus' time, had gained influence and control over the temple and its priesthood. The Essenes stressed community life, strict observance of the Law, and asceticism. They were very likely the people behind the Dead Sea Scrolls. There were also activist insurgent groups that engaged in armed resistance to the Roman occupiers, and there were end-time visionaries, scribes, chief priests, tax collectors, and "sinners" (Jews who by choice or occupation did not observe the Mosaic law).

We can say with some confidence that Jesus lived as an observant Jew. His quarrel was more with the traditions attached to the Law than with the Law itself. We can also say that among the various Jewish groups he was closest to the Pharisees in that they shared an interest in such topics as resurrection, Sabbath observance, and the relative importance of ritual purity, and in that he frequently entered into debate with them. Moreover, they occasionally invited him to their houses for meals (see Luke 7:36–50, 14:1–24).

What is beyond doubt is that Jesus had some connection with the movement begun by John the Baptist. That Jesus underwent John's baptism is a well-established fact. Since John's baptism was associated with repentance for the forgiveness of sins, this was not something that early Christians would have created. It is also likely that John served as a mentor for Jesus, especially with regard to his vision of the coming kingdom of God and how to prepare for it. Moreover, according to John 1, some of Jesus' first disciples were drawn from John's movement and became members of his inner circle of the twelve apostles.

Nevertheless, Jesus eventually went his own way. Whereas John adopted an ascetic and world-denying lifestyle, Jesus celebrated festive meals and preached to all kinds of people. Whereas John emphasized the future coming of God's kingdom, Jesus also stressed its present dimensions. And whereas John preached moral renewal as a way to get ready for God's judgment, Jesus invited sinners to throw themselves on the grace and mercy of God in the here and now.

THE KINGDOM OF GOD

In the context of first-century Judaism, the kingdom of God referred especially to God's future display of power and judgment and to the final establishment of God's rule over all creation; then all peoples and all creation will recognize and acknowledge the God of Israel as the only God and Lord. When that day comes, the will of God will be done perfectly on earth just as it is done in heaven. Jesus' own prayer, the Lord's Prayer (Matt 6:9–13 and Luke 11:2–4), is first and foremost a prayer for the coming of God's kingdom in its fullness ("Thy kingdom come").

While sharing the hopes of his Jewish contemporaries for the future manifestation of God's kingdom, Jesus also insisted that the kingdom is present now, even if in a small way, as his parables about seeds, yeast, hidden treasure, and the pearl (see Matt 13:1–53) indicate. Also, several sayings that very likely reflect the views and words of the historical Jesus—Luke 11:20/Matt 12:28; Matt 11:12/Luke 16:16; and Luke 17:21—suggest that God's kingdom has a present dimension all around us if only we look hard enough to find it. The Synoptic Gospels assume that God's kingdom was especially present in the person and ministry of Jesus himself. That is, he was the embodiment or incarnation of the kingdom of God. The belief that Jesus was the present manifestation of the kingdom of God may help to explain why in John's Gospel the focus is more on Jesus as the revealer and revelation of God than on the kingdom of God itself.

THE TEACHER

The kingdom of God and how to prepare for it were the central themes of Jesus' teaching. As a wise teacher, he used the methods that wise teachers use—short stories, memorable sayings, and symbolic actions. His primary audience was made up of ordinary persons who lived in first-century Galilee. For them he had a message of hope.

The problem Jesus the teacher faced was the nature of his main topic, the kingdom of God. How does one talk about something that is beyond human comprehension and control, and whose fullness is future? Jesus used parables, analogies that seek to illuminate an important and even transcendent reality by appealing to something in nature or everyday life that is better known. Thus he taught about the future and present dimensions of God's kingdom in terms of stories about farming, fishing, cooking, and housecleaning. Jesus' parables can be found in the Synoptic Gospels in the collections in Mark 4:1–34, Matt 13:1–53 and 24:32–25:46, Luke 8:4–15, and elsewhere in their narratives.

Much of Jesus' so-called ethical teaching concerns the values and virtues most appropriate for those who wish to enter the kingdom of God and so reach their goal of eternal happiness with God. The Sermon on the Mount in Matt 5:1–7:29 and the Sermon on the Plain in Luke 6:20–49 contain various sayings with a high degree of probability of emanating from Jesus himself. In them Jesus uses the literary forms that Jewish wisdom teachers customarily used: beatitudes, woes, admonitions, analogies, proverbs, prohibitions, and so on. Other literary devices for teaching include the controversy story or debate (or *chreia*), the misunderstanding, and the long discourse (especially in John's Gospel).

Jesus also taught by means of symbolic actions. In doing so, he followed the example of the great biblical prophets Isaiah, Jeremiah, Ezekiel, and Hosea. Examples of this mode of teaching include Jesus' "triumphal" entry into Jerusalem in Mark 11:1–11 and his cleansing of the temple there in Mark 11:15–19. By such symbolic actions Jesus confirmed his identity as the prophet of God's kingdom and his continuity with Israel's prophets of the past while fulfilling their own prophecies.

THE MIRACLE WORKER

The common definition of "miracle" today is an event that is an exception to the laws of nature. In the Bible, however, what we call miracles are described more loosely as "signs and wonders," or acts of power, that are attributed to God. In the Old Testament, Moses and the prophets Elijah and Elisha are especially prominent as miracle workers.

The Gospels are full of reports about Jesus' miraculous activities. Almost one third of Mark's Gospel is devoted to Jesus' miracles. By one estimate (counting repeated passages only once), the Synoptic Gospels contain seventeen healings, six exorcisms, and eight nature miracles. The first half of John's Gospel features seven miracle stories known as "signs," ranging from Jesus turning water into wine at the wedding feast at Cana to his raising his friend Lazarus from the dead.

The miracle stories present special problems for modern historians, who generally operate on the following three assumptions: (1) The past is basically the same as the present; (2) Historical events can and should be interpreted only within the realm of earthly cause and effect, and no supernatural interventions are allowed as explanations; and (3) There are no unique historical figures. Of course, these were not the assumptions of the Evangelists or of anyone else in antiquity. Nor are they the assumptions of most people today. Ultimately affirming or denying an event as a miracle involves a philosophical or theological judgment.

The Gospel writers had no doubt that Jesus was a miracle worker. Moreover, according to them, unlike other biblical miracle workers, Jesus acted on his own authority and power, not merely as a mediator between God and other persons. Nevertheless, Jesus' acts of power are portrayed by them not simply as spectacular displays or even as proofs of his divinity. Rather, their significance is captured best in the saying attributed to Jesus in Luke 11:20: "If it is by the finger of God that I cast out demons, then the kingdom of God has come to you." In other words, his miracles are best understood to be anticipations and present manifestations of the kingdom of God.

The accounts of Jesus' healings and exorcisms in the Gospels provide only minimal information about the person's medical condition. There is never anything like a complete diagnosis. How physicians today might interpret or explain these conditions is a matter of speculation. In most instances, the sick person (or his or her friends) approaches Jesus in a spirit of faith and asks for healing. Jesus responds with words or sometimes with a gesture, and the healing is immediate and complete. According to the Gospels (see Mark 3:22–30), Jesus' opponents in his own time did not deny his ability to heal and cast out demons. Their questions concerned the power by which he performed these miracles: Was it by God or Satan?

The nature miracles—the stilling of the storm, feeding crowds of 4,000 and 5,000 persons, walking on the water, changing water into wine, and so on—are among the most spectacular displays of power on Jesus' part and mark him as unique among humans and even suggest his divinity. The ways in which the nature miracles are presented in the Gospels evoke many biblical motifs and precedents, and highlight the theological significance of Jesus' person and actions. Even more than the healings and the exorcisms, they are vehicles of early Christian theology. Thus, it is often very difficult to determine what might have been the historical core (if there was one) behind these narratives.

Even more problematic for modern historians are the accounts about Jesus raising persons from the dead: the daughter of Jairus (Mark 5:35–43), the son of the widow of Nain (Luke 7:11–17), and Lazarus (John 11:1–44). These narratives foreshadow what is perhaps the most problematic miracle of all, the resurrection of Jesus himself. It is this area especially where the assumptions of modern critical historiography and Christian faith come into conflict.

WOMEN AND SEXUALITY

The society in which Jesus lived and taught was patriarchal and hierarchical. That is, the husband or father was the head of the household, and the women, children, and servants/slaves were subordinate to him. The various tasks and roles were clearly divided between men and women. Jesus and his first followers were people of their particular time and place. Nevertheless, in comparison with other Jewish religious leaders of his day, Jesus seems to have been remarkably open to the participation of women in his movement.

In the Gospels, Mary, the mother of Jesus, is especially prominent in the infancy narratives in Matthew 1–2 and Luke 1–2. According to John, her words at the wedding feast at Cana prompted Jesus' first "sign" of turning water into wine, and she appears again at the foot of the cross with the Beloved Disciple. According to Acts 1, she was present with the followers of Jesus as they gathered in Jerusalem after his death and awaited the Holy Spirit at Pentecost. In 8:1–3, Luke names three women followers of Jesus—Mary Magdalene, Joanna the wife of Chuza, and Susanna—and adds that there were many other women who provided for Jesus and his male disciples. Likewise, Mark in 15:41 mentions women who provided for Jesus and his disciples when they were in Galilee and who came up to Jerusalem with them.

During Jesus' public ministry, women were often the recipients of his healing power. For example, he healed Peter's mother-in-law, the daughter of Jairus, the woman with the flow of blood, and the daughter of the Syrophoenician woman. From his encounter with the Syrophoenician woman (a non-Jew), Jesus seems to have learned that his mission was not to be limited to fellow Jews. With his prohibition of divorce, Jesus gave protection to women in a society in which a husband could divorce his wife merely by giving her a legal document and sending her out of his household (see Deut 24:1–4).

The women followers of Jesus are especially prominent in the Gospels' account of Jesus' death and resurrection. They see Jesus die, they see where he was buried, and they find his tomb empty on Easter Sunday morning. Their fidelity contrasts with the infidelity and flight of his male disciples in the passion narratives. The most prominent woman in these accounts is Mary of Magdala, a village on the western shore of the Sea of Galilee. She is generally named first on the lists of women witnesses, and according to Matthew and John she was the first to see the risen Jesus on Easter Sunday morning. She seems to have been the recipient of an exorcism, very likely performed by Jesus (see Luke 8:2). Her reputation as a prostitute rests on the unwarranted identification of her with the sinful woman in Luke 7:36–50. She is better understood as a witness to the risen Jesus and the one commissioned by him to tell the good news to the apostles (and so she is often called "the apostle to the apostles"). That Mary Magdalene was the lover or wife of Jesus has no foundation in ancient texts.

Despite the prominence of women in the ancient sources about Jesus, there is no evidence that he had a wife. The practice of celibacy (abstaining from sexual relations and marriage) was unusual in ancient Judaism, though there were exceptions (such as the Therapeutae, Essenes, John the Baptist, and Paul). It appears that Jesus refrained from marriage primarily out of total dedication to his mission of proclaiming God's kingdom (see Matt 19:12). Celibacy undertaken "for the sake of the kingdom" fits well with what we know to have been the focus of Jesus' life and preaching. There is no hint of contempt for the body or for marriage and sexual activity in his teaching.

SOCIAL AND POLITICAL ISSUES

In his teachings about wealth and poverty, Jesus stood in the great biblical tradition of social justice and concern for the poor. On the one hand, he emphasized the need for the rich to share their material possessions with the poor of this world while they still have time to do so (see Luke 16:19–31). On the other hand, when sending his disciples out to carry on his mission of preaching God's kingdom, he insisted that they adopt a simple lifestyle (Luke 9:3; Matt 10:5–15; Mark 6:6–13). At several points he warns that no one can serve both God and money/Mammon (Matt 6:24), and that excessive concern with material possessions can be an obstacle to entering the kingdom of God (Mark 10:21, 10:23). He even goes so far as to declare the poor to be "blessed" or "happy" (Luke 6:20; Matt 5:3), on the grounds that they are in a better position to recognize their total dependence on God.

Jesus was a popular teacher who drew crowds of Jews, many of whom were looking forward to the coming kingdom of God. Even though the thrust of Jesus' teaching was against violence and there is no evidence that he was in sympathy with violent Jewish revolutionary groups, his popularity among members of a subject people made him suspect to the Roman officials and to some Jewish leaders who wished to preserve the status quo. To them, the religious movement that centered on Jesus looked like a political, and perhaps even a military, movement. To them, Jesus' message that God alone is king and that his kingdom will soon be made manifest to all creation sounded like a call for revolution. However, in the "render to Caesar" passages (Mark 12:13–17; Matt 22:15–22; Luke 20:20–26), Jesus displays a cautious acceptance of the reality of Roman rule while remaining true to his principle that God is the real king and deserves more respect and service than any earthly ruler does.

CONDEMNATION AND DEATH

The accounts of Jesus' passion and death in the four Gospels agree on many basic points. They tell us that Jesus was arrested, underwent two hearings or trials, was sentenced to death by crucifixion, and died on a cross. Mark's passion narrative seems to have been the earliest. Indeed, large blocks of it probably existed before he composed his Gospel around 70 CE. Matthew and Luke independently used Mark's account as a source and included material from other traditions. While agreeing with Mark's narrative on many points, John's passion narrative represents a separate tradition. None of the Evangelists set out to write a detailed chronicle of the day on which Jesus died, though each of them provides some reliable historical details. Their major interest lay in the theological significance of Jesus' death and how his death took place in accord with OT prophecies. The major debate among historians is the extent to which these sources are mainly "history remembered" or mainly "prophecy historicized."

The Gospels suggest that the Jewish leaders were the prime movers in getting Jesus executed and that Romans only ratified what they set in motion by their "trials." However, it is also possible that historically the Romans were the prime movers and that the Jewish authorities reluctantly gave into pressure. What is clear is that Jesus was executed "under Pontius Pilate" and that the Jewish officials at Jerusalem played some role. Nevertheless, the manner of Jesus' death (crucifixion), the legal system in force (with Pilate having ultimate responsibility in capital cases), the official charge against Jesus ("the King of the Jews"), and the persons being executed along with him (most likely insurgents or revolutionaries) all point to the conclusion that the ultimate legal and moral responsibility for Jesus' death lay with the Roman prefect/ governor, Pontius Pilate.

RESURRECTION

The first followers of Jesus believed that Jesus, having died on the cross on Good Friday and having been buried in the tomb owned by Joseph of Arimathea, was miraculously restored to life on Easter Sunday and appeared to them as alive again. If historians have difficulty in dealing with claims about the miracles of Jesus, how much more difficult are the claims about his resurrection! At the very least, however, historians can describe the effects of the early Christians' belief in Jesus' resurrection.

Some Jews in Jesus' time, especially the Pharisees, expected that the resurrection of the dead would take place at the end of human history, as part of the full coming of God's kingdom and in preparation for the general judgment. According to Mark 12:18–27, Jesus sided with the Pharisees in this belief, rather than with the Sadducees. The early Christians claimed that on Easter Sunday morning the tomb of Jesus was found empty, that this fact was best explained by the claim that Jesus had been restored to life after his death, and that he appeared as alive once more to those who saw him die or knew that he was dead. These beliefs in turn transformed some followers who had previously abandoned Jesus and even denied knowing him (such as Peter) into fearless preachers of the "good news" about Jesus' death and resurrection: "that Christ died for our sins in accordance with the scriptures, that he was buried, and that he was raised on the third day in accordance with the scriptures, and that he appeared to Cephas, then to the twelve" (1 Cor 15:3–4). That formula freely mixes historical facts and theological interpretation, and so it is typical of what one finds throughout the New Testament. Thus it illustrates very effectively the problem of getting to the historical Jesus.

NOTE

In this introductory essay, I have drawn on and adapted some material from my book *Jesus: A Historical Portrait* (Cincinnati: St. Anthony Messenger, 2007).

The Dictionary

–A–

ABBA. The definite or emphatic form of the Aramaic noun for "father" (*'ab*), which is used by Jesus in his **prayer** in **Gethsemane** according to Mark 14:36 ("Abba, Father"). It is thought to express concisely the special bond of intimacy with **God** (respect in return for God's loving care) that Jesus experienced. The simple address ("Father") in the version of the **Lord's Prayer** in Luke 11:2–4 seems to reflect that relationship and serves as an invitation to Jesus' followers to enter into a similar relationship as **children** of their heavenly Father. Its occurrences in Rom 8:15 and Gal 4:6 ("Abba! Father!") suggest that early Christians used the formula in their prayer.

ABGAR. The **apocryphal** correspondence between Jesus and King Abgar of Edessa appears in the Syriac *Doctrine of Addai* and in Greek in Eusebius' *Ecclesiastical History* 1.13 (see 2.1.6–8). Allegedly a contemporary of Jesus, Abgar initiates the correspondence by noting the wonderful things he has heard about Jesus and asking that Jesus come to Edessa and heal him. Jesus replies that he cannot come just now. Instead, he promises that after his **ascension** he will send one of his **disciples** to heal Abgar. While charming, the exchange of letters is better understood as a later explanation for Edessa's conversion to Christianity than as providing any solid historical information about Jesus.

ABOMINATION OF DESOLATION. The traditional term now translated as "the desolating sacrilege." Based on the Hebrew expression in Dan 9:27, 11:31, and 12:11, the phrase appears in Greek in Matt 24:15 and Mark 13:14. In **Daniel** it referred to the desecration

of the **temple in Jerusalem** in 167 BCE under the Syrian king Antiochus IV Epiphanes in transforming it into what seemed like a pagan
shrine. In the **Gospels** it is used to refer to some horrendous future (or
recent) event that would cause flight and confusion. The parenthetical comment ("Let the reader understand") suggests an analogy with
the events of the second century BCE without specifying to what it
referred for the first readers of the Gospels.

ABRAHAM. In **Matthew's genealogy of Jesus** (1:1–17), which
emphasizes Jesus' roots in Jewish history, Abraham appears first
and serves as one of the three benchmarks (along with **David** and
the exile) in the three series of 14 generations. In recognition of
Zacchaeus' generous hospitality, Jesus praises him as "as a son
of Abraham" (Luke 19:9; see also Gen 18). In Matt 8:11 (see also
Luke 13:28), Jesus pictures the **kingdom of heaven** as a great feast
at which Abraham, Isaac, and Jacob will be present. And in the **parable** of the **Rich Man and Lazarus** (Luke 16:19–31), the blissful
resting place of the **righteous** after death is portrayed as being in
"Abraham's bosom." In John 8:39–59, when Jesus is debating with
his adversaries about who are the true **children** of Abraham, Jesus
asserts that "before Abraham was, I am" (8:58).

ADAM. In Gen 1–3 Adam is the first human created by **God**, and his
disobedience to God's commandment constitutes the original sin.
In Luke's **genealogy of Jesus** (3:23–38), which moves backward
and highlights Jesus' significance for all of humankind, Adam is
described at the end as "**son of God.**" In Rom 5 and 1 Cor 15, **Paul**
portrays Adam and Jesus as bearers of two different destinies for
humankind (sin versus grace), and stresses the superiority of Jesus as
the representative of the new creation inaugurated by his death and
resurrection.

ADOPTIONISM. The view that Jesus was simply a human person
whom **God** favored and adopted as the "**Son of God**" at some point
in his life, either at his **baptism** or his **resurrection**. Proponents of
this view have pointed to the **voice from heaven** at Jesus' baptism
("you are my Son," Mark 1:11) or to the profession of faith quoted by
Paul ("declared to be Son of God . . . by resurrection from the dead,"

Rom 1:4). However, early Christian hymns (Phil 2:6; Col 1:15) and the other **Gospels** insist that Jesus was the Son of God from his birth (and even before).

ADVOCATE. An English translation of the Greek word *parakletos,* which refers to a mediator, helper, or intercessor. The term appears prominently in Jesus' **farewell discourse** in John 14–16 and serves as a synonym for the **Holy Spirit**. There, Jesus describes the Spirit as "another Advocate" (14:16), suggesting that the Spirit will function as his replacement by teaching and reminding his followers of what he said (14:26), testifying on Jesus' behalf (15:26), convicting the world (16:7), and guiding the community "into all truth" (16:13). In 1 John 2:1, Jesus is described as our "Advocate with the **Father**," indicating a legal connotation to the word (a defense attorney) and suggesting that he continues in this role even after his **ascension**.

AGRAPHA. Literally meaning "things not written down," the term refers to sayings not written down in the four **canonical Gospels** but attributed to Jesus elsewhere. A good example is Acts 20:35, where **Paul** says, "remembering the words of the **Lord** Jesus, for he himself said: 'It is more blessed to give than to receive.'" Other examples can be found in Paul's letters (1 Cor 7:10, 9:14; 1 Thess 4:15–16), though these may be loose quotations or paraphrases of sayings also found in the canonical Gospels. Many other examples can be found in NT manuscripts, the **apocryphal Gospels** (especially the *Gospel of Thomas*), and patristic writings. Determining which, if any, of these sayings are authentic words of Jesus is very difficult.

ALLEGORY. Allegorical interpretation finds spiritual meanings in biblical texts by identifying most or all of their details with major figures or institutions in **salvation** history. Examples of allegorical interpretation appear with reference to Jesus' **parables** of the **Sower** in Matt 13:18–23 and of the **Wheat and the Weeds** in Matt 13:36–43. The approach is based on methods developed in Alexandria in Egypt by pagan interpreters of Homer's *Iliad* and *Odyssey*, as well as by Philo who brought insights from Platonic philosophy to bear on Old Testament texts. Its application to the Christian Scriptures is often associated with the **Church** Fathers of Alexandria, especially Clement and Origen.

ALMSGIVING. In the OT a pious person was expected to act as a benefactor for the **poor** and needy (see Deut 14:28–29, 24:19–22; Isa 58:6–8; Prov 14:21, 14:31; Job 29:12, 29:16). According to Matt 6:2–4, Jesus assumes that his followers will give alms. His warning there is aimed against ostentation when doing so in order to win a public reputation for holiness rather than doing it simply to please and worship **God**. In the **Last Judgment** scene in Matt 25:31–46, acts of beneficence toward the most needy provide the criteria for end-time rewards and punishments.

AMEN. Derived from the Hebrew root *'aman* ("be faithful, trust"), the word "Amen" appears frequently in the Hebrew Bible as an expression of acceptance or confirmation (as in Deut 27:15–26). A double "Amen" occurs in Ps 89:53 and Neh 8:6. Likewise in the NT, "Amen" often functions as a response to an important theological statement or praise of **God** (see Rom 1:25, 9:5, 11:36, 15:33, 16:24, 16:27). In Rev 3:14 ("the words of the Amen"), it even serves as a title for Jesus, suggesting that he is the expression and confirmation of God's will. In the **Gospels**, however, "Amen" appears frequently (about 50 times in the **Synoptic Gospels** and about 25 times in **John**) at the beginning of a sentence. In the Synoptic tradition, the usual formula is "Amen, I say to you" (usually plural), while in John there is often the double formula "Amen, amen, I say to you." All these sayings are attributed to Jesus and deal with important topics such the **unforgivable sin** (Mark 3:28–29), the refusal to give a **sign** (Mark 8:12), approval of the faith shown by a non-Jew (Matt 8:10), the imminence of the coming **kingdom** (16:28), Jesus' words to the good thief (Luke 23:43), the promise of seeing the glorious **Son of Man** (John 1:51), and the assurance that God will answer the **prayers** of Jesus' followers (John 16:23). The introductory "Amen" formula calls attention to the special importance to what follows. Efforts at finding convincing parallels in the Hebrew Bible, **rabbinic** writings, and Greek literature have not gained general scholarly approval. Its restriction to sayings of Jesus in the Gospels suggests that it was one of his own characteristic ways of speaking.

ANDREW. One of the **twelve apostles,** he was from Bethsaida in **Galilee** (John 1:44), a brother of Simon **Peter** and a **fisherman** (Matt 4:18; Mark 1:16; Luke 6:14; John 1:40), one of the first four **disciples** called by Jesus, and always listed among the first four **apostles** (Matt 10:2; Mark 3:18; Luke 6:14; Acts 1:13). Andrew is also among the four apostles who question Jesus about the destruction of the **temple in Jerusalem** (Mark 13:3). In **John's Gospel** (1:35–41), Andrew is one of **John the Baptist's** disciples who follows Jesus when John identifies him as "the **Lamb of God,**" tells his brother Peter that Jesus is the **Messiah,** and brings Peter to Jesus. In John 6:8, Andrew informs Jesus about a boy who has five barley loaves and two **fish,** and in 12:20 he informs Jesus that some Greeks wish to see him.

ANGELS. In the Bible, angels are spiritual beings who serve as messengers from **God.** In the **Gospels** they are most prominent in the **infancy narratives.** In Matt 1–2, an "angel of the **Lord**" guides **Joseph** in accepting Jesus as his **child** and keeping him safe (1:20, 1:24, 2:13, 2:19). In Luke 1–2, the angel **Gabriel** announces the births of both **John** and Jesus, and the shepherds hear about Jesus' birth through angels. Mentions of angels elsewhere in the Gospels cluster around texts dealing with **eschatological** matters in which angels will play a part (see Mark 13, Matt 24–25, and Luke 12). While **Mark** identifies the messenger in the empty **tomb of Jesus** as a "young man" (16:5), **Matthew** calls him an angel (28:5). Here and elsewhere in the Bible it is difficult to know whether the angel is really to be understood as a specific spiritual being or simply as a dramatic literary convention to describe a communication from God.

ANGER. Some manuscripts state that in Mark 1:41, Jesus was moved with anger (rather than compassion) at the plight of a man with **leprosy.** In Mark 3:5, Jesus displays anger at the hardness of heart shown by those in the **synagogue** at **Capernaum** who object to his healing the man with the withered hand. In 10:14, Jesus grows angry with his **disciples** for trying to prevent the **children** from coming to him. For further displays of Jesus' emotions, see Mark 1:43, 8:12, 8:17–21, and 9:19. The other Evangelists tend to omit references to Jesus' anger and frustration, presumably because they regarded them as inappropriate or not worth mentioning.

ANNA. (1) According to Luke 2:36–38, Anna, the daughter of Pha-
nuel and of the tribe of Asher, was an elderly woman (84 years
old), having been widowed after seven years of **marriage**, and also
a **prophetess**. Like **Simeon**, she frequented the **Jerusalem temple**,
was there for the presentation of the **child** Jesus, and pointed to his
significance for all like herself "who were looking for the redemption
of **Jerusalem**." (2) According to *Protevangelium of James*, Anna
was the name of the mother of **Mary**, the mother of Jesus, and thus
of the grandmother of Jesus.

ANOINTING. The application of olive oil or some other ointment to
a person or thing. According to Matt 26:6–13 and Mark 14:3–9, an
unnamed woman anoints Jesus on his head with a large amount of
expensive ointment at the beginning of the **passion narrative**, thus
symbolically identifying him as the **Messiah** (the "Anointed One")
and preparing his body for **burial**. A similar incident is placed by
Luke during Jesus' **Galilean** ministry (7:36–50) in which "a sinful
woman" anoints Jesus' feet as a token of her **love** and gratitude for
the **forgiveness of her sins**. In John 12:1–8, Mary of Bethany anoints
Jesus' feet and wipes them with her hair, at the end of Jesus' public
ministry. This anointing, the accounts of which may be variations
of a single event, emphasizes the dignity of Jesus and his identity as
the Messiah. In Mark 6:13, we are told that Jesus' **disciples** were to
anoint the sick and cure them as part of their mission. The medicinal
aspect of anointing the sick underlies the early **church**'s ritual described in Jas 5:14–15.

APHORISM. A concise statement of a principle, a brief formulation
of a truth or sentiment. In contrast to a proverb, an aphorism is a saying attributed to a specific person and understood within the context
of his particular **wisdom** and activity. Examples of Jesus' aphorisms
include his sayings in **Mark's Gospel** about old and new wineskins
(2:22), the **Sabbath** as made for humans (2:27–28), saving and losing
one's life (8:25), and the impossibility of a camel going through the
eye of a needle (10:25). The aphorisms of Jesus, like his **parables**
and **miracles**, generally concern some aspect of the **kingdom of
God**.

APOCALYPSE, APOCALYPTIC. An apocalypse is a literary genre in which a seer or **dreamer** is granted a revelation (*apokalypsis* in Greek) of the future and/or the heavenly realm. Since the content of an apocalypse is often the "last things," the adjective "apocalyptic" is often used to refer to end-time or **eschatological** events. The books of **Daniel** and **Revelation** are at least in part apocalypses within the biblical canon. The most prominent Jewish apocalypses outside the **canon** are the books known as *1 Enoch*, *4 Ezra*, and *2 Baruch*. There are apocalyptic elements in many of the **Dead Sea Scrolls** and in some early Christian works (*Shepherd of Hermas*). Within the **Synoptic Gospels**, Jesus' final discourses in Matt 24–25, Mark 13, and Luke 21 are sometimes called the "little" or "Synoptic" apocalypse. In these passages Jesus foretells certain historical and cosmic events leading up to the climactic appearance of the glorious **Son of Man**. However, he leaves uncertain the precise timing of these events, and so urges constant vigilance and adequate preparation for them: "Beware, keep alert; for you do not know when the time will come" (Mark 13:33).

APOCRYPHAL GOSPELS. Derived from the Greek word "hidden," these noncanonical early Christian texts (from the late second century onward) include narratives about Jesus' birth and **childhood** and about his **death** and **resurrection**, as well as various sayings attributed to Jesus. For Jesus' **infancy**, the most important resources are *Protevangelium of James* and *Infancy Gospel of Thomas*. For Jesus' **passion**, death, and resurrection, the most significant texts are the *Gospel of Peter*, *Gospel of Judas*, and *Gospel of Nicodemus* (or *Acts of Pilate*). These works purport to answer questions arising from the four **canonical Gospels** and to fill in gaps perceived to have been left by them. They pretend to give eyewitness accounts from early followers of Jesus. However, if one wants solid and reliable historical information about Jesus, they are of little or no value. But they are very useful as witnesses to the imagination of early Christians, perhaps on the margins of the mainline, or catholic, **church** from the late second to the seventh century. The *Gospel of Thomas* provides 114 sayings attributed to Jesus. While many of these sayings reflect **gnostic** perspectives, there may be among them some **teachings** in forms that antedate the versions in the canonical Gospels. The apocryphal Gospels also include several "lost" Gospels known only from quotations (usually negative and even hostile) found in the writings of the Church Fathers, such as the *Gospel according to the Hebrews*, *Gospel of the Nazaraeans*, *Gospel of the Ebionites*, and *Gospel of the Egyptians*. The texts of all these apocryphal Gospels and many other apocryphal texts can be found in good English translations in J. K. Elliott's *The Apocryphal New Testament* (1993).

APOSTLE. An apostle is someone who is "sent" as a representative of a prominent person or a community. Jesus' saying in Matt 10:40 ("whoever welcomes you welcomes me, and whoever welcomes me welcomes the one who sent me") views Jesus as **God**'s own "apostle" and his **disciples** as Jesus' representatives (see also John 5:23, 12:44–45, 13:20). The term was not originally limited to the **twelve apostles**, as the examples of **Paul** and Barnabas, as well as that of Andronicus and Junia (Rom 16:7), show. Lists of the twelve apostles appear in Matt 10:2–4, Mark 3:16–19, Luke 6:24–26, and Acts 1:13. Luke is especially concerned to present the twelve apostles as principles of continuity between the time of Jesus and that of the **Holy Spirit**/early **church**.

APPEARANCES. The experiences of the risen Jesus by his followers are presented in the NT as proofs that he had been really **raised from the dead**. The earliest NT list of them comes from Paul in 1 Cor 15:5–8 and includes as recipients Cephas (**Peter**), the **twelve apostles**, 500 others, **James**, and **Paul** himself. **Matthew** provides reports about the risen Jesus' appearances to **Mary Magdalene** and the "other Mary" in Jerusalem (28:9–10) and to 11 apostles in **Galilee** (28:16–20). **Luke** describes appearances to two **disciples** on the way to Emmaus (24:13–35) and to 11 apostles in **Jerusalem** (24:36–49). In John 20, the risen Jesus appears in Jerusalem to Mary Magdalene (20:11–18), the disciples (20:19–23), and the disciples and **Thomas** (20:24–29), while in John 21 he appears in Galilee to seven of the apostles and converses at length with Peter. Mark 16:9–20 is generally viewed as a second-century summary of the appearances found in the other **Gospels**. The exact nature of these appearances (real events, visions, dreams, or hallucinations?) and the lack of agreement among them, as well as the whole idea of **resurrection** of a dead person, present many problems for historians and believers alike.

ARCHAEOLOGY. The excavation and scientific analysis of the material culture in Jesus' time in Palestine, while telling us little directly about Jesus in particular, greatly illuminate the world in which Jesus lived. For example, recent excavations at **Nazareth** give a glimpse of a neighborhood in which Jesus may have grown up. The **Dead Sea Scrolls** provide the library of a Jewish sect (possibly the **Essenes**) contemporary with Jesus. Extensive excavations at **Caesarea Maritima** on the Mediterranean coast show the degree to which a city in ancient Palestine had been Hellenized and Romanized under **Herod the Great**. Explorations in **Jerusalem** give us a sense of many places mentioned in the **Gospel passion narratives**. The scientific reconstruction of the skeleton of a crucified man whose bones were found near Jerusalem may clarify how Jesus met his **death**. And the **burial** caves surrounding Jerusalem and the ossuaries within them can help us visualize the **tomb** in which Jesus was buried.

ARREST OF JESUS. In the **Synoptic Gospels**, the arrest of Jesus takes place in **Gethsemane** where Jesus went to pray and school himself to accept the fate that awaited him (Matt 26:36–46; Mark 14:43–52; Luke 22:47–53). It occurs when **Judas** arrives with a band of soldiers who seize Jesus despite a **disciple**'s resistance (Matt 26:47–56; Mark 14:43–52; Luke 22:47–53). Jesus offers no resistance on the grounds that the Scriptures and thus **God**'s will for him were being fulfilled. A similar account appears at the beginning of **John**'s **passion narrative** in 18:1–12. The term translated "robber" (*lestes* in Greek) in Matt 26:55, Mark 14:48, and Luke 22:52 may carry a political connotation (like "insurgent" today) and reflect how Jesus was perceived by the Jewish leaders and Roman officials. Of course, Jesus and the Evangelists denied the truth of this charge.

ASCENSION. With regard to Jesus, the term refers to the belief that after his **resurrection** from the dead, the risen Jesus was taken up into **heaven** where he remains in glory until his second coming or **Parousia**. The OT precedents include Enoch (Gen 5:24) and **Elijah** (2 Kgs 2:11). The key NT text is Acts 1:6–11, where 40 days after

Easter the risen Jesus is said to have been "lifted up, and a cloud took him out of their sight." Luke 24:50–51 locates the ascension in **Bethany** near **Jerusalem** and states that Jesus "was carried up into heaven." The longer ending of Mark claims that Jesus "was taken up into heaven and sat down at the right hand of **God**" (16:19), thus fulfilling Ps 110:1 (the OT text quoted most frequently in the NT). In John 20:17, the risen Jesus forbids **Mary Magdalene** to touch him on the grounds that he had "not yet ascended to the Father." Then he commissions Mary to tell the **disciples**, "I am ascending to my Father and your Father, to my God and your God." The ascension as narrated by **Luke** and referred to by the other **Gospels** obviously goes beyond the canons of modern **historical criticism**. The accounts raise questions for any reader of the Bible: What and where is heaven? How does Jesus get there? Is he the first "spaceman"? Where is he now? In what form will he come back? While some take it as simply as an actual historical event, others view it (skeptically) as a mass hallucination on the disciples' part, and still others interpret it (positively) as a dramatic or theological portrayal of the spiritual reality of Jesus passing from the earthly realm to God.

ATONEMENT. A prominent early Christian interpretation of Jesus' **death** as being "for us" and "for our sins," and thus bringing about reconciliation between **God** and humankind. The NT concept is rooted in the OT rituals of **sacrifice**, especially those concerned with the Day of Atonement (see Lev 16). The concept is well expressed in Jesus' saying in Mark 10:45: "For the **Son of Man** came not to be served but to serve, and to give his life as a **ransom** for many." The atoning death of Jesus is a major theme in the NT Epistles (see 1 Cor 15:3; Rom 3:25; 1 Pet 2:24, 3:18, etc.). The **letter to the Hebrews** (chaps. 4–10) contains an extended meditation on the atoning significance of Jesus' death and its superiority to the OT rituals associated with the Day of Atonement.

– B –

BANQUET. One of the recurrent criticisms of Jesus by his opponents in the **Gospels** was the charge that he often ate with **tax collectors** and **sinners** (see Mark 2:15–16, etc.). This charge seems to reflect the earthly Jesus' practice of sharing meals with all kinds of people, especially socially and religiously marginal persons, as a symbol of what life will be like in the fullness of **God's kingdom** (see Matt 8:11; Luke 13:28). It is in this context that we need also to interpret Jesus' miraculous **feedings** of large **crowds** (Mark 6:30–44, 8:1–10 parr. [parr. = parallel texts in the Gospels]), his own **Last Supper** (Mark 14:17–25 parr.), and his meals with his **disciples** after his **resurrection** (Luke 24:13–49; John 21:1–14). While undoubtedly an important feature of Jesus' earthly ministry to marginal persons, these meals were especially important vehicles (enacted **parables**) in his theological agenda of proclaiming open commensality (**table fellowship**) in **God**'s kingdom.

BAPTISM OF JESUS. That Jesus underwent baptism by John is among the most certain historical facts in the **Gospels**. Since it could suggest some dependence on John and even inferiority to him on Jesus' part, it is not the kind of story that early Christians would have invented. Nevertheless, while there is no doubt about the historicity of the event, the Evangelists in their accounts were clearly more interested in proclaiming the theological significance of Jesus and his relationship of superiority to **John the Baptist**. According to Mark 1:9–11, Jesus came from **Nazareth** to be with John by the Jordan River. As he was coming up from the water, Jesus experienced a divine revelation symbolized by the opening of the **heavens**, the **dove**-like descent of the **Holy Spirit**, and the **voice from heaven** that identifies him as the **Son of God** (Ps 2:7), **God**'s Beloved (Gen 22:2, 22:12, 22:16 [Isaac]), and the **Servant of God** (Isa 42:1–2). The account in Matt 3:13–17 seeks to cover over the possible embarrassment about Jesus undergoing John's baptism "for **repentance**" (3:11) by inserting in 3:14–15 a dialogue that tries to explain why it was appropriate for Jesus to be baptized ("to fulfill all **righteousness**"). **Luke** in 3:19–20 describes John's **arrest** before narrating the baptism of Jesus in 3:21–22, probably reflecting his distinctive theology of **salvation** history, according to which John belonged to the time of **Israel** and Jesus' public ministry inaugurated the middle or center of time (see Luke 16:16). In John 1:29–34, John the Baptist looks back on Jesus' baptism and testifies that Jesus really was "the Son of God" (see also John 1:6–7, 15).

BARABBAS. The prisoner released by **Pontius Pilate** instead of Jesus (see Matt 27:16; Mark 15:7; Luke 23:18–19; John 18:40). According to **Mark**, Barabbas was a rebel or insurgent who had committed murder. His name means "son of Abba," and **Abba** means "Father." In some manuscripts he is called "Jesus Barabbas." That would mean that the **crowd** before Pilate had to choose between Jesus Barabbas (a political rebel and murderer) and Jesus of **Nazareth** (the real "Son of the Father" [**God**]).

BARTIMAEUS. The blind beggar whose sight was restored by Jesus according to Mark 10:46–52. The name is explained as meaning "son of Timaeus" in Mark 10:46. The miraculous healing takes place in **Jericho** when Bartimaeus repeatedly calls upon Jesus as "**Son of David**" and asks for mercy. His persistence is rewarded, and he begins to see immediately and completely. The note that he followed Jesus "on the **way**" suggests that he became a **disciple** of Jesus and joined Jesus and his companions on their journey to **Jerusalem**.

BAUER, BRUNO (1809–1882). From his early research on **John's Gospel**, Bauer concluded that it was a purely literary creation and had no historical foundation. Likewise, when he examined **Mark** and the other **Synoptic Gospels**, he decided that they too had no historical basis. Thus he was driven to conclude that there never was any **historical Jesus**. That is, everything that was said about Jesus in the **Gospels** belonged to the world of the imagination, was invented by the early Christian community, and had nothing to do with a real historical person. **Albert Schweitzer** regarded Bauer's signal achievement to have been setting forth clearly the difficulties involved in reconstructing the life of the historical Jesus.

BEATITUDES. A beatitude declares someone blessed, fortunate, or happy. As a Jewish **wisdom** teacher focusing on the **kingdom of God**, it is very likely that Jesus used this literary form. The OT beatitudes generally appear in the third person ("Happy is the one who . . . ," Ps 1:1) and in a wisdom context. In the NT, the declaration is often **eschatological**; that is, the person is promised a share in **God**'s end-time reign or **salvation**. Jesus' four beatitudes in Luke 6:20–23 are expressed in the second person plural ("Blessed are you") and promise blessedness to the **poor**, hungry, weeping, and persecuted. His nine beatitudes in Matt 5:3–12 are in the third person plural ("Blessed are they who") and exhibit a spiritualizing tendency at some points ("poor in spirit," "hunger and thirst for **righteousness**"). These beatitudes introduce Jesus' **Sermon on the Plain** (Luke 6:20–49) and **Sermon on the Mount** (Matt 5–7), respectively. Seven beatitudes appear at various points in the book of **Revelation** (1:3, 14:13, 16:15, 19:9, 20:6, 22:7, 22:14).

BEELZEBUL/BEELZEBUB. The name "Baal-zebul" in ancient times may have meant "**Lord** of **Heaven**." However, in 2 Kgs 1:2, 1:6, King Azariah inquires of "Baal-zebub," the god of Ekron, whose name means "Lord of the Flies." While that name may have alluded to the god's control over diseases, the OT form was probably a sarcastic parody on Baal-zebul. In Matt 12:24 and Luke 11:15, Beelzebul is called "the ruler of the **demons**." Jesus is charged by his opponents with being possessed by Beelzebul (Mark 3:22), is called Beelzebul by his enemies (Matt 10:25), and is accused of performing **exorcisms** by the power of Beelzebul (Matt 12:27; Luke 11:18). While Jesus' opponents did not deny his ability to cast out demons, they attributed it to the **evil** forces.

BELOVED DISCIPLE. The unnamed figure who appears only in **John's Gospel** and is a witness to several major events in the last week of Jesus' life: the **Last Supper** (John 13:23–25), his **trial** before the high **priest** (18:15), crucifixion (19:25–27), empty **tomb** (20:1–10), and appearance to the **Galilean fishermen** (21:7). In the epilogue (21:24), he seems to be identified as the primary source of John's Gospel's distinctive witness to Jesus. He is traditionally identified as **John the son of Zebedee**, though some have argued that he was **Lazarus** (see John 11:3, 11:11, 11:36). Still others have interpreted him as merely a symbol for the ideal **disciple** of and witness to Jesus.

BENEDICTUS. The hymn attributed to **Zechariah**, the father of **John the Baptist**, in Luke 1:68–79 is customarily known by the first word in its Latin version, *Benedictus*, meaning "blessed." Using many biblical phrases and allusions, the hymn celebrates the birth of John the Baptist as a divine visitation. However, its real focus is the birth of Jesus, who is from the house of **David** (1:69) and is portrayed as **God**'s special intervention for the **salvation** of his people **Israel** in accord with the promises contained in Scripture. The hymn draws John the Baptist into the dynamic of God's action in Jesus and makes clear John's subordinate role with regard to Jesus.

BETHANY. A village some 3 km (2 mi.) east of **Jerusalem**, perhaps meaning "House of the Afflicted/**Poor**." It was the home of Simon the **leper** (Mark 14:3; Matt 26:6) and of **Lazarus** and his sisters **Martha and Mary** (John 12:1). There Jesus was **anointed** before his **passion** began. According to Luke 24:50, his **ascension** took place near **Bethany**. The precise location of the place called "Bethany beyond the Jordan" (John 1:28) where John was baptizing is disputed.

BETHLEHEM. A village in Judea, 7–8 km (5 mi.) south of **Jerusalem**, perhaps meaning "House of Bread." It was the home of King **David** (1 Kgs 17:12, 20:6) and was expected to be the home of the future **Messiah** (Mic 5:1). According to various NT passages (Matt 2:1–12, 2:16; Luke 2:4, 2:15; John 7:42), it was where Jesus was born. There was also a village in **Galilee** named Bethlehem, 11 km (7 mi.) northwest of **Nazareth**.

BETRAYAL. While **Judas** is regularly identified in the **Gospels** as the one who betrayed or "handed over" Jesus, the motif of "handing over" (Greek *paradidomi*) serves often as a shorthand reference to Jesus' **arrest**, with echoes of Isaiah 53 (the **Suffering** Servant) and of early Christian confessions of faith (Rom 4:25, 8:32; 1 Cor 11:23; Gal 1:4, 2:20). The implication is that these events were taking place not merely because of Judas' treachery but also and especially in accord with **God**'s will and plan. That is, to some extent the **Father** was involved in the handing over of Jesus.

BINDING AND LOOSING. The power bestowed by Jesus first on **Peter** in Matt 16:19 and then on the **disciples** as a group in 18:18. The expression has been interpreted in various ways: laying down rules and making exemptions, imposing and lifting excommunications, forgiving and not forgiving sins (see John 20:23), or perform-ing **exorcisms**. The assumption is that **God** will stand behind these decisions and/or actions.

BLASPHEMY. The use of this term in the **Gospels** need not be re-stricted to the improper use of the divine name YHWH as in Lev 24:11. Rather, the term is used generically to refer to offensive reli-gious speech. The charge of blasphemy is first made against Jesus in Mark 2:7, when he declares forgiven the sins of a paralyzed man (see also 3:28–29, 7:22, 15:29). In Mark 14:64, in the **trial of Jesus** be-fore the Jewish council, the high **priest** accuses Jesus of blasphemy because of his affirmation of his identity as **Messiah**, **Son of God**, and **Son of Man**.

BLOOD AND WATER. According to John 19:34, when Jesus died, a soldier pierced his side (see Zech 12:10), and "at once blood and water came out." While this statement may merely have sought to confirm that Jesus was really dead, it has attracted many different symbolic and theological interpretations. Perhaps the best approach is to link it with John 7:38: "out of his heart shall flow rivers of living waters." In this context, the blood expresses Jesus' physical **death**, and the water symbolizes the giving of the **Holy Spirit** (see John 19:30; 1 John 5:6–8).

BOANERGES. The nickname given by Jesus to **James** and **John**, the sons of **Zebedee** (Mark 3:17). Derived from Hebrew or Aramaic, it may mean "**sons of thunder**" or even "sons of **anger**."

BOAT. Since Jesus used **Capernaum** as a base and his first **disciples** were **fishermen**, the **Gospels** contain many references to boats (Mark 1:20, 4:36–37, etc.). The kind of boat we are to imagine in these texts has been illuminated by the recovery in 1986 of an ancient boat from the **Sea of Galilee** and by the mosaic of a boat at Magdala-Taricheae in **Galilee**. The Galilean fishing boat would have been about 26 feet long and 8 feet wide, and capable of holding 12 to 15 persons. Chiefly through the episode of Jesus stilling the storm at sea in Mark 4:35–41 and Matt 8:18–27, the boat became a symbol of the **church**.

BORNKAMM, GÜNTHER (1905–1990). Professor of NT exegesis at the University of Heidelberg, his book *Jesus of Nazareth* (1956, German; 1960, English) was an important contribution to the renewal of the **quest for the historical Jesus** in the mid-twentieth century. While admitting that no one is in a position to write a life of Jesus, he was convinced that the **Gospels** and the traditions behind them allow and demand historical inquiry into what Jesus taught (about the **kingdom of God**, the will of **God**, **discipleship**, **suffering** and **death**, etc.) and what he was trying to accomplish.

BRIDEGROOM. In Mark 2:19 (Matt 9:15), Jesus responds to a question from **John's** **disciples** and the **Pharisees** about why his disciples were not fasting by comparing himself to a bridegroom and the time of his public ministry to a great wedding feast (that is, a time of joy and celebration) when **fasting** would be inappropriate. But he adds immediately that when he is taken away (anticipating his **death**), then his disciples will fast. In the **parable** of the **Ten Maidens** (Matt 25:1–10) the bridegroom whose coming is delayed is clearly a reference to belief in Jesus' return as the glorious **Son of Man**. In Eph 5:22–33, the relationship between the risen Christ and the **church** is imagined in terms of bridegroom and bride.

BROTHERS AND SISTERS. According to Mark 3:21, the family of Jesus suspects that "he has gone out of his mind." And so in 3:31–35 Jesus ignores their presence and redefines his real family as those who do the will of **God**. In Mark 6:4 the people of **Nazareth** name four brothers of Jesus—James, Joses, Judas, and Simon—and refer in general to his "sisters." From antiquity on, their precise relationship to Jesus has been debated. Were they true siblings of Jesus, the other **children** of **Mary** and **Joseph** (Helvidius)? Or were they Joseph's children from an earlier **marriage**, and so Jesus' stepbrothers and stepsisters (Epiphanius)? Or were they close relatives such as cousins (Jerome)? After Jesus' **death**, the "family" of Jesus, at least **James** and **Jude**, became prominent in the early Christian **church** at **Jerusalem**. Two NT epistles bear the names of James and Jude.

BROWN, RAYMOND E. (1928–1998). A prominent American Catholic biblical scholar and **priest**, Brown in *The Birth of the Mes-*

siah (1977; rev. ed. 1993) gave particular attention to the influence of Old Testament texts in shaping the language and concepts of the accounts of Jesus' birth and **infancy** in Matthew 1–2 and Luke 1–2. In his two-volume *The Death of the Messiah* (1994), he provided detailed literary and historical analyses of the **passion narratives** in all four **Gospels**. These studies remain comprehensive and classic treatments of the literary sources pertaining to Jesus' birth and **death**.

BULTMANN, RUDOLF (1884–1976). In *The History of the Synoptic Tradition* (1919), Bultmann investigated the literary forms and the process of transmission by which the **teachings** associated with Jesus were handed down in the early **church**. The subject of his 1926 book *Jesus* was not so much the life and personality of Jesus as it was the message of Jesus. He discerned three major themes: the coming of **God's kingdom** and the need to decide for or against it; doing **God**'s will; and God as both near (immanent) and remote (transcendent). Bultmann is also famous for his proposal to "demythologize" the **Gospels**, that is, to interpret various narratives such as Jesus' **baptism**, healings, **nature miracles**, and **resurrection** not so much as external events visible to all but rather as **myth**, internal happenings accessible to the eyes of faith and concerned mainly with human existence. In this project he was influenced strongly by the existentialist philosophy of Martin Heidegger.

BURIAL OF JESUS. The **Synoptic Gospels** (Matt 27:57–61; Mark 15:42–47; Luke 23:50–56) and John (19:38–42) agree that **Joseph of Arimathea** took charge of Jesus' burial and that the **women** at the **cross** saw where he was buried. Given the circumstances of Jesus' **death** (crucifixion) and the time constraints of **Passover** and the **Sabbath**, the burial of Jesus took place in haste in a cave outside the walls of **Jerusalem**. Whether Joseph was already a disciple of Jesus or simply acted out of Jewish piety (see Deut 21:22–23), or both, is not clear. Likewise, this is the case with **Nicodemus**, who according to John 19:39–40 assisted Joseph. The **Gospels** insist that the women, who were certainly **disciples** of Jesus, saw Jesus die, saw where he was buried, came to the right **tomb** on Easter, and found it empty.

– C –

CAESAREA MARITIMA. A major port city on the Mediterranean coast (the meaning of Maritima is "by the sea"), about 40 km (25 mi.) north of Tel Aviv, built by **Herod the Great** and named in honor of the emperor Augustus Caesar. It was a full-scale Hellenistic city and was used as headquarters by the Roman prefects (governors) of Judea. **Pontius Pilate** would have made his base there, going to **Jerusalem** only occasionally for pilgrimage feasts such as **Passover** to maintain the peace. This city is especially prominent in Acts.

CAESAREA PHILIPPI. A city in northern **Israel**, located near Mount Hermon. It was once known as Paneas (after the Greek god Pan) and was renamed Caesarea (after the Roman emperor) by Philip, one of **Herod**'s sons. In the **Gospels** it is the place where **Peter** identified Jesus as the **Messiah** (Mark 8:27–30; Matt 16:13–20) and from which Jesus and his **disciples** began their final journey to **Jerusalem**.

CAIAPHAS. The Jewish high **priest** between 18 and 36 CE, and the son-in-law of Annas (John 18:13) who held that office from 6 to 15 CE. According to the **Gospels**, Caiaphas played an important role in the plot to **arrest** Jesus (Matt 26:3; John 11:49–50) and presided over a hearing/**trial** concerning Jesus that led to his condemnation (Matt 26:57; John 18:24). In John 11:47–53, Caiaphas (ironically) utters a prophecy about Jesus and his saving significance for others: "It is better for you to have one man die for the people."

CALVARY. The Latin equivalent (*calvaria*, meaning "skull") for the Aramaic **Golgotha** and the Greek *kranion*. It refers to the place where Jesus was executed outside the walls of **Jerusalem**—"the place of the skull," according to Matt 27:33, Mark 15:22, Luke 23:33, and John 19:17. It was so called probably for both geographical (a hilly place) and legal (an execution site) reasons.

CANA. A village in **Galilee**, whose precise location is disputed. According to John 2:1–11 (see 4:46), this was where Jesus performed his first **miracle** by turning water into **wine** at a wedding feast. In

John 21:2, Jesus' **disciple Nathanael** is said to have come from Cana.

CANON. The word "canon" derives from the Greek *kanon*, which refers to a reed or measuring stick. In Christian theology the canon of Scripture is the list of approved or sacred books that serves as the rule or norm of Christian faith and practice. Of course, the Bible of the early **church** was what is now called the Old Testament. By 200 CE there was widespread acceptance in the churches of the four narratives about Jesus attributed to **Matthew, Mark, Luke,** and **John** as among the core books of the NT canon. While the criteria for inclusion were not made explicit, it appears that orthodoxy of content, some association with the **apostles,** and use in and acceptance by the churches were important factors. This development was probably accelerated by reactions to Marcion's proposal to accept only an abbreviated version of **Luke's Gospel** and by the **gnostic** production of other (secret) **Gospels.** While there was some dispute about boundaries, the 27 books of the present NT canon were generally recognized as Sacred Scripture by around 400 CE.

CAPERNAUM. A fishing village on the northwestern shore of the **Sea of Galilee,** identified with Tell Hum. Jesus' first followers were **fishermen** at work in Capernaum (Mark 1:16–20; Matt 4:18–22), and the **tax/toll collector** Levi/**Matthew** seems to have had his booth there (Matt 9:9). Much of Jesus' early activities centered on Capernaum (Mark 1:21–34, 2:1–3:6), and it served as his center of operations in **Galilee** (Mark 2:1). Nevertheless, according to Matt 11:23–24, Jesus' reception there was mixed at best, and in frustration he pronounced a curse upon it for its lack of faith in him ("you will be brought down to **Hades**").

CARPENTER. The traditional rendering of the Greek word *tekton,* which can refer more generically to someone who builds or does construction work. According to Mark 6:3, the people of **Nazareth** referred to Jesus as "the carpenter," while according to Matt 13:55 they called him "the carpenter's son." Some have speculated that **Joseph** and Jesus may have worked as craftsmen in the building of Sepphoris, not far from Nazareth.

CELIBACY. The practice of celibacy (refraining from sexual relations and **marriage**) was not common in ancient Judaism. Indeed, in the Babylonian Talmud, **Rabbi** Eliezer says, "Any Jew who does not have a wife is not a Jew." However, it appears that in Jesus' time members of some religious groups (**Essenes** and Therapeutae) who lived a communal life similar to that of monks were celibate. There is no indication in the **Gospels** that either **John the Baptist** or Jesus was married or had **children**. The idea that **Mary Magdalene** was Jesus' wife has no foundation in the ancient sources and is the invention of modern novelists. It appears that Jesus refrained from marriage primarily out of dedication to his mission of proclaiming **God's kingdom**. In Matt 19:10–12, Jesus observes that celibacy is a gift from **God** and must be voluntary on the **disciple**'s part. Celibacy undertaken "for the sake of the kingdom" fits well with what was the focus of Jesus' life and preaching. There is no contempt for the body or for marriage and sexual intimacy in his **teachings**.

CENSUS. Derived from the Greek word *kensos*, this term refers in the **Gospels** to the tax imposed on Jews that is mentioned in Jesus' statement on paying taxes to the Roman emperor (Mark 12:12; Matt 22:17, 22:19), and more specifically to the tax paid by Jews first for the upkeep of the **Jerusalem temple** (see Matt 17:24–27) and then after 70 CE for the upkeep of the Temple of Jupiter in **Rome** (called the *fiscus Iudaicus* in Latin). For "census" in the sense of a listing of the population, see **Quirinius**.

CENTURION. The commander of 100 men in a Roman **legion**. According to Matt 8:5–13 and Luke 7:1–10 (see also John 4:46–54), Jesus marveled at the faith of a centurion in him and healed his servant. In Mark 15:39, the centurion in charge of Jesus' crucifixion confessed that "truly this man was **God**'s Son," and in 15:44–45 he confirms to **Pilate** that Jesus was really dead. It is ironic that the only person who correctly identifies Jesus as the **Son of God** in **Mark's Gospel** should be a **Gentile** soldier presiding at Jesus' **death** on the cross. According to Acts 10, the Roman centurion Cornelius becomes the first Gentile Christian.

CHIEF PRIESTS. A collective term for the leaders among the Jewish priests, who exercised control over the **temple in Jerusalem.** Annas was the high **priest** from 6 to 15 CE, while his son-in-law **Caiaphas** was the high priest between 18 and 36 CE. In **Mark's Gospel** (and the others) the chief priests are hostile to Jesus from his entry into **Jerusalem** (Mark 11:18, 11:27, 12:12) and take the lead in getting Jesus **arrested** and tried before **Pilate** (Mark 14:1, 14:10–11, 14:43, 14:53, 15:1, 15:11, 15:31). They had been mentioned previously in two of Jesus' **passion predictions** (Mark 8:31, 10:33), thus suggesting that he foresaw their opposition.

CHILD. In two cases Jesus uses a child to impart a lesson about life in his movement and in the **kingdom of God.** In Mark 9:33–37 (Matt 18:1–5; Luke 9:46–48), when his **disciples** are arguing about greatness among them, Jesus takes a little child into his arms and declares that whoever welcomes such a child welcomes him and his **Father.** In Jewish society of the time, small children had little or no political or social importance. The lesson is that greatness in Jesus' movement consists in the service of the least significant members of society. In Mark 10:13–16, when the disciples try to prevent children from coming to him, Jesus claims that **God's kingdom** belongs to those who (like children) receive the kingdom as a gift from **God** rather than as something that they earn or is owed to them. In **Mark**'s narrative Jesus restores to life Jairus' 12-year-old daughter and heals the **Syrophoenician woman**'s daughter (5:35–43) and the epileptic boy (9:14–29).

CHILDHOOD OF JESUS. Little is known about Jesus' life between his birth and the beginning of his public ministry at the age of around 30 (Luke 3:23). According to Matt 2, Jesus was born in **Bethlehem** of Judea, was honored by the **Magi** as an infant, and embarked with **Mary** and **Joseph** on a dangerous journey from Bethlehem through Egypt to **Nazareth** in **Galilee** where he lived until he began his public activity. According to Luke 2, Mary and Joseph had to travel from Nazareth to Bethlehem where Jesus was born. Then, 40 days later, Jesus was brought to the **temple in Jerusalem** for his presentation and the purification of his mother, and they returned to Nazareth where "the **child** grew and became strong, filled with **wisdom**; and the favor of **God** was upon him" (2:40). Then at the age of 12 he and his parents went to **Jerusalem** for **Passover**. There he became separated from his parents and was found by them in the temple area, conversing with the great scholars (2:41–50). Afterwards, he returned to Nazareth, was obedient to his parents, and "increased in wisdom and in years, and in divine and human favor" (2:51–52). According to Matt 13:55, Jesus was "the **carpenter**'s son," and according to Mark 6:3 he himself was "the carpenter" in the eyes of the people at Nazareth. Here "carpenter" probably had the broad sense of builder or construction worker. For some fantastic accounts about Jesus' exploits between 5 and 12 years of age, *see Infancy Gospel of Thomas.*

CHREIA. A teaching serving as the climax in a brief narrative; it is also known as the pronouncement story, controversy story, or apothegm. For example, in Mark 12:13–17 some **Pharisees** and **Herodians** approach Jesus with a (hostile) question about whether it was lawful to pay taxes to the Roman emperor. Jesus then asks for a coin and elicits from his questioners the admission that it belongs to the emperor. All this leads up to Jesus' climactic saying, "Give to the emperor the things that are the emperor's, and to **God** the things that are God's." Widely used in Greco-Roman schools, the *chreia* is a prominent discourse form in the **Synoptic Gospels** for conveying Jesus' **teachings** and his personal cleverness. It was one of the several small literary formats in which Jesus' teachings were expressed and handed on in early Christian circles. They served as important sources for **Mark** in writing his first connected narrative about Jesus.

CHRISTOLOGY. The study of the titles and theological interpretations applied to Jesus in the NT and other early Christian documents. Early Christian hymns about Jesus as the **Servant of God** (Phil 2:6–11), the **Wisdom** of God (Col 1:15–20), and the Word of God (John 1:1–18) are quoted in various parts of the NT. In the opening verse of 1 Thessalonians (written in 50 CE), **Paul** refers to Jesus as "the **Lord** Jesus Christ," and looks forward to his second coming in 4:13–5:11. Throughout his letters, Paul focuses especially on the saving significance of Jesus' **death** and **resurrection** "for us" and "for our sins." The **letter to the Hebrews** is an extended theological reflection on

Jesus as the perfect (in the sense of truly effective) **sacrifice** for sins and as the great high **priest** (because he offered himself willingly). The **Synoptic Gospels** portray Jesus as the **prophet** of **God's kingdom**, a wisdom teacher, and a **miracle** worker, while John presents him as the definitive revealer and revelation of **God**.

CHRONOLOGY. (1) Jesus' birth: According to Matt 2:1 and Luke 1:5, Jesus was born during the reign of **Herod the Great** over **Judea**, and according to Matt 2:15 and 2:19–20, Herod died when Jesus was an infant. That would place Jesus' birth in 5 or early 4 BCE. (2) Jesus' ministry: According to Luke 3:1–2, the ministries of **John the Baptist** and Jesus began in the 15th year of the Roman emperor Tiberius (= 29 CE). According to Luke 3:23, Jesus was then "about thirty years old." John mentions three **Passovers** in his account of Jesus' ministry (2:13, 2:23, 6:4, 11:55), while the **Synoptic Gospels** mention only one (Matt 26:17; Mark 14:1; Luke 22:1). On the historical level, John's three-year ministry seems more likely. (3) Jesus' **death**: John places Jesus' death on the day before Passover began in the evening, whereas the Synoptic Gospels place it within the period of Passover. Again John's chronology seems more likely. Jesus was most likely crucified on Friday, the 14th of Nisan (early April), in 30 (or 33) CE.

CHURCH. In the **Gospels** the Greek word for "church" (*ekklesia*) appears only in Matt 16:18 and 18:17. Jesus' primary task was proclaiming **God's kingdom**. He was a charismatic **prophet** and showed little interest in establishing a highly structured organization or a new religion. However, Jesus' **teachings** and practices as well as his circle of early **disciples** provided the preparation and continuities for the emergence of the church after his **death** and **resurrection**. The church is the community of aspirants to **God**'s kingdom gathered in Jesus' name and led by the **Holy Spirit**. The crucial event in the founding of the church was Jesus' death and resurrection. Through **baptism**, Christians share in that foundational event and become members of God's people in Christ.

CIRCUMCISION. The removal of the foreskin from the penis, usually performed on a Jewish infant boy eight days after his birth. In Jesus' time, circumcision had become one of the identity markers (along with ritual and food **purity** rules and **Sabbath** observance) for Jews in the Greco-Roman world and was sometimes even referred to as "the **covenant**." According to Luke 1:59 and 2:21, both **John the Baptist** and Jesus underwent this ritual without any objection from their parents. During his earthly ministry according to the **Gospels**, Jesus never raised any objection to circumcision. It became an issue for early Christians only after the mission to the **Gentiles** began (Gal 2:1–10; Acts 15:1–29).

CLEAN AND UNCLEAN. According to modern anthropologists, what is clean or **pure** is in its proper place, while what is unclean or impure is out of place. Impurity can be physical, ritual, or moral. While treated in various parts of the OT, these topics are dealt with in a concentrated way in Lev 11–15. Although Jesus in the **Gospels** does not abrogate explicitly the biblical laws about clean and unclean (Mark 7:19 is the Evangelist's parenthetical comment), he does criticize the traditions that the **Pharisees** developed to safeguard their observance (Mark 7:1–23; Matt 15:1–20). Moreover, Jesus does not hesitate to touch those who are ritually unclean such as **lepers** (Mark 1:40–45; Luke 17:11–19), the woman with the flow of blood (Mark 5:25–34), and the dead (Mark 5:35–43; Luke 7:11–17; John 11:1–44).

CLEANSING OF THE TEMPLE. *See* TEMPLE, CLEANSING OF THE.

COMMANDMENT, NEW. In John 13:34–35, Jesus identifies as a "new commandment" that his **disciples** should love one another (the so-called **Love Command**). Since Jesus in **John's Gospel** repeatedly urges his disciples to love one another and since love of neighbor is commanded in the OT (Lev 19:18) and is prominent in the **Synoptic Gospels** (Matt 22:39; Mark 12:31; Luke 10:27) and the NT Epistles (1 Thess 4:9; Gal 5:14; Rom 13:9), it is hard to grasp what exactly is new about it. Perhaps it is the emphasis on the loving service of others within the community, the explicit link to Jesus' own love for them, and the idea that love within the community will be the distinguishing feature of Jesus' followers to outsiders (see 1 John 3:11–17).

COMMISSIONING STORIES. In the **Synoptic Gospels**, Jesus attracts **disciples** and eventually commissions them to carry on and extend his own mission of proclaiming **God's kingdom** in word and deed. In Mark 6:7–13 (Matt 10:1–15; Luke 9:1–6, 10:1–12), Jesus provides detailed instructions about the content and lifestyle of their mission. They are to proclaim **repentance** in the face of the coming kingdom and to live simply in the service of their mission. The final commissioning occurs in Matt 28:16–20 when the risen Jesus instructs the eleven **apostles** (minus **Judas**) to make disciples of all nations by **baptizing** and **teaching** them. The Johannine **farewell discourse** in chapters 14–17 provide instructions for Jesus' disciples to carry on his mission by belief in Jesus, **love** within the community, and openness to the guidance of the **Holy Spirit**.

CORBAN. A Hebrew/Aramaic word meaning "offering" or "gift," used in Mark 7:11 to refer to something consecrated as a gift to **God** and therefore excluded from ordinary or secular use. In Mark 7:9–13, Jesus uses the practice to illustrate the **hypocrisy** of the **Pharisees** and **scribes** in allowing adult children to declare their wealth or property as dedicated to God (*corban*) as a way of avoiding the biblical commandment to honor (and support) one's aging parents.

CORNERSTONE. According to Ps 118:22 "the stone that the builders rejected has become the cornerstone." In Mark 12:10 (Matt 21:42; Luke 20:17), these words are applied to Jesus as the **Son of God** and foreshadow the pivotal significance of his **death** on the **cross**. There is a debate among scholars as to whether the Greek expression *kephale gonias* ("head of the corner") refers to the cornerstone in the foundation of a building or to the capstone placed at the top of an arch as a sign of the building's completion. In either case, the stone (Jesus) rejected by the builders (the Jewish leaders) has become essential to the building's survival (the people of **God**).

COVENANT, NEW. Covenant is a major biblical term for **God's** relationship with God's people **Israel**. While not necessarily a religious word, the concept of covenant provides the background for many key biblical terms (know, fear, **love**, serve, fidelity, justice, **righteousness**), ideas (God as **lord**, God's mighty acts, laws and attitudes, threats of punishment), and public worship (blessings and curses, **heaven** and earth as witnesses, **sacrifices** and common **meals**). The covenant theme is prominent in the **Gospels'** accounts of Jesus' **Last Supper** and his institution of the Eucharist (Matt 26:28; Mark 14:24; Luke 22:20). The idea of the "new covenant" is mentioned in 1 Cor 11:25, developed at some length in Heb 8:6–13 on the basis of Jer 31:31–34, and is central to **Paul**'s argument in 2 Cor 3. The traditional title for the collection of Greek writings sacred to Christians is the "New Covenant" (or Testament). The adjective "new" in these expressions need not be taken as an outright rejection or dismissal of the "old" covenant. The Christian claim is that the one covenant made by God with Israel ("I will be your God, and you shall be my people") has been brought to a new phase or fullness through Jesus. According to Paul, God's covenant with Israel has not been revoked (Rom 11:29), and in the end he expects that "all Israel will be saved" (Rom 11:26).

CRITERIA OF AUTHENTICITY. How can one distinguish between the **teachings** of the historical Jesus and the possible modifications and adaptations of it by early Christians and the Evangelists? Some criteria for making such distinctions have been developed and proven useful in the modern **quest for the historical Jesus**: (1) Double dissimilarity or discontinuity—a saying that cannot be ascribed to contemporary Judaism or to the early **church** may be ascribed to Jesus (e.g. "Do not swear at all," Matt 5:34). (2) Embarrassment—if an action (e.g., Jesus receiving **John**'s **baptism**) or a saying (such as Mark 13:32) might have embarrassed early Christians, it has a good chance of being authentic Jesus material. (3) Multiple attestation—if a specific teaching is ascribed to Jesus in several different sources (**Mark, Q, M, L, John, Paul**), it probably can be attributed to Jesus. (4) Palestinian coloring—if a teaching makes sense only when translated from Greek into Aramaic or Hebrew, or reflects the distinctive customs and life-setting of Palestine in Jesus' time, then it is at least possible that it came from Jesus, who spoke Aramaic and lived in Palestine. (5) Factors in Jesus' **death**—if an action (Jesus **cleansing the temple**) or a saying (threats about destroying the temple) might have so offended the Roman officials and/or Jewish leaders that it contributed to Jesus' death, it may well reflect the activity of the historical Jesus. (6) Coherence—if a teaching coheres with or is consistent with teachings attributed to Jesus by the other criteria, it may well be an authentic teaching of Jesus. Not one of these criteria is without obvious logical problems. However, taken together, they can tell us some things about what Jesus did and stood for.

CROSS-BEARING. Crucifixion was a public punishment visited upon rebels and slaves. The one being executed was forced to carry the horizontal cross-beam to the site of execution. According to Mark 15:21, **Simon of Cyrene** was compelled to carry Jesus' cross, presumably because Jesus lacked the physical strength to do so because of the abuse he had suffered. In Mark 8:34 (see Matt 16:24; Luke 9:23), Jesus challenges his prospective followers to "take up their cross" and come after him. While the reference to the cross evokes in readers today (and surely in **Mark**'s first readers) a remembrance of Jesus' own crucifixion, it is not impossible that Jesus used such imagery during his public ministry, since crucifixion was known in his time and place as the ultimate punishment. In either a pre-Easter or a post-Easter setting, the saying indicates that prospective **disciples** of Jesus must be willing to follow the "**way**" of Jesus as the suffering **Messiah**.

CROWDS. Throughout the **Gospels**, the crowds (*ochlos/ochloi*) are present as onlookers at Jesus' public activities, **miracles**, and **teachings**. Their reactions range from wonder and praise to ambivalence and even hostility. They represent the mass of uncommitted persons, and Jesus has to struggle for their allegiance with the **scribes**, **Pharisees**, **chief priests**, and other groups. They marvel at him on **Palm Sunday** but join in the chorus demanding his **death** on Good Friday.

CROWN OF THORNS. According to Mark 15:17 (Matt 27:29; John 19:2), the soldiers who abused Jesus before his execution put "a crown of thorns" on his head. Their action was probably intended both to inflict pain on Jesus and to **mock** the claims about him being the **King of the Jews**. For the first readers of the **Gospels**, however, the irony was that in their view Jesus really was the King of the Jews.

CUP. At several points in the **Gospels** the image of the cup is best understood in terms of the OT theme of the cup of **suffering** (Jer

25:15–29; Ps 75:8; Isa 51:17, 51:22, etc.). In Mark 10:38, Jesus challenges his **disciples** to be prepared to "drink the cup that I drink," that is, the cup of suffering. Likewise, in **Gethsemane** Jesus prays that **God** might "remove this cup from me" (Mark 10:36), while in John 18:11 he expresses his willingness "to drink the cup that the **Father** has given me." This understanding of the cup surely underlies Jesus' invitation at the **Last Supper** to drink from his cup (Mark 14:23; Matt 26:27; Luke 22:17).

CYNICS. In the ancient Mediterranean world, philosophies and religions were spread primarily by traveling missionaries. The Cynics were known especially for their street-corner oratory and ascetic (countercultural) lifestyle. Their name derived from the Greek word for "dog" (*kyon*) in the sense of one who is "dogged" (or persistent) and "barks" at others (is confrontational). While there are some interesting parallels between Cynic values and practices and Jesus' **teaching** and lifestyle and his instructions to his **disciples**, it is dubious that he himself was or was perceived as a Cynic during his lifetime. Rather, he fits more comfortably in the framework of first-century Palestinian Judaism and its background in biblical religion and Jewish **eschatology**. His emphasis on **God's kingdom** as the future display of divine power and sovereignty is especially different from the "hippie" utopia for which the Cynics hoped and worked.

– D –

DANIEL. The book of Daniel is the only **apocalypse** in the Hebrew Bible. Its text appears partly in Hebrew (chaps. 1, 8–12), and partly in Aramaic (chaps. 2–7). Its content and language find many echoes and allusions in Jesus' **teaching** according to the **Synoptic Gospels**. The coming of **God's kingdom**, which according to Mark 1:15 (and Matt 4:17) was the focus of Jesus' teaching, evokes the idea of an eternal kingdom to be established by **God** (Dan 2:44) and to be received and possessed by the "holy ones of the Most High" (Dan 7:1). Jesus' **parables** about God's kingdom find a partial model in the visions spread throughout Daniel, especially in their use of the term "mystery" and in the format of a narrative followed by its interpretation (see Mark

4:1–20; Matt 13:1–23, 13:24–30, 13:36–43, 13:47–50). The climax of a parable of the **Mustard Seed** in Mark 4:32 ("so that the birds of the air can make nests in its shade") is often traced to the vision of King Nebuchadnezzar in Dan 4:9, 4:21. The vision of "the one like a son of man" in Dan 7 is especially prominent in the **Gospel** sayings about a pivotal figure in the events associated with the full coming of God's kingdom. According to Mark 8:38, the **Son of Man** "when he comes in the glory of his **Father** with his holy **angels**" will be ashamed of those who have been ashamed of him and his teachings. Mark 13:26 places the manifestation of the glorious Son of Man as the climax in the series of events that constitute the future unfolding of God's plan for **salvation**. At the **trial** scene, Jesus in Mark 14:62 not only accepts the titles "**Messiah**" and "Son of the Blessed" but also identifies himself as the glorious Son of Man in terms taken from Dan 7:13–14. Other expressions in the Synoptic Apocalypse (Mark 13 parr.) allude to the book of Daniel. The "desolating sacrilege" (traditionally known as the "**abomination of desolation**") in Mark 13:14 has its roots in a Hebrew expression found in Dan 9:27, 11:31, and 12:11 that referred originally to the pagan altar erected by order of King Antiochus IV Epiphanes in the **Jerusalem temple** in 167 BCE. And mention of the "**great tribulation**" in Mark 13:19 echoes Dan 12:1: "There shall be a time an anguish, such as has never occurred since nations came into existence." The description of the **resurrection of the dead** in Dan 12:1–3 provides part of the biblical background for Jesus' argument with **Sadducees** in Mark 12:18–27 and his **passion-resurrection predictions** in Mark 8:31, 9:31, and 10:33–34. The critical issue involves deciding what aspects of Daniel's language and themes came from Jesus and what came from the early **church**.

DARKNESS AT THE CRUCIFIXION. According to the **Synoptic Gospels** (Matt 27:45; Mark 15:33; Luke 23:44), there was "darkness over the whole land" from the sixth hour (noon) to the ninth hour (3:00 p.m.) before Jesus' **death**. Whether the Evangelists understood "the whole land" as **Jerusalem**, the land of **Israel**, or the whole world is not clear. The darkness has been interpreted as due to a sandstorm or an eclipse (Luke 23:45). In the background may be Amos 8:9: "On that day, says the Lord **God**, I will make the sun go down at noon and darken the earth in broad daylight." The idea seems to be that all creation enters into mourning at the death of God's Son.

DAVID, SON OF. The greatest king in ancient Israel, David came from **Bethlehem** and established the monarchy at **Jerusalem** around 1000 BCE. The **Gospels** trace Jesus' ancestry from David through **Joseph**, and thus they frequently refer to him as "Son of David." In the **genealogy of Jesus** in Matt 1:1–17, David along with **Abraham** and the exile serve as major benchmarks in **Israel**'s history. The title "Son of David" is especially prominent with regard to Jesus' ministry as a healer (Matt 9:27, 12:23, 15:22, 20:30–31), thus evoking the figure of **Solomon**, another Son of David with a reputation as a healer. However, the point of Mark 12:35–37 (Matt 22:41–46; Luke 20:41–44) seems to be that as **Lord** and **Son of God** Jesus is greater than David or any other Son of David.

DAY OF THE LORD. In the OT (especially the Prophets) the expression refers to **God**'s decisive future visitation that will bring judgment on the wicked and **salvation** for the faithful remnant (see Zech 12–14). In the NT it refers primarily to the second coming or **Parousia** of Jesus (1 Thess 5:2; 1 Cor 1:8; 2 Cor 1:14; 2 Pet 3:10–13, etc.), at which the wicked will be justly punished and the **righteous** will be vindicated and rewarded. Although certain events must take place beforehand (Mark 13:1–27 parr.; 2 Thess 2:1–13, etc.), its precise timing remains uncertain and so it demands constant vigilance on the part of the faithful (Mark 13:32–37 parr.; Rom 13:11–14). *See also* LAST JUDGMENT.

DEAD SEA SCROLLS. The term refers to a series of manuscript discoveries in the late 1940s and 1950s at various sites near the Dead Sea. The largest and most important manuscript discovery was made at Khirbet **Qumran** where ancient texts were found in 11 caves surrounding a central complex of buildings. The Qumran scrolls are generally understood to be the remnants of the library of a Jewish "monastic" community identified as **Essenes**. Most of the Qumran manuscripts can be dated confidently between 150 BCE and 70 CE. Reports about the discovery of NT texts at Qumran or references to NT figures (Jesus, **Paul, James**, etc.) have no solid basis, nor does there seem to have been any direct relationship between the Essenes and Jesus and his movement, unless it was through **John the Baptist**. However, the Qumran scrolls do offer many interesting parallels to (and contrasts with) what the **Gospels** say about Jesus with regard to the coming **kingdom of God**, **table fellowship**, **baptism**, **marriage**, **divorce**, and so on.

DEATH OF JESUS, MEDICAL CAUSES OF THE. All the Evangelists describe the **death of Jesus** simply. With eloquent understatement, they write that he "breathed his last" (Matt 27:50; Mark 27:37; Luke 23:46) and "gave up his spirit" (John 19:30). Without ignoring the intense **suffering** that crucifixion involved, they were apparently more interested in the theological significance of Jesus' death ("for us" and "for our sins") than in the medical details. Modern medical analysis, however, may be helpful in thinking about how and why Jesus died on the cross. The most prominent causes of death by crucifixion were hypovolemic shock and exhaustion asphyxia. Other possible contributing factors included dehydration, stress-induced arrhythmias, and congestive heart failure with the rapid accumulation of pericardial and perhaps pleural effusions. It remains unsettled whether Jesus died of cardiac rupture or of cardio-respiratory failure (see W. D. Edwards, W. J. Gabel, and F. E. Hosmer, "On the Physical Death of Jesus Christ," *Journal of the American Medical Association* 255 [1986]: 1455–63).

DEATH OF JESUS, NT ACCOUNTS OF. The only ancient sources for Jesus' death are the **passion narratives** in Mark 14–15, Matthew 26–27, Luke 22–23, and John 18–19. They agree that Jesus was **arrested** in **Jerusalem** around **Passover** time (probably in the early spring of 30 CE), underwent hearings or **trials** before Jewish and Roman authorities, was subjected to abuse and **mockery**, was sentenced to die by crucifixion, and died a painful death on the **cross**. The **Gospels** suggest that the Jewish leaders were the prime movers against Jesus and that the Roman official (**Pontius Pilate**) eventually ratified their decision. In the context of Passover (the Jewish celebration of liberation from slavery in Egypt under **Moses**), the Jewish officials and Pilate apparently regarded Jesus as some kind of political insurgent who might use religion to stir up the people. In their eyes it was in the best interests of both parties to keep the peace in Jerusalem during the **festival**. According to Mark 14:53–65, there were two charges raised against Jesus in the Jewish trial: He threatened to destroy the **Jerusalem temple**, and he claimed to be "the **Messiah, the Son of the Blessed One**." The official Roman charge against Jesus appears on the cross, "the **King of the Jews**" (Mark 15:26; John 19:19). This **title** suggests that Pilate viewed Jesus as another in a series of Jewish religious-political revolutionaries eager to destroy the Roman Empire and to disturb the status quo in Jerusalem in the name of the **kingdom of God**. In Jesus' time, crucifixion was a Roman punishment inflicted on slaves and revolutionaries. The usual Jewish mode of execution was stoning (see Acts 6–7). As a public punishment, crucifixion was meant to shame the victim and to deter others from doing what he had done. Jesus did not die alone. Rather, he was crucified along with men described in various translations as "thieves," "bandits," "rebels," or "revolutionaries." Jesus seems to have died rather quickly (Mark 15:44; John 19:33).

DECALOGUE. Also known as the Ten Commandments, the series of divine commands concerning **Israel**'s relationship to **God** and relationships within the community of Israel. In Exod 20:1–17 they are the words that God speaks to Israel on Mount Sinai, whereas in Deut 5:6–21 they are the words of **Moses** as he reveals what God said to him on Mount Horeb. Jesus seems to regard the Ten Commandments as foundational, often quotes or alludes to them, and never contests their validity (while urging his followers to go to the root of what they command, as in Matt 5:21–48). The second part of the Decalogue appears in its most concentrated form in Jesus' dialogue with the rich young man (Matt 19:18–19; Mark 10:19; Luke 18:20). In that encounter Jesus suggests that keeping those commandments qualifies him to enter **God's kingdom** and enjoy eternal life.

DECAPOLIS. The predominantly **Gentile** federation or league of "10 cities" (the meaning of Decapolis), east of the Jordan River (except Scythopolis), in northern Jordan and southern Syria. Though there are some variations in the ancient lists, they included Damascus, Philadelphia, Raphana, Scythopolis, **Gadara**, Hippos, Dion, Pella,

Gerasa, and Canatha. The Decapolis is mentioned in Matt 4:25 and Mark 5:20, 7:31, without comment.

DEMONS. While in Greek *daimonion* refers (often positively) to a semi-divine spirit somewhere between the gods and humans, in the **Gospels** and Jewish writings of Jesus' time demons are generally malevolent or unclean spirits who are agents of **Satan**, harm humans, and engage in combat with Jesus. They are responsible for various sicknesses, and enter into and take over persons' lives (Mark 1:23–26, 5:1–20, 7:24–30, 9:14–29). In the face of criticism from his opponents, Jesus has to establish that he is the enemy of Satan and the demons (Matt 12:25–37; Mark 3:23–30; Luke 11:17–23). His ability to overcome demons is taken as a **sign** that **God**'s **kingdom** is already present in his ministry (Matt 12:27–28; Luke 11:20).

DESTRUCTION OF JERUSALEM. In Matt 23:32–39 Jesus foretells the destruction of **Jerusalem** and its **temple** ("your house is left to you, desolate"), and the context suggests that this was to be the result of the city's mistreatment of Jesus and his **apostles** as well as the **prophets** of old. Likewise in Luke 21:20–24, Jesus describes in some detail the city's destruction and the dominance of the **Gentiles** over it until their times are fulfilled. In forecasting the destruction of Jerusalem and its temple, Jesus stands in line with the great prophets **Isaiah**, **Jeremiah**, and Ezekiel who made similar statements. However, since those two **Gospels** were not written until Jerusalem had been destroyed by the Romans in 70 CE, it is hard to know to what extent these texts have been influenced by events that had already happened.

DIBELIUS, MARTIN (1883–1947). Professor of NT exegesis at the University of Heidelberg, his 1919 book on the **form criticism** of the **Gospels** (English, *From Tradition to Gospel*, 1934) was one of the pioneering works in the literary and historical analysis of the **Synoptic Gospels**. He contended that the Synoptic Gospels were intended as popular literature and that the Evangelists are best understood as collectors, transmitters, and editors of traditional materials associated with Jesus and handed on in small packets (**parables,**

miracle stories, etc.) in early Christian circles and often shaped to meet their own pastoral needs. His most famous saying was, "In the beginning was the sermon," suggesting that much of the material attributed to Jesus arose in the homiletic activity of the early **churches**.

DISCIPLES/DISCIPLESHIP. Followers and pupils of a **teacher** or religious leader in the Jewish and Greco-Roman worlds. The disciples of Jesus include three entities: the relatively large group of men and **women** who followed him; the **twelve apostles** who were called directly by Jesus (Mark 3:16–19); and the inner circle of three apostles constituted by **Peter**, **James**, and **John** (Mark 9:2–13, 14:32–42). The names of the 12 are listed in Matt 10:2–4, Mark 3:16–19, Luke 6:13–16, and Acts 1:13. The life of discipleship involves special challenges and demands (Mark 8:34–9:1 parr.; Matt 8:19–22; Luke 9:57–62, etc.). But those who remain faithful can expect great rewards in this age and the age to come (Mark 10:29–30; Matt 19:28–29; Luke 18:29–30, 22:28–30).

DISHONEST MANAGER, PARABLE OF THE (LUKE 16:1–8). The **parable** appears in the context of Jesus' **teachings** about the proper attitudes toward material possessions in Luke 16. When a rich man learns that his manager (also known as the Unjust Steward) has been squandering his property, he demands an accounting and fires the manager. The manager in turn devises a scheme in which he writes off some percentage of the debts owed to his employer. Whether he was involving the debtors in a dishonest scheme or simply forgoing his own commission is not clear. What is surprising is that the employer praises the manager for his cleverness. The parable illustrates how much more shrewd and resourceful the people of this (secular) world are in financial dealings than the **children** of **light** (sincerely religious persons) are with regard to seeking the **kingdom of God**. Attached to the parable in Luke 16:9–13 are various sayings about the proper use of wealth.

DIVORCE. In Jesus' time, **marriages** among Jews (and many other peoples) were often arranged between the heads of the families. After an engagement period (see Matt 1:18–25), a legal contract would be signed and the bride would be brought to the household of the

bridegroom or his family (see Matt 25:1–13). Divorce was allowed on the basis of Deut 24:1–4. If the husband found "something objectionable" in the wife, he need only write out a certificate of divorce, give it to the wife (thus allowing her to marry someone else), and send her out of his household. The debate among Jewish teachers of Jesus' time concerned the grounds for divorce (see Mishnah *Gittin* 9:10). The School of Shammai gave a restrictive interpretation to "something objectionable" (probably sexual misconduct on the wife's part), while the School of Hillel interpreted it broadly (if she was a bad cook) and **Rabbi** Aqiba treated it even more broadly (if he found someone more beautiful). More radical than any of his contemporaries, Jesus questions the institution of divorce itself. The highly restrictive version of his **teaching** appears in Luke 16:18, taken over from the Sayings Source **Q**: "Anyone who divorces his wife and marries another commits adultery, and whoever marries a woman divorced from her husband commits adultery" (see the similar teachings in Mark 10:11–12 and Matt 5:32). Likewise **Paul** in 1 Cor 7:10–11 claims to have his teaching from the **Lord** (Jesus) "that the wife should not separate from her husband . . . and that the husband should not divorce his wife." In Mark 10:2–9, Jesus engages in a hostile debate with some **Pharisees** about whether it is lawful for a man to divorce his wife. It was a trap, since they knew it was lawful according to Deut 24:1–4 and they also knew Jesus' radical views on the topic. Jesus, however, dismisses Deut 24:1–4 as allowing divorce "because of your hardness of heart" and appeals instead to Gen 1:27 and 2:24 as expressing the original will of **God** that "the two shall become one flesh" and that "therefore what God has joined to together, let no one separate." These texts all indicate that Jesus took a very restrictive position (no divorce) on this matter and were based on the very positive view of marriage ("one flesh"), which gave some legal, social, and economic protection to the wife. However, it also appears that various NT writers introduced exceptions. For example, Paul in 1 Cor 7:15 allows divorce in a mixed marriage if the pagan spouse wishes to dissolve the marriage. And **Matthew** in 5:32 and 19:9 includes the phrase "except for unchastity," which probably refers to sexual misconduct on the wife's part (as in the ruling of the House of Shammai). These exceptions raise the question about the nature of Jesus' teaching (whether it is an ideal to be pursued or a law to be followed), and about the relationship between Jesus' absolute teaching and the exceptions made in some early Christian circles.

DODD, CHARLES HAROLD (1884–1973). In *The Parables of the Kingdom* (1935; rev. ed., 1961), Dodd showed the value of reading the **Gospel** parables as vehicles for Jesus' **teachings** about the **kingdom of God** and as a source for knowledge about Jesus' historical career. He argued that Jesus emphasized **realized eschatology**; that is, he was convinced that the kingdom of **God** had already arrived and that "future" eschatology was due to Jesus' use of **prophetic** imagery or was the product of later (incorrect) Christian teaching. He also demonstrated that in handing on Jesus' **parables** of the kingdom, early Christians used them in new contexts and altered their applications. In *Historical Tradition in the Fourth Gospel* (1963), Dodd traced the solid topographical and historical information in **John's Gospel** to the Evangelist's use of a Jewish-Christian source from before 70 CE. In *The Founder of Christianity* (1970), Dodd dealt with Jesus' personal characteristics and teachings, his place within Judaism and the titles applied to him in the Gospels, and his story as it appears in the Gospels. Throughout his long scholarly career Dodd regarded the Gospels as both witnesses to the **church**'s faith and historical documents whose authors were interested in facts.

DONKEY. A domesticated animal, used as a beast of burden. According to Mark 11:1–10 (Matt 21:1–9; Luke 19:28–38; John 12:12–19), Jesus entered **Jerusalem** on **Palm Sunday** while riding on the colt of a donkey, thus fulfilling Zech 9:9: "Lo, your king comes to you; triumphant and victorious is he, **humble** and riding on a donkey, on a colt, the foal of a donkey." Matthew in 21:2, 21:7 seems to have envisioned Jesus riding astride two animals—the donkey and her colt, on the basis of an excessively literal reading of Zech 9:9. In Luke 13:15, Jesus uses the action of untying one's donkey and giving it water as an example of work customarily done on the **Sabbath** without any objection.

DOVE. A small bird of the *columbidae* family that was domesticated in biblical times. The image of the dove is used in connection with the descent of the **Holy Spirit** on Jesus at his **baptism** by **John** (Matt 3:16; Mark 1:10; Luke 3:22; John 1:32) and may have evoked memories of the OT creation account (Gen 1:2) and flood narrative (Gen 8:8–12). The Spirit's dove-like descent stands alongside the images of the opening of the **heavens** and the **voice from the heavens** to develop the theme of the new and better communication between **God** and humankind made possible through Jesus.

DREAMS. In the OT, dreams are often used as vehicles of divine communication from Jacob (Gen 28:10–22) and Joseph (Gen 37:5–11) to **Daniel**, though in some other texts (Deut 13:1–5; Sir 34:7) dreams are regarded with suspicion. In the NT dreams are most prominent in **Matthew's Gospel**. In the **infancy narrative, God** communicates by dreams with **Joseph** (Matt 1:20, 2:13, 2:19, 2:22) and the **Magi** (2:12). And in Matt 27:19, **Pilate**'s wife sends word to him during the **trial of Jesus**, "Have nothing to do with that innocent man, for today I have suffered a great deal because of a dream about him."

– E –

ELIJAH. The ninth-century BCE **prophet** whose exploits are described in 1 Kings 17–19 and 21, and 2 Kings 1–2. The account of his assumption into **heaven** (2 Kgs 2:1–12) led to speculations about his return before "the great and terrible **day of the Lord**" (Mal 4:5–6). In the **Gospels** Elijah is expected by some to be the **Messiah** (Matt 6:14–15; Mark 8:27–28; Luke 9:7–8) or at least to prepare the way for the Messiah. By his dress and diet, **John the Baptist** placed himself in the tradition of Elijah (Mark 1:6; Matt 3:4), and according to Luke 1:17 the **angel Gabriel** prophesied that John would be the precursor of the Messiah even before he was born. In Luke 4:25–26, Jesus cites Elijah's example in ministering to non-Jews (1 Kgs 17:8–16), and Elijah along with **Moses** appears as a witness at the **transfiguration** of Jesus (Matt 17:3; Mark 9:4; Luke 9:30).

ELISHA. The **disciple** of and successor to **Elijah**. His exploits as a **prophet** and **miracle** worker are described mainly in 2 Kgs 2–8 (see also 1 Kgs 19:19–21 and 13:14–21). In Luke 4:27 Jesus cites Elisha's healing the **leprosy** of Naaman the Syrian (see 2 Kgs 5:1–19) as a precedent for a Jewish prophet ministering to a non-Jew, thus preparing for the story of the spread of Jesus' movement described in Acts.

ELIZABETH. The wife of **Zechariah** the **priest** and mother of **John the Baptist.** According to Luke 1:5–7, she belonged to a priestly family and was religiously very observant, but was sterile and getting on in years. She attributed her conception of John to divine favor (1:25). On being visited by her relative **Mary** (1:36), Elizabeth declared Mary to be "blessed among **women**" and addressed her as "the mother of my **Lord**" (1:39–45). At John's **circumcision** (1:59–66), Elizabeth gave him the name "John," and her choice was affirmed by her husband Zechariah.

EMMANUEL. A Hebrew name meaning "**God** [= *El*] is with us [= *immanu*]), taken over from the quotation of Isa 7:14 in Matt 1:23 and applied to Jesus at his **virginal conception**. Its translation as "God is with us" prepares for the risen Jesus' promise at the end of **Matthew's Gospel**, "I am with you always, to the end of the age" (Matt 28:20).

ENTRY INTO JERUSALEM. According to Matt 21:1–9, Mark 11:1–10, Luke 19:28–38, and John 12:12–19, Jesus entered **Jerusalem** at the beginning of Holy Week (**Palm Sunday**) in a triumphal procession while riding a young **donkey**. This symbolic action served to fulfill the **messianic** prophecy in Zech 9:9, "Lo your king comes to you, triumphant and victorious is he, **humble** and riding on a donkey, on a colt, the foal of a donkey." According to the **Gospel** accounts, Jesus was received with great rejoicing on the **crowd's** part, who greeted him with the words of Ps 118:25–26 and spread palm branches before him. The detailed planning of the event on Jesus' part suggests that it was intended as a prophetic demonstration in line with the tactics of the great OT **prophets**. While the Evangelists give the impression of a very large crowd, it is more likely that only a small percentage of the population of Jerusalem witnessed the event. However, it surely would have come to the attention of both the Jewish and the Roman officials, and contributed greatly to Jesus' **arrest** and execution.

EPHPHATHA. An Aramaic imperative verb meaning "be opened." It appears in Mark 7:34, in the account of Jesus healing a man who was deaf and barely able to speak. While it may well represent the actual word of Jesus, in the context of the Greek **Gospel** of **Mark** it seems to function as something like a "magic word."

ESCHATOLOGICAL DISCOURSE. The last extensive speech of Jesus in the **Synoptic Gospels** (Mark 13; Matthew 24–25; Luke 21) is often called the "Little **Apocalypse**" in distinction from the Great Apocalypse (the book of **Revelation**). In **Mark**'s version Jesus describes the course of future events and a climactic cosmic transformation issuing in the coming of the glorious **Son of Man**, the general **resurrection**, and the **Last Judgment**. At the end he urges constant vigilance, since "about that day and hour no one knows" (13:32). While taking over much of the material in Mark 13, **Luke** urges his readers to see in these events their own vindication "because your redemption is drawing near" (21:28). **Matthew** also draws extensively on Mark 13 but supplements it with a series of **parables** about the need for constant watchfulness and concludes with the judgment scene in Matt 25:31–46. Many scholars believe that Mark has used a Palestinian apocalyptic scenario as his base text and integrated it into his **Gospel**. The major critical question is, How much of this material came from Jesus? There is no consensus about the precise form and extent of that source.

ESCHATOLOGY. Derived from the Greek word for "last things" (*eschata*), the term in the context of Judaism in Jesus' time and the NT refers to the end of human history and the **resurrection of the dead**, the **Last Judgment**, rewards and punishments, and eternal life in the **kingdom of God**. These teachings are often conveyed in **apocalypses** such as the book of **Daniel**, *1 Enoch, 4 Ezra* (2 Esdras 3–14), and *2 Baruch*, as well as the Synoptic Apocalypse (Mark 13; Matt 24–25; Luke 21) and the book of **Revelation**. Moreover, eschatological thinking permeates the **Dead Sea Scrolls**, other early Jewish writings, and the NT as a whole. The central theme of Jesus' **teaching** and activity—the kingdom of **God**—is an eschatological concept. Much of his teaching concerned how best to prepare for the coming kingdom. His **miracles** and other activities are best understood as previews or anticipations of that kingdom (see Luke 11:20, 17:21). Mark 1:15 is an apt summary of Jesus' ministry in terms of eschatology: "The time is fulfilled, and the kingdom of God has come near; **repent** and believe in the good news."

ESSENES. A Jewish religious movement active in the Land of **Israel** from 150 BCE to 70 CE. Although many etymologies have been offered, those associating the Essenes with the "pious" and "healers" seem most likely. They were variously described by Philo, **Josephus**, Pliny, Hippolytus, and Epiphanius. The group that lived at **Qumran** and preserved the most important of the **Dead Sea Scrolls** was identified in the mid-twentieth century as Essenes, and most scholars today accept that identification. Thus some of the various community rules found at Qumran may provide firsthand accounts of Essene life and history (*Rule of the Community, Damascus Document, Thanksgiving Hymns, Pesharim*, etc.). While there are many parallels between the Qumran scrolls and the **Gospels**, and while **John the Baptist** may have been associated with them (Luke 1:80), there are no clear references to the Essenes in the Gospels and no evidence of their direct influence on Jesus.

ETHICS. Taken from Greek philosophy, the term refers to customs, norms, and behaviors that will presumably lead one to personal happiness and the common good. Jesus in the **Gospels** seems mainly concerned with character formation rather than setting forth precise rules and regulations. Central to his ethical program are the two OT commandments about **love** of **God** (Deut 6:5) and love of neighbor (Lev 19:18). On these two principles hang all the Law and the Prophets (Matt 22:34–40; Mark 12:28–34; Luke 10:25–37). The **Sermon on the Plain** (Luke 6:20–49) and the **Sermon on the Mount** (Matt 5:1–7:29) are often taken as summaries of Jesus' ethical **teachings**. However, these teachings cannot be separated from the narratives about Jesus (the Gospels) in which he appears as the best example of his own teachings. In teaching his followers, Jesus makes no sharp distinction between law and love. And the horizon and goal of his ethical teachings is hope for the fullness of life in **God's kingdom**.

EVIL. In the OT evil refers to human or communal corruption and immorality and is often associated with idolatry and violation of **God**'s **covenant** with **Israel**. Likewise, in the **Gospels** the term "evil" refers often to moral corruption. For Jesus, evil originates in the person's heart and manifests itself in evil deeds (Mark 7:20–23; Matt 15:18–20). He distinguishes between good and evil persons (Matt 7:15–20, 12:33–37) and describes his opponents as belonging to "an evil and adulterous generation" (Matt 12:39). But the Gospels (and other Jewish writings of the time) assume the existence of **Satan** as "the Evil One" and the **demons** as his subordinates, and that these figures are Jesus' ultimate opponents in the cosmic and **eschatological** combat that will issue in the full coming of **God's kingdom** and the abolition of evil entirely. It is difficult to know whether to interpret the final petition in the **Lord's Prayer** in Matt 6:13 as a **prayer** for deliverance from "evil" or from "the Evil One."

EXORCISM. In **Mark's Gospel** there are four substantial narratives in which Jesus performs an exorcism: the man with the unclean spirit in the **synagogue** (1:23–26), the **Gerasene** demoniac (5:1–20), the **Syrophoenician woman**'s daughter (7:24–30), and the boy with the unclean spirit (9:14–29). Exorcisms are also mentioned in various summaries of Jesus' actions (1:34, 1:39, 3:11, etc.). In the extended narratives there is some struggle, and the **demons** recognize Jesus' power over them (1:24, 5:12). Jesus heals the possessed persons immediately and completely. According to Matt 12:28 and Luke 11:20, Jesus' ability to cast out demons is a **sign** that "the **kingdom of God** has come upon you." When Jesus' followers perform exorcisms (Luke 10:17–20; Acts 16:16–18), they do so "in the name of Jesus." The ultimate power by which Jesus performs his exorcisms—**God** or **Satan**?—becomes a topic of debate between him and his opponents (Matt 12:25–37; Mark 3:23–30; Luke 11:17–23).

– F –

FAITH. In the **Synoptic Gospels** the terms "believe" and "faith" occur frequently in **miracle** stories with regard to Jesus' power to bring healing (Mark 3:25, 5:34, 9:23–24, 10:52, etc.). They also refer to the authority of Jesus as **Messiah** and **God**'s Son and his message ("believe in the good news," Mark 1:15). Yet even those close to Jesus struggle with faith in him. In **Mark's Gospel**, his family thinks that he is "out of his mind" (3:21). And when Jesus stills the storm, he upbraids his **disciples** for their lack of faith (4:40; see also 8:14–21). In **Matthew's Gospel** the disciples are accused repeatedly of having only "little faith" (Matt 6:30, 8:26, 14:31, 16:8, 17:20). However, having faith even as small as a **mustard seed** is acknowledged as capable of producing great results (Matt 17:20). In **John's Gospel** the verb "believe" appears nearly a hundred times, and its object is generally Jesus himself and the relationship to his **Father** that he brings. There is a lively debate among scholars today about whether **Paul**'s expression "the faith of Christ" refers to faith in Christ (objective genitive) or the faith or trust that Jesus himself displayed in his Father and his plan (subjective genitive).

FAREWELL DISCOURSE. In Jewish writings in Jesus' time, the farewell discourse or testament was a common literary form. In a testament a dying hero looks into the future and offers advice to his listeners on how to conduct themselves here and now. In his **Last Supper** narrative **Luke** has constructed a brief testament for Jesus out of traditional materials (Luke 22:24–39). But the most extensive farewell discourses of Jesus appear in John 14–17. After washing his **disciples**' feet and prophesying about his disciples' **betrayals** of him in John 13, Jesus provides a series of four farewell discourses. He first assures his disciples about the importance of faith and **love**, and promises that they will receive divine help in his physical absence (14:1–31). Next he stresses that love should prevail within the community of his followers and warns them about the hatred they will experience from outside (15:1–16:4). Then he reflects on why it is good for them that he depart, on their sorrow at his departure and their joy over his return, and on his use of figurative and plain speech (16:5–33). Finally he prays for himself, for his disciples, and for those who come to believe through them (17:1–26). Throughout these speeches Jesus explains how his disciples can carry on the movement he began. They can do so through faith in Jesus, through love for one another, and through the help of the **Advocate**/Paraclete (that is, the **Holy Spirit**). He promises that the Advocate "will teach you everything, and remind you of all that I have said to you" (John 14:26). The Spirit will serve as the stand-in or replacement for the earthly Jesus. The Johannine Christians did not make sharp distinctions between the words of the earthly Jesus, those of Spirit-inspired **prophets** who spoke in Jesus' name, and the work of transmission and interpretation that went on in the Johannine school or circle. The critical historical question regarding the Johannine farewell discourses is, How much goes back to the earthly Jesus, and how much is the product of the Johannine community?

FASTING. While the only regular fast prescribed in the OT is on the Day of **Atonement**, fasts were undertaken on special occasions or crises (see Joel 1:14, 2:12, 2:15) or as a sign of special devotion (Isa 58:3). In the **Gospels**, Jesus fasts for 40 days and nights (Matt 4:2) before undertaking his public ministry. Both the **Pharisees** and the **disciples** of **John the Baptist** undertook devotional fasts (Mark 2:18), and in Luke 18:12 the Pharisee boasts in his **prayer** that he fasts twice a week. In Matt 6:16–18 Jesus approves fasting but insists that it not be done ostentatiously merely in order to gain a public reputation for holiness. In Mark 2:18–20, Jesus defends his disciples when their failure to fast is questioned by Pharisees and disciples of John the Baptist. He contends that his time is a special moment of joy and celebration (like a wedding party) but allows that when he (the **bridegroom**) is taken away, then his followers can and will fast. The early Christian writing called the *Didache* in 8:1 directs Christians to fast on Wednesdays and Fridays, but not on Mondays and Thursdays as the **hypocrites** (Pharisees) do.

FATHER. *See* ABBA.

FEEDING MIRACLES. The OT model is the prophet **Elisha**'s miraculous feeding of 200 persons in 2 Kgs 4:42–44. Jesus' miraculous feeding of 5,000 persons appears in all four **Gospels**: Matt 14:13–21,

Mark 6:32–44, Luke 9:10–17, and John 6:1–15. His **miraculous** feeding of 4,000 persons is described in Matt 15:32–39 and Mark 8:1–10. In each case a **crowd** had been with Jesus for some time, and there was apparently not enough food in the area to feed them. When Jesus tells his **disciples** to feed the crowd, all they can find are five loaves and two **fish** in the first case and seven loaves and a few fish in the second case. Nevertheless, Jesus miraculously multiplies the food, feeds the crowd, and has a large amount of leftovers. The two feedings seem to be doublets or twin versions of the same event. The fact that all four Evangelists included the narrative in their Gospels (and two of them did it twice) indicates that they regarded this episode as very significant. However, the precise nature of the event (and its historicity) is hard to pin down. On the one hand, the idea that Jesus simply persuaded a crowd to share their food with one another seems shallow and rationalistic. On the other hand, there is clearly much theological symbolism in these accounts, and they obviously point forward to the **Last Supper** and to the **messianic** banquet as an image of fullness of life in **God's kingdom** (see Matt 8:11–12, 22:1–10).

FESTIVALS. The OT calendar of Jewish festivals appears in Lev 23. The **Gospels** portray Jesus as observing and participating in the celebration of the **Sabbath** (e.g., Luke 4:16–30). His quarrel with the **Pharisees** concerns what exactly constitutes work on the Sabbath (e.g., Matt 12:1–14). In Luke 2:41–52 the boy Jesus along with his parents makes a pilgrimage to **Jerusalem** at **Passover**. In the **Synoptic Gospels** the adult Jesus and his **disciples** make only one pilgrimage to Jerusalem at Passover, while in **John's Gospel** there are three Passovers during Jesus' public ministry (John 2:13, 2:23, 6:4, 11:55). Chapters 5–10 in John's Gospel correlate events in Jesus' public ministry with the Sabbath (5:1–47), Passover (6:1–71), Tabernacles (7:1–10:21), and Dedication/Hanukkah (10:22–39), respectively. All the Gospels place the **death of Jesus** at Passover.

FIG TREE. Common in ancient **Israel**, fig trees are often mentioned in the OT alongside vines, pomegranates, and olive trees. In John 1:48–50, Jesus impresses **Nathanael** with his knowledge that he had seen Nathanael under a fig tree. In teaching about **God**'s patience and loving care in awaiting the **repentance** of **sinners**, Jesus in Luke 13:6–9 tells a **parable** about a barren fig tree brought back to fertility. In his **eschatological discourse** (Matt 24:32; Mark 13:28; Luke 21:29), Jesus assumes that his listeners are familiar with the growth cycle of the fig tree. All this background makes especially puzzling the episode of Jesus cursing a fig tree in Mark 11:12–14, 11:20–21 (Matt 21:18–20). One could expect that a fig tree in Palestine would have leaves in April but fruit only in June. However, in not finding fruit on a fig tree at **Passover** time (early April), Jesus curses the tree ("May no one ever eat fruit from you again"), and on the next day it is found withered from the root. His destructive and apparently irrational action is the only "**miracle**" that he performs in **Jerusalem** according to the **Synoptic Gospels**. Perhaps the best explanation is that the withered fig tree symbolizes the failure by many in Israel to accept Jesus as God's messenger and his message about **God's kingdom**. The "event" may have originated from something like the parable of the barren fig tree in Luke 13:6–9.

FIRE. In the **Gospels**, "fire" appears frequently as either a natural agent of destruction (Matt 3:12, 7:19, 13:40, etc.) or a symbolic representation of **suffering** for the wicked in "hell" (Matt 18:8–9; Mark 9:43, etc.). However, in Matt 3:11/Luke 3:16, **John the Baptist** points forward to the one (Jesus) who will baptize "in the **Holy Spirit** and fire." Here the reference seems to be to the refining fire of the **day of the Lord** in Zech 13:9 (see 1 Cor 3:13–15). For the connection between the Holy Spirit and fire, see the Pentecost account in Acts 2:3.

FISH. Since much of Jesus' public ministry took place near the **Sea of Galilee** (then as now a major fishing center), it is not surprising that Jesus would refer to fish in his **teachings** about **God**'s willingness to answer **prayers** of petition (Matt 7:10/Luke 11:11) and about the divine judgment what will accompany the **kingdom of God** (Matt 13:47–50). Fish are served in the various accounts of the multiplication of the loaves (Mark 6:30–44 parr.) and at **meals** where the risen Jesus appears to his **disciples** (Luke 24:42; John 21:9–14). In early Christian circles the fish became a symbol for Jesus on the basis of an acrostic formed by the letters of the Greek word for "fish" (*ichthus*), which was taken to mean "Jesus Christ, God's Son, **Savior**."

FISHERMEN. The first disciples of Jesus—**Peter** and **Andrew**, **James** and **John**—were fishermen (Matt 4:18; Mark 1:16; Luke 5:2). According to Luke 5:1–11, Peter and the others followed Jesus on the basis of a **miraculous** catch of **fish** that he directed. The first **disciples** were commercial fishermen, presumably capable of reading and writing at least at the level of their business needs. The description of Peter and John in Acts 4:13 as "uneducated and ordinary men" should not be taken too literally. Jesus' commission of them to become "fishers of men" (Matt 4:19; Mark 1:17) not only alludes to their occupation but perhaps also to Jer 16:16 ("I am now sending many fishermen, says the **Lord**"). In Matt 17:24–27, Jesus directs Peter to catch a fish with a coin in its mouth to pay the temple tax. And in John 21:1–14 the risen Jesus meets seven disciples (including Peter, James, and John) who had returned to fishing in the **Sea of Galilee**, and performs for them another miraculous catch of fish.

FOOTWASHING. At the beginning of the **Last Supper**, according to John 13:1–20 only, Jesus, knowing that **Judas** had **betrayed** him and that he was going to die, laid aside his outer garment and proceeded to wash the feet of his **disciples**. Such an action was proper to a slave or lowly servant, not to a distinguished religious teacher like Jesus. As a prelude to Jesus' **passion** and **death**, his action receives two interpretations. First, when **Peter** refuses to let Jesus wash his feet, Jesus uses it to illustrate the necessity of being willing to accept the **salvation** that will become available through his shameful death on the **cross** (13:6–11). Then he interprets the footwashing as an example of his own ideal of leadership as the **humble** service of others (13:12–17).

FORGIVENESS OF SINS. In the OT it is **God** who forgives sins (Exod 34:7). In both versions of the **Lord's Prayer** (Matt 6:12; Luke 11:4), Jesus urges his followers to pray for the forgiveness of their sins and in return to be willing to forgive one another's sins. The interrelationship between the two is dramatized in the **parable** of the Unforgiving Servant in Matt 18:23–35. In Mark 2:1–12, Jesus' declaration that the sins of the paralyzed man are forgiven leads the **scribes** to accuse him of **blasphemy**. Again in Luke 7:36–50, Jesus' declaration that the "sinful woman" has been forgiven inspires questions about his real identity ("Who is this who even forgives sins?"). The power to forgive sins is handed on to the community by the earthly Jesus in Matt 18:21–22 and by the risen Jesus in John 20:23. The **unforgivable sin** (Mark 3:28–29) seems to involve attributing the work of the **Holy Spirit** (active in and through Jesus) to **Satan** or some other **evil** force.

FORM CRITICISM. Applied to the **Gospels** and the historical study of Jesus, form criticism refers to the process of identifying the literary forms in which the traditions about Jesus incorporated in the Gospels were formulated and handed on in early Christian circles. It also seeks to establish the history of how, where, when, and why these small units originated and were transmitted in written and oral forms. The discourse forms include **parables**, proverbs, **aphorisms**, prophetic and **apocalyptic** sayings, **beatitudes**, **prayers**, warnings, apothegms, and so on. The narrative forms include healings, **exorcisms**, and **nature miracles**. In research on Jesus, form criticism has been more successful as a literary tool in illuminating the rhetorical devices with which Jesus in the Gospels communicates his message than as a historical tool for determining the history of the early **church** and of events in Jesus' life. *See also* ORAL TRADITION.

FRINGES. According to Num 15:38–39 and Deut 22:12, Jews were to wear fringes (or tassels) on the corners of their outer garments. According to Matt 9:20 and 14:36, Jesus observed this commandment. He does, however, criticize the **scribes** and **Pharisees** in Matt 23:5 for "making their fringes long," thus calling undue attention to themselves as especially religious persons.

FUNK, ROBERT W. (1926–2005). Professor of NT at Vanderbilt Divinity School and the University of Montana, and founder of the **Jesus Seminar**. In *Honest to Jesus: Jesus for a New Millennium* (1996), Funk defined the goal of the **quest for the historical Jesus** as "to set Jesus free, to liberate him from prevailing captivities," which include the Christian theological tradition, biblical scholars, popular piety, and the NT itself. For Funk, the proper starting point for the "renewed" quest for Jesus is the corpus of non-**apocalyptic parables** along with the proverbs and **aphorisms** attributed to Jesus in the

Sayings Source **Q** and the *Gospel of Thomas*. Jesus was certain that **God**'s rule was already present, and his task was to help people see it. According to Funk, central to Jesus' program were **love** of enemies, an unbrokered (or unmediated) relationship with God, and trust in God's ability and desire to provide for human needs.

– G –

GABBATHA. The place of the judge's bench in **Jerusalem** where according to John 19:13 **Pilate** sat and acceded to the **crowd**'s wishes to have Jesus condemned and crucified. While clearly an Aramaic word, its etymology is disputed, though there is some connection with an elevated area or ridge. *Gabbatha* was most likely a raised, paved area outside of **Herod the Great**'s palace at the western edge of the city, where the Roman governor stayed during **Passover** and other **festivals**. The place was also known as "Lithostratos," a Greek term meaning "Stone Pavement."

GABRIEL. The **angel** who reveals end-time mysteries in Dan 8:15–26 and 9:21–27, and announces the births of **John the Baptist** and Jesus in Luke 1:11–20 and 1:26–38, respectively. He describes John as destined to become like **Elijah** (1:17), and Jesus as chosen to be the Davidic **Messiah** and **Son of God** and to be born of the **Holy Spirit** (1:32–33, 1:35).

GADARA. A city of the **Decapolis**, identified with modern Umm Qeis, some five to six miles southeast of the **Sea of Galilee**. According to Matt 8:28–34, Jesus performed an **exorcism** there on two men possessed by **demons** and drove a herd of pigs (now possessed by the demons) into the sea. How the demons got to the sea from Gadara is hard to imagine, unless a vague use of "Gadarene territory" is supposed. The problem is even greater in Mark 5:1–20 (and Luke 8:26–39) where the same or similar event takes place at **Gerasa**, more than 30 miles southeast of the sea.

GALILEE. The northern part of ancient **Israel**, bounded by Lebanon and Syria on the north, the Mediterranean Sea to the west, **Samaria**

to the south, and the **Sea of Galilee** and the Jordan River to the east. Jesus was raised in **Nazareth** in Galilee (Mark 6:1; John 1:46), and much of his early public ministry took place in Galilee, with **Capernaum** serving as his headquarters (Mark 2:1). Those who lived in the district were called "Galileans" and could be recognized by their distinctive dialect or accent, at least in the case of **Peter** (Mark 14:70; Luke 22:59).

GALILEE, SEA OF. A freshwater lake in northern **Israel**, part of the Jordan River system, 14.5 km (9 mi.) long and 8 km (5 mi.) wide. It is harp-shaped (and thus the alternative names Chinnereth and Gennesarat) and was a fertile fishing area. Jesus' first **disciples** were **fishermen** based in **Capernaum** (Mark 1:16–20), and much of his early ministry took place around the Sea of **Galilee**. According to Mark 4:35–41 and Matt 8:18–27, Jesus displayed divine power in stilling a sudden and fierce storm at sea there.

GEHENNA. The term referred first to the "Valley of Hinnom," situated west and south of **Jerusalem** and running into the village of Silwan. In OT times, it seems to have functioned as a place of pagan worship and even **child sacrifice** (2 Kgs 23:10; Jer 32:35), and perhaps eventually became a dump. However, by NT times, "Gehenna" had become in Jewish circles a term for what we call "hell" or "hell-fire," the place of punishment to which **sinners** go after their death. This is the sense that it carries in various sayings attributed to Jesus; see Matt 5:22, 5:29–30, 10:28, 18:9, 23:15, 23:33; Mark 9:43, 9:45, 9:47; Luke 12:5.

GENEALOGY OF JESUS. A genealogy is the record of a person's heritage from a series of ancestors. It may be segmented (taking account of several figures in a single generation) or linear (listing one figure in each generation). The most important OT (linear) genealogies appear in Genesis and Chronicles. It is always important to reckon with the particular function or purpose that a genealogy serves. The two genealogies of Jesus in Matt 1:1–17 and Luke 3:23–38 are linear in form. **Matthew** highlights Jesus' roots in **Israel**'s history and his identity as the descendant of **Abraham** and the **Son of David**. With regard to Matthew's genealogy, the most important OT

sources are in 1 Chr 2–3 (for names from Abraham to the Babylonian exile) and Ruth 4:18–22 (for names from Perez to David, and for the formal pattern of "A was the **father** of B"). It consists of three sections with 14 members each (7 x 2 = 14): from Abraham to David, from David to the exile, and from the exile to Jesus. This neat pattern is interrupted by the inclusion of four **women**—Tamar, Rahab, Ruth, and the wife of Uriah (Bathsheba)—whose surprising stories prepare for the most unusual (**virginal**) **birth** of Jesus from **Mary**. **Luke** presents Jesus as the Son of **Adam** and **Son of God**, thus stressing his universal significance for humankind. His genealogy moves backward from Jesus to Adam, traces Jesus' descent from David through Nathan rather than **Solomon**, and gives **Joseph**'s father's name as Eli rather than Jacob. Both genealogies present Joseph as a descendant of David and the legal father of Jesus but suggest that he was not his biological father. Efforts at reconciling or harmonizing all the details in the two genealogies have never been totally convincing.

GENERATION. In the **genealogy of Jesus** (Matt 1:1–17) and Mary's *Magnificat* (Luke 1:46–55), "generation" is used in its neutral sense of a time-span of some 30 or 40 years. However, in many of Jesus' sayings in the **Synoptic Gospels** "this generation" carries a negative connotation (Mark 8:12; Matt 11:16; Luke 7:31, etc.) and is sometimes qualified with adjectives such as "**evil**," "adulterous," "faithless," and "perverse" (Matt 12:39, 17:17, etc.). The expression refers to those who fail to understand and accept Jesus' message, and its contexts suggest some frustration on his part. In the three versions of his **eschatological discourse**, Jesus promises that "this generation will not pass away until all these things have taken place" (Mark 13:30; Matt 24:34; Luke 21:32). The most obvious meaning seems to be that it refers to the imminent return (**Parousia**) of Jesus as the glorious **Son of Man**.

GENNESARAT. The name of the plain south of **Capernaum** (Mark 6:53; Matt 14:34), which is also applied in Luke 5:1 to the lake adjacent to it ("the Lake of Gennesarat" or the **Sea of Galilee**).

GENTILES. A general term for non-Jewish persons. In **Matthew's Gospel** it is sometimes used pejoratively (6:7, 18:17), though that

same Gospel reaches its climax with the risen Jesus' commission in 28:19 to make **disciples** of "all the nations" (*panta ta ethne*). During his public ministry, however, the Matthean Jesus warns his disciples to "go nowhere among the Gentiles" (10:5). The four **Gospels** agree that Jesus confined his ministry generally to the Land of **Israel** and his fellow Jews. A notable exception is Jesus' encounter with the **Syrophoenician**/Canaanite woman (Mark 7:24–30; Matt 15:21–28) when Jesus in **Tyrian** territory gets bested in debate by a Gentile woman and agrees to heal her daughter. Likewise, in healing a **centurion**'s servant (Matt 8:5–13; Luke 7:1–10; see John 4:46–54), Jesus accedes to a Gentile's request and remarks that "not even in Israel have I found such faith." Moreover, his vision of the coming **kingdom of God** included persons from all over the world, joining the great **banquet** with all the saints of Israel (Matt 8:11–12; Luke 13:28–29).

GERASA. A city of the **Decapolis**, identified with modern Jerash in Jordan, north of Amman. According to Mark 5:1 and Luke 8:26, it was the site of Jesus' **exorcism** of the man possessed by many **demons** ("**Legion**"). In Matt 8:28 the name is changed to **Gadara**. In either case, the place is outside the traditional boundaries of **Israel** and a substantial distance from the **Sea of Galilee** (as is Gadara).

GETHSEMANE. The place on or near the **Mount of Olives**, east of **Jerusalem**, where Jesus offered his **prayer** after his **Last Supper** and before his **arrest** and **betrayal** (Mark 14:32; Matt 26:36). The name means "oil press."

GNOSTICISM. The term has been used since the eighteenth century to describe a variety of ancient and modern religious and philosophical movements characterized by their attempts to transcend material limitations by retrieving their spark of divinity and returning to the highest god through reception of genuine knowledge about the human condition (spirit immersed in matter) and the possibility of restoration to the true god. The designation has been applied to many of the mainly early Christian documents discovered at **Nag Hammadi** in Egypt, which are mainly Coptic translations of Greek originals from the second and third centuries, and found in several other codices (Askew, Bruce, Berlin). Indirect testimonies include the somewhat hostile descriptions of various gnostic groups by Irenaeus, Hippolytus, Epiphanius, and other orthodox writers. These brands of gnosticism combine threads from Neoplatonism, Judaism, and Christianity in various proportions. These documents are more important for understanding Christianity in the second and third centuries than for gaining knowledge about Jesus. However, some scholars have suggested that **John, Paul**, and other NT writers may have had contact with such movements in their very early phases.

GOD. The God revealed in the Hebrew Scriptures, especially in Isa 40–55, is the God and Father of Jesus Christ—that is, creator, **lord**, and god of all things—who has entered into a covenantal relationship with **Israel** as the people of God. The central theme of Jesus' preaching and activity was the **kingdom of God**, that moment when all creation will acknowledge and proclaim God as the all Holy One (see Mark 1:15; Matt 6:9–13). The **Gospels** emphasize repeatedly that Jesus referred to God as his Father (**Abba**) and that he encouraged his followers to use similar language and to relate to God as their Father too. Their insistence on these points suggests that Jesus enjoyed a particularly intense and intimate personal relationship with God to the point that he apparently regarded himself as "the **Son of God**" in a very special **way** and taught others to share in that relationship of intimacy. While regarding the kingdom of God as at least in part a present reality (Luke 11:20, 17:21), he also urged his followers to hope for something far greater from God in the future ("Thy kingdom come").

GOD'S KINGDOM. *See* KINGDOM OF GOD/HEAVEN.

GOLDEN RULE. The traditional title given to Jesus' saying in Luke 6:31: "Do to others as you would have them do to you." A somewhat elaborated version appears in Matt 7:12: "In everything do to others as you would have them do to you; for this is the law and the prophets." What is often put forward as unique to Jesus is in fact rooted in the OT and has many parallels in Jewish and other writings from Jesus' time. The theological basis of the Golden Rule is found in Lev 19:18: "You shall **love** your neighbor as yourself." A negative formulation appears in Tobit 4:15 ("Do to no one what you yourself dislike"), and a similar teaching is attributed to **Rabbi** Hillel. This is sometimes called the "Silver Rule." Theologians and philosophers debate the extent to which the Golden Rule goes beyond enlightened self-interest and how it fits with Jesus' more challenging **teaching** about love of enemies (see Luke 6:32–36).

GOLGOTHA. The place of Jesus' crucifixion and **death** in **Jerusalem** according to Matt 27:33, Mark 15:22, Luke 23:33, and John 19:17. The word means "the place of a skull" in Aramaic (= Calvaria in Latin), and probably refers both to its hilly terrain and its use as a place of execution. While in Jesus' time it was outside the city walls, it has been identified since the fourth century CE as within the city walls, in the Church of the Holy Sepulcher. *See also* CALVARY.

GOOD SAMARITAN, PARABLE OF THE (LUKE 10:25–37). When a lawyer asks Jesus how he might inherit eternal life, Jesus elicits from him the two great biblical commandments of loving **God** (Deut 6:4–5) and loving the neighbor (Lev 19:18). When the lawyer inquires, "Who is my neighbor?" Jesus tells the story of a man traveling from **Jerusalem** to **Jericho** who is beaten, robbed, and left for dead. He is first passed by and ignored by a Jewish **priest** and a Levite. But a **Samaritan** (someone whose Jewishness was suspect) not only stops and tends to his wounds but also brings him to an inn and agrees to pay his expenses during recovery. Jesus then elicits from the lawyer the answer that the one who helped the wounded man (the Samaritan) proved to be his neighbor. Jesus in turn challenges the lawyer to "go and do likewise." Thus the parable expands the biblical understanding of "neighbor" beyond fellow Jews to include everyone in need of help.

GOSPEL. The traditional rendering of the Greek term *euangelion* ("good news"), a word used frequently by **Mark** (see 1:1, 1:14, 1:15, 8:35, 10:29, 13:10, 14:9) to describe the good news about what **God** has done through Jesus' life, **death**, and **resurrection**. There are precedents for the term in the Greek OT (2 Sam 4:10, 18:19–20; Isa 40:9, 52:7) as well as in secular Greek in relation to the birthday of the Roman emperor Augustus. **Paul** used the term frequently to summarize the significance of Jesus (1 Thess 1:2–9; 1 Cor 15:1–11, etc.). It is likely that Mark knew the Pauline tradition, and so he included the word in the heading of his own work, "The beginning of the good news of Jesus Christ, the **Son of God**" (1:1). Through Mark's usage, the word came to describe the early Christian literary genre of a connected and substantial narrative about Jesus. While the Gospels include elements from the Greco-Roman biographical tradition, their literary models also included the narrative sections of the OT about **Moses**, Samson, Samuel, **David**, and **Elijah** and **Elisha**. The four Gospels contained in the Christian **canon** of Scripture are associated with the names of **Matthew**, Mark, **Luke**, and **John**. These substantial narratives about Jesus were written from the perspective of beliefs about his identity as the Son of God and about the saving significance of his death and resurrection. Although the Evangelists regarded Jesus as a good example, he was to them far greater than that. The **apocryphal Gospels** generally fill in perceived "gaps" in the **canonical Gospels**, especially with regard to Jesus' birth and **infancy** and to his **passion** and death. The **Nag Hammadi Gospels** purport to reveal Jesus' "secret" or esoteric teachings, often in a postresurrection setting.

GOSPEL OF TRUTH. This **gnostic** meditation on the person and work of Jesus was preserved in a Coptic version in the **Nag Hammadi** codices. It is "**gospel**" in the sense of "good news" about Jesus as the eternal and divine Son, the Word who reveals the **Father** and passes on knowledge, especially self-knowledge. By means of such knowledge, gnostics learn that they are of divine origin and that their knowledge of the Father brings them joy and wholeness. While not a narrative like the four **canonical Gospels**, this work alludes to them and reads them from a gnostic perspective. The Greek original was probably produced in Valentinian gnostic circles in the latter half of the second century. It tells us little or nothing about the historical figure of Jesus.

GOSPELS, CANONICAL. Derived from the Greek word for "good news" (*euangelion*), the four canonical Gospels—**Matthew, Mark, Luke**, and **John**—tell the story of Jesus' life, **death**, and **resurrection**. None of the four Gospels explicitly identifies its author; the traditional ascriptions seem to have been added to the manuscripts in the second century. According to Christian tradition, Matthew and John were members of the **twelve apostles**, and Mark was associated with **Peter** and **Paul** and Luke with Paul. The four **Gospels** look like biographies of Jesus, and in antiquity readers would have assumed that they were such (though the claims made about Jesus transcended the conventions of the biography genre). The first three Gospels offer a "common view " of Jesus and so are called "**Synoptic**," while John represents an independent tradition with a different cast of characters, reflects a different **chronology**, and portrays Jesus as speaking in long discourses.

GREAT SUPPER, PARABLE OF THE. In Luke 14:15–24 Jesus tells the story of a man who prepared a great feast and invited many people. But those invited gave various excuses and refused to come. Angered at their rejection, the host orders that all kinds of persons be brought in and declares that "none of those who were invited will taste my dinner" (14:25). The **parable** highlights the importance of accepting the invitation to **God's kingdom** being offered by Jesus. In the version preserved in Matt 22:1–10, the **banquet** becomes a royal wedding banquet for the king's son (the **Messiah**), the excuses are flimsy, the invitees abuse and kill the king's messengers (the **Prophets**), the king has the city destroyed (**Jerusalem** in 70 CE), and the hall is filled with other guests. The **Matthean** version is generally understood to be the Evangelist's rewriting of the parable in light of Jesus' **death** and the destruction of Jerusalem. The parable of the **Wedding Garment** is added on in Matt 22:11–14.

GRIESBACH HYPOTHESIS. Associated with the eighteenth-century German scholar J. J. Griesbach and revived in the second half of the twentieth century, this solution to the problem of the relationships among the **Synoptic Gospels** proposes that **Matthew** was the first written **Gospel**, that **Luke** used Matthew, and that **Mark** used both Matthew and Luke. While effective in explaining the agreements on a logical level, on the historical level it makes Mark into something of a dunce. Why would Mark omit either the **infancy narrative**, the **Sermon on the Mount**, great parables like the **Good Samaritan** and the **Prodigal Son**, and so on? Why would Mark insert so many unnecessary details, stylistic redundancies, and duplications? Most scholars today prefer the **two-source theory**, according to which Matthew and Luke independently used Mark and the Sayings Source **Q**, along with other traditions to which they alone had access (**M** and **L**).

– H –

HADES. The Greek abode of the dead named for the god of the netherworld; the name was then used to describe the place of the dead. The Hebrew equivalent is Sheol. In Hellenistic times both Hades and Sheol began to be understood as places of punishment for the wicked (hell). According to Matt 16:18, Jesus promised **Peter** that "the gates of Hades" will not prevail against his **church**. According to 1 Pet 3:19–20 and 4:6, the risen Jesus visited the abode of the dead and proclaimed the good news there. In Rev 1:18 the risen Jesus claims to possess the "keys (power over) of Death and Hades."

HEAVEN. In OT cosmology, heaven is the area above the earth (in the sky), separated by a dome from whose sluice gates the rains descend (Gen 1:6–8). It is also understood to be the dwelling place of **God** and the place of his heavenly court. In his **teaching**, Jesus assumes the three-level Hebrew cosmology and speaks frequently about God as "your [or my] Father in heaven" (Matt 5:16, 5:45, 6:1, 6:9, 7:11, 7:21, etc.). In **John's Gospel**, Jesus is described as the one who came down from heaven (John 3:13, 3:31, 6:38, 6:42, 6:50). **Matthew** often uses "heaven" as a synonym for God, especially in the phrase "the **kingdom of heaven**" (Matt 3:2, 4:17, 5:3, 5:10, 5:19–20, 7:21, 8:1, etc.) According to Matt 24:30–31, the risen Jesus will return from heaven as the glorious **Son of Man** and send out **angels** to gather the elect for the **Last Judgment** and their reward of eternal life with God and the risen Christ.

HEBREWS, LETTER TO THE. Despite a few epistolary features (in 13:22–25), Hebrews is better understood as an elaborate sermon in written form, composed perhaps in **Rome** in the late first century CE. It is an extended commentary on the early Christian confession that "Christ died for our sins in accord with the Scriptures" (1 Cor

15:3). After establishing Jesus' identity as the **Son of God** through various OT texts (1:1–4:13), it describes the priesthood and **sacrifice** of Christ (4:14–10:18) and encourages perseverance in Christian life (10:19–13:25). Central to Hebrews is the conviction that Jesus' **death** was the perfect (in the sense of truly effective) **sacrifice** for sins, and that he is a **priest** because he willingly offered himself as a sacrifice. However, because Jesus was from the tribe of Judah rather than Levi, he could never have been a Jewish priest on earth (Heb 7:13–14). And so the author constructed another (older and superior in his mind) priesthood that he traced back to the ancient priest-king Melchizedek (Gen 14:17–20; Ps 110:4).

HERMENEUTICS. The term derives from the Greek verb which means "to interpret." It can describe the whole process of interpreting a **Gospel** text, including **textual**, **literary**, and **historical criticisms**. Or it can be used narrowly to refer to what one does with a Gospel passage (or any other) text after it has been subjected to critical analysis. In that latter sense, hermeneutics concerns the significance, appropriation, and application of the text for a person or a group to-day. The ongoing interaction between the text and the interpreter is sometimes described as the hermeneutical circle or spiral.

HEROD ANTIPAS. A son of **Herod the Great** and ruler over **Galilee** from 4 BCE to 39 CE (see Luke 3:1, 3:19). According to the **Gospels**, he was responsible for the execution of **John the Baptist** when John challenged him about his **marriage** to Herodias (Matt 14:1–12; Mark 6:14–29; Luke 9:7–9). In Mark 8:15, Jesus warns his **disciples** about "the **yeast**" of Herod (in the negative sense of a corrupting agent). On his way to **Jerusalem** (Luke 13:31–32), Jesus on being warned that Herod Antipas was trying to kill him refers to him disparagingly as "that fox." According to Luke 23:6–12, **Pontius Pilate** sent Jesus to Herod (who was in Jerusalem for **Passover**) since as a Galilean Jesus fell under Herod's jurisdiction. But the hearing quickly turned into a **mockery** of Jesus, and Herod sent him back to Pilate.

HEROD THE GREAT. King of Judea from 37 to 4 BCE, he was from an Idumean family that married into the Jewish high priestly family, gained control over Judea and **Jerusalem**, was a client of the Roman emperor Augustus, and became famous for his many building projects and infamous for his personal and family life. According to Luke 1:5, the births of **John the Baptist** and Jesus took place late in his reign. According to Matt 2:1–12, Herod regarded the infant Jesus as a potential rival for the title "**King of the Jews**" and sought to have him killed. This in turn forced **Joseph** to flee to Egypt with **Mary** and the **child** (2:13–15). In a desperate effort to kill off his rival, he ordered that all boys under two years of age in the vicinity of **Bethlehem** be killed (2:16–18). Only when Herod died in 4 BCE did Joseph and his family return from Egypt and settle in **Galilee** (2:19–23).

HERODIANS. Supporters of the Herod family, and in particular of **Herod Antipas** in Jesus' time. In Mark 3:6 (in **Galilee**) and in Mark 12:13 and Matt 22:16 (in **Jerusalem**), they join forces with the **Pharisees** to plot against and trap Jesus. To what extent they formed an organized movement or party in Jesus' time is not clear.

HISTORICAL CRITICISM. Applied to the **Gospels** and the historical study of Jesus, historical criticism involves charting the history of the text, placing the text in its historical and cultural contexts, and trying to determine the shape of the events behind the text. Historical criticism takes account of the circumstances in which the Gospels were written: author, date, audience, language, purpose, content, structure, and theology. It also demands attending to what can be known about the cultural and historical circumstances in which they were composed. Archaeological excavations and other discoveries such as the **Dead Sea Scrolls** have greatly illuminated the intellectual and spiritual world in which the Gospels took shape. Determining exactly what happened behind the texts (e.g., regarding the birth of Jesus, his **nature miracles**, his **resurrection** appearances) forces the historian to act as a detective and so to deal necessarily only in the realm of the probable or possible. Much will also depend on the philosophical and theological assumptions that the historian brings to the task, with regard to questions such as, Is **virginal conception** possible? Do **miracles** happen? Can dead persons come back to life?

HISTORICAL JESUS. *See* QUEST FOR THE HISTORICAL JESUS.

HOLY SPIRIT. In the **Gospels** the term refers to **God**'s presence and power in action. In the **infancy narratives**, Jesus' **virginal conception** is attributed to the Holy Spirit (Matt 1:20; Luke 1:35), and the Spirit inspires **Elizabeth, Zechariah**, and **Simeon** to prophesy (Luke 1:41–42, 1:67, 2:25–26). At Jesus' **baptism**, the Holy Spirit descends upon Jesus (Mark 1:10; Matt 3:16; Luke 3:22), and the Spirit then leads Jesus into the **wilderness** where he overcomes testing by **Satan**. During his public ministry, Jesus acts out of the power of the Holy Spirit, and it is as if all the energy of the Spirit is concentrated in him. To think otherwise is to commit the **unforgivable sin** (Mark 3:28–30) of attributing Jesus' healings and **exorcisms** to Satan and other **demonic** forces. In John 14–16, Jesus repeatedly promises to send the Holy Spirit (the **Advocate** or Paraclete) who will take Jesus' place and carry on his mission. When Jesus takes his last breath on the **cross**, he "gave up his spirit" (John 19:30), suggesting ironically that with his **death** the new age—the age of the Holy Spirit—was beginning (see Acts 2).

HORSLEY, RICHARD A. (1940–). Professor emeritus of religious studies at the University of Massachusetts at Boston, Horsley in *Jesus and the Spiral of Violence* (1986), *Jesus and Empire* (2003), and many other books has sought to counter what he describes as "the unhistorical quest for an apolitical Jesus." He insists that the context of Jesus' ministry was the "spiral of violence" created in Jewish Palestine by the increasing colonizing presence of the **Romans** from Maccabean times onward. The major elements in this spiral included institutionalized injustice, protest and resistance, repression, and revolt. In this setting Horsley argues that the **kingdom of God** was a political metaphor and symbol, that the goal of Jesus' preaching and activity was the liberation and welfare of his people, and that Jesus looked forward to the renewal of **Israel** where egalitarian, non-exploitative, and non-authoritarian social relations would prevail. The primary audience for Jesus, according to Horsley, was the oppressed peasantry in the towns and villages of Galilee. Convinced that God would soon end the spiral of violence, Jesus preached a social revolution. While not a pacifist, Jesus was opposed to violent resistance. However, the Roman and Jewish leaders regarded him as a political threat (and he was), and so he was executed as a rebel against the Roman order.

HOSANNA. A shout derived from a Hebrew term (see Ps 118:25–26), which means "Save, I pray," or "Help." While in the OT "Hosanna" is a cry for divine aid, in the NT (Matt 21:9, 21:15; Mark 11:9–10; John 12:13), it becomes a term of praise and an expression of joy at the triumphal entrance of Jesus into **Jerusalem** at the beginning of Holy Week (**Palm Sunday**).

HUMILITY. In Mediterranean culture where honor had a very high value, Jesus' **teachings** in Matt 23:12 and Luke 14:11, 18:14, that those who exalt themselves will be humbled and those who humble themselves will be exalted would have been highly unusual. While there is a certain earthly **wisdom** to this strategy, these sayings are most likely meant to be taken in the context of the coming **kingdom of God** (which is **God**'s to give). In Matt 18:4, Jesus challenges his **disciples** to become "humble like this **child**" in order to become "the greatest in the kingdom of **heaven**." In Jesus' society, children had no special social status or political significance. The point is that only by becoming a "nobody" and disregarding social status and personal honor can one expect to become great in God's kingdom. As the servant of all (Mark 10:45), Jesus best embodies his own ideal. And on **Palm Sunday** he defines his **messianic** identity in terms of Zech 9:9: "Look, your king is coming to you, humble, and mounted on a **donkey**" (Matt 21:5).

HUMOR. While some scholars have discovered hundreds of examples of humor in the **Gospels**, most readers today find little or none. Humor is culturally dependent to a large extent, and it is especially difficult to discern when all we have to go on are books written almost 2,000 years ago. However, it is fair to say that Jesus' first Jewish onlookers would have enjoyed and found humor in his driving a "**legion**" of **demons** into a herd of pigs (Mark 5:13) and in his bizarre image of a camel trying to pass through the eye of a needle (Mark 10:25). And **John's Gospel** is full of word plays and ironies from **Nicodemus**' confusion about being born "again" or "from above"

(John 3:3–5) to the Evangelist's interpretation of Jesus being "lifted up " on the **cross** as the beginning of his exaltation to the **Father**.

HYPOCRITE. Derived from a Greek word that designates an actor who performed behind a mask, the term took on the meaning of someone who pretends to be someone else or something he or she is not. It is used in the **Synoptic Gospels** with regard to the opponents of Jesus, especially in **Matthew's Gospel** with reference to those who perform acts of piety only to be seen by others (6:2, 6:5, 6:16) and to the **scribes** and **Pharisees** who are brutally attacked as hypocrites by Jesus in chapter 23 for their failure to practice what they preach (23:13, 23:15, 23:23, 23:25, 23:27, 23:29).

– I –

"I AM" SAYINGS. The unique identity and authority of Jesus are brought out especially in **John's Gospel** by the frequent use of the Greek formula *ego eimi* ("I am"), which occurs around 30 times. In some cases there is a clear predicate: "the bread of life" (6:35, 6:41, 6:48, 6:51), "the **light** of the world" (8:12, 9:5), "the good shepherd" (10:11, 10:14), and so forth. In other instances, the predicate is left uncertain (6:20, 18:5), and in still other passages "I am" seems to function as a title on its own (8:24, 8:28. 8:58, 13:19). These uses of the "I am" formula echo **God**'s self-revelation to **Moses** on Sinai ("I am who I am," Exod 3:13–14) and God's self-identifications in Isa 43:25, 51:12, and 52:6. The reaction of those **arresting** Jesus in John 18:6 ("When Jesus said to them, 'I am he,' they stepped back and fell to the ground") suggests that to them the formula served to affirm Jesus' status as divine.

INCARNATION. The term in general refers to the embodiment of a deity or spirit in human form. When used with reference to Jesus, it concerns the preexistent **Son of God** or Word of **God** taking on human flesh and human nature as Jesus of **Nazareth**. The two most important NT witnesses are hymns about Christ in Phil 2:6–11 and John 1:1–18. According to the very early Christian hymn quoted by **Paul**

in Phil 2:6–11, Jesus put aside his equality with God and "emptied himself, taking the form of a slave, being born in human likeness." Moreover, Jesus so fully appropriated human nature that he suffered a shameful **death**, "even death on the **cross**." Likewise, according to the prologue to **John's Gospel**, Jesus the Word (or **Wisdom**) of God who was with God and was God and so existed before all the rest of creation "became flesh and lived among us" (1:14). Thus he was able to fulfill his role as the revealer and the revelation of God. For other NT passages about Jesus as the preexistent Wisdom of God, see Col 1:15–17 and Heb 1:3. These texts (especially John 1:1–18) figured prominently in early Christian reflection on and debate about the two natures of Christ (divine and human) and about relations among the persons of the **Trinity**. In some theological circles today, they provide the criteria of theological orthodoxy about Christ.

INFANCY GOSPELS. Matthew and **Luke** preface their accounts of Jesus' public ministry with narratives about his birth and infancy. They combine historical facts, biblical fulfillments and allusions, and theological statements about Jesus. It is often difficult, however, to distinguish one kind of element from another. The infancy narrative in Matt 1–2 emphasizes Jesus' roots in Judaism, focuses on **Joseph** as a central character, describes the miraculous **(virginal) conception** of Jesus as fulfilling Isa 7:14, portrays the **Magi** as coming to pay homage to the infant Jesus, and traces the Holy Family's escape from the murderous intent of **Herod the Great** by their journey from **Bethlehem** through Egypt to **Nazareth**. The infancy narrative in Luke 1–2 compares the birth announcements and birth narratives of **John the Baptist** and Jesus, so as to emphasize the superiority of Jesus. It takes **Mary** as a central character and portrays her along with **Zechariah** and **Elizabeth**, the shepherds, and **Simeon** and **Anna** as representing the best in **Israelite** piety. It includes the hymnal passages known as Mary's *Magnificat* (Luke 1:46–55), Zechariah's *Benedictus* (1:69–79), and Simeon's *Nunc Dimittis* (2:29–32). It concludes with the episode in which the 12-year-old Jesus is found teaching the **teachers** in the **Jerusalem temple**. The two major apocryphal infancy Gospels, *Protevangelium of James* and *Infancy Gospel of Thomas*, are from the late second century at the earliest, clearly depend on the two canonical infancy **Gospels**, and purport to fill in gaps and answer questions that arise in them. The *Protevangelium of James* describes the births and infancies of Mary and Jesus, while insisting on Mary's virginity and explaining the "**brothers**" of Jesus as **children** from the first **marriage** of Joseph the elderly widower. The *Infancy Gospel of Thomas* describes the fantastic exploits of the child Jesus between 5 and 12 years of age. While he appears to be a petulant boy-wonder, the real point seems to be that the powers Jesus displayed as an adult were already present in his **childhood**. Later **apocryphal Gospels** such as *Gospel of Pseudo-Matthew*, *Arabic Infancy Gospel*, *History of Joseph the Carpenter*, and so on, drew heavily on both the canonical and apocryphal sources, and expanded them with even more tales about the infant Jesus and his family.

INFANCY NARRATIVES. *See* INFANCY GOSPELS.

ISAIAH. The name of the eighth-century **prophet** based in **Jerusalem**. The OT book that bears his name reflects conditions in Jerusalem in the eighth century (chaps. 1–39), in Babylon in the mid-sixth century (40–55), and in Jerusalem in the late sixth century (56–66). Passages from this book appear frequently in the **Gospels** as having being fulfilled by Jesus. For examples, see Matt 3:3, 4:14, 8:17, 12:17, 13:14, 15:7; Mark 1:2, 7:6; Luke 3:4, 4:17; and John 1:23, 12:38–41.

ISRAEL. In NT times, "Israel" was primarily a Jewish self-designation, while "Jews" was the name more familiar to outsiders. Israel was not so much a geographical term as it was a social and religious designation. Jesus' statement about his being sent to "the lost sheep of the house of Israel" (Matt 15:24) suggests both his identification with Israel and his mission to Israel and on Israel's behalf. His choice of **twelve apostles**, with its obvious symbolism of the 12 tribes of Israel, indicates that he may well have regarded his movement as a remnant within Israel, just as other Jewish sectarian groups of his time did. While he criticized and warned those in Israel who were outside his movement (in "this **generation**"), it seems to have been his hope to draw them to himself so that eventually Israel would be renewed on a larger scale and **God**'s will might "be done on earth as it in **heaven**" (Matt 6:10).

– J –

JAMES, BROTHER OF THE LORD. The "**brother**" of Jesus, and a prominent figure in the early **Jerusalem** church. Whether "brother" means full sibling, stepbrother, cousin, or some such relative has been debated for many centuries. While not a follower during Jesus' lifetime, James was a recipient of an **appearance** by the risen Jesus (1 Cor 15:7) and gradually became a leader in the **church** at Jerusalem as **Paul** attests (Gal 1:19, 2:9, 2:12) and Acts also bears witness (12:17, 15:13, 21:18). He is the implied (if not the real) author of the **letter of James**. He died a martyr's death under the high **priest** Ananus shortly before the Jewish revolt in 66 CE.

JAMES, LETTER OF. While having some features of a letter (in 1:1), this NT writing is in fact a **wisdom** instruction that moves rapidly with its advice on various topics. The implied author is meant to be James "the **brother** of the **Lord**," though many scholars regard it as a pseudonymous composition from around 80 CE. In either case, it was clearly written by a Jewish Christian for a Jewish Christian audience. It mentions Jesus only twice (1:1, 2:1), and then in a formulaic (though reverential) manner as the "Lord Jesus Christ." It contains several close parallels with sayings in **Matthew's Gospel**, such as the prohibition of swearing **oaths** in Jas 5:12 and Matt 5:34, without explicitly attributing them to Jesus.

JAMES, PROTEVANGELIUM OF. An imaginative account of the births of **Mary** and Jesus, based largely on 1 Sam 1–2 (for Mary) and Luke 1–2 and Matt 1–2 (for Jesus). The epilogue attributes the work to **James** in **Jerusalem**, presumably "the **brother** of the **Lord**." But it most likely originated in Syria or Egypt in the late second century CE. It purports to fill in gaps and answer questions about the origins of Mary and Jesus, and harmonizes the NT **infancy narratives** into what has come to be known as "the Christmas story." It names Mary's parents as Joachim and **Anna**, and traces her lineage to the "tribe of David," thus reinforcing Jesus' identity as the **Son of David**. It portrays Mary as living in the **Jerusalem temple** precincts from age 3 to 12, when she is entrusted to the care of **Joseph**, an elderly widower with sons from a previous **marriage** (including James, the implied author). It situates the birth of Jesus to Mary (at 16) in a cave near **Bethlehem**, and insists on Mary's **virginity** before and after Jesus' birth on the basis of **Salome**'s testimony. And it identifies the father of **John the Baptist** (see Luke 1:5–25) with the **Zechariah** mentioned in Matt 23:35 as having been murdered in the temple area.

JAMES, SON OF ZEBEDEE. A Galilean **fisherman** who along with his brother **John** was among the first **disciples** called by Jesus (Matt 4:18–22; Mark 1:16–20). He is frequently named with **Peter** and John as constituting the inner circle among the **twelve apostles** (Mark 1:29, 3:17, 5:37, 9:2, 13:3, 14:33; Luke 5:10, 8:51, 9:28). In Luke 9:54, James and John express indignation at the **Samaritans'** lack of respect toward Jesus, and in Mark 10:35–40 they ask Jesus for special places of honor in the **kingdom of God**. According to Acts 12:2, this James (a son of **Zebedee**) was executed under Herod Agrippa I in 44 CE.

JEREMIAH. A Judean **prophet** active in the late seventh and early sixth century BCE, who focused especially on the imminent threat to **Jerusalem** and its **temple** from the Babylonians. The book that bears his name is quoted in Matt 2:17 and 27:9. According to Matt 16:14, some people thought that Jesus was Jeremiah brought back to life. Both Jeremiah and Jesus were rejected prophets.

JEREMIAS, JOACHIM (1900–1979). Professor of NT at the University of Göttingen, he was best known for his research on the tradition of the **Synoptic Gospels** and on the original Aramaic wording of Jesus' **teachings**. His *Parables of Jesus* (1966) sought to go behind the Greek texts of the **Gospels** to reconstruct not only the Aramaic wording of Jesus' sayings but also their original **Galilean** context. His goal was to help us hear the "voice" of Jesus once more and thus to appreciate better his message of **God**'s coming kingdom and its manifestation in his own ministry. In *The Eucharistic Words of Jesus* (1966) he tried to reconstruct the oldest text and to clarify the original meaning: **table fellowship** with Jesus as an anticipatory gift of the final consummation. His *New Testament Theology*, Vol. 1, *The Proclamation of Jesus* (1971), provided a defense of the reliability of the tradition of Jesus' sayings, and then used these sayings to reconstruct Jesus' positions on the **kingdom of God** and his own place in God's plan.

JERICHO. A very ancient city, 16 km (10 mi.) north of the Dead Sea, near a crossing of the Jordan River. It is mentioned in Jesus' **parable** of the **Good Samaritan** (Luke 10:30) and seems to have been the home of **Zacchaeus** the **tax collector** (Luke 19:1–10) and **Bartimaeus** the blind beggar (Mark 10:46–52).

JERUSALEM. Located in the hill country of Judea, Jerusalem served as the capital city of **Israel** from the time of King **David** onward (around 1000 BCE) and was the site of the **temple** built under King **Solomon** that became the central shrine of the people of Israel. According to Luke 2, Jesus visited Jerusalem as an infant to undergo the rites of presentation and purification (2:22–40), and as a 12-year-old boy on a **Passover** pilgrimage (2:41–51). In **John's Gospel**, Jesus makes several visits to Jerusalem, where he **cleanses the temple** (2:13–25), ministers to **Nicodemus** (3:1–21), heals a paralyzed man (5:1–18), preaches during the **festival** of Booths (7:1–8:59), heals a man born blind (9:1–41), preaches during the festival of Dedication/Hanukkah (10:22–42), restores **Lazarus** to life and is **anointed** for **burial** (11:1–12:11), and enters the city where he delivers **farewell discourses** to his **disciples**, undergoes **arrest** and execution, and appears as alive again to some of his followers (chaps. 13–20). By contrast, the Synoptic Evangelists follow **Mark**'s geographical outline and envision only one visit to Jerusalem, a short ministry there during "Holy Week," and Jesus' **passion**, **death**, and **resurrection**.

JERUSALEM TEMPLE. *See* TEMPLE IN JERUSALEM.

JESUS, NAME OF. The name Jesus is a Greek form of the Hebrew names "Yeshua" and "Yeshu," which are shortened forms of Joshua. These names were based on the Hebrew root *yasha* meaning "save," and they mean "Y$_{HWH}$ saves." The interpretation of Jesus' name in Matt 1:21 ("for he will save his people from their sins") connects his name with what would be his mission as an adult. The name was customarily bestowed at the **circumcision** of the male **child**, on the eighth day after his birth (Luke 1:59, 2:21). Either parent could give the name. According to Matt 1:25, **Joseph** gave Jesus his name, though in Luke 1:31 **Mary** is supposed to name him Jesus.

JESUS SEMINAR. Founded by **Robert W. Funk** and inaugurated in 1985, the Jesus Seminar consists mainly of professors of religious studies at U.S. universities who meet regularly to analyze the sayings and actions of Jesus as they are presented in the **canonical Gospels** and other ancient sources. They have given particular attention to the Sayings Source **Q** and the *Gospel of Thomas*, which many members regard as the oldest and purest sources for reconstructing the **historical Jesus**. For voting on the authenticity of the sayings of Jesus, the seminar adopted a color scheme: red—Jesus said it or something like it; pink—Jesus probably said something like it; gray—these are not Jesus' words but the ideas are close to his own; and black—Jesus did not say it. A similar scheme is applied to reports about Jesus' actions: red—historically reliable; pink—probably reliable; gray—possibly reliable; and black—improbable and may be fictive.

JEWISH INTERPRETATIONS OF JESUS. The earliest traditions about Jesus were formulated and handed on by Jews, and were eventually put into the form of **Gospels** that celebrated Jesus as the fulfillment of **God**'s promises to **Israel**. If the core of **Josephus**' testimony to Jesus in his *Jewish Antiquities* 18.63–64 is authentic, then it provides a positive description of Jesus from a first-century Jew who was not one of his followers. In the early phases of the rabbinic movement there was mainly silence about Jesus from Jews. Only in later Talmudic texts are there hostile references to Jesus as a bastard, magician, deceiver, and apostate. These negative traditions were eventually (in the ninth–tenth centuries and later) put together in the *Toledot Yeshu* texts, which convey a highly negative picture of Jesus. The European Enlightenment in general and the emergence of classical Jewish scholarship in the nineteenth century made it possible for Jews to produce critical historical accounts of Jesus' life and teachings. In some cases there was also a religious or nationalistic motive to reclaim Jesus and bring him "home' to his Jewish roots. Abraham Geiger in *Das Judentum und seine Geschichte* (1864–1865) was the first modern Jewish scholar to produce a detailed historical analysis of Jesus from an explicitly Jewish perspective. He classified Jesus as a **Pharisee** and interpreted early Christianity as a paganization and ultimate **betrayal** of Jesus' Jewish message. In *Jesus of Nazareth* (1925), **Joseph Klausner** produced in modern Hebrew the first objective study of Jesus for his fellow Jews in Palestine, and argued that Jesus remained faithful to the **Torah** and that his **ethical** teachings were within the parameters of Judaism. In *We Jews and Jesus* (1965), Samuel Sandmel, while confessing to seeing no originality in Jesus' authentic teachings, concluded that Jesus was a Jewish loyalist, a martyr to his Jewish patriotism, and a leader sufficiently singular for his followers to say that he had been **raised from the dead**. The very title of Schalom ben-Chorin's *Brother Jesus* (German 1967; English, 2001) marked an important positive step in the Jewish reclamation (or homecoming) of Jesus as one of their own. In *Jesus* (German 1969; English, 1969), David Flusser sought to prove that the **Synoptic Gospels** present a reasonably faithful picture of Jesus as a Jew of his own time, more a Jewish **teacher** and **miracle** worker than the redeemer of humankind. **Geza Vermes** in *Jesus the Jew* (1974) and many other subsequent publications classified Jesus as a **Galilean** charismatic healer and teacher in light of striking similarities with his Galilean Jewish contemporary, Hanina ben Dosa. Pinchas Lapide in *Israelis, Jews, and Jesus* (1979) affirmed that Jesus was "no lukewarm, uprooted Jew" but rather one who stood in mainstream of the Jewish **prophetic** tradition. In *Jesus the Pharisee* (1985), Harvey Falk argued that Jesus' criticisms of Jews and the Pharisees were directed at the School of Shammai, not at the School of Hillel, and that Jesus had no intention of abolishing Judaism. Focusing on various texts in **Matthew's Gospel**, Jacob Neusner in *A Rabbi Talks with Jesus* (1993) explained why, if he had been in the Land of Israel in the first century CE, he would not have joined the circle of Jesus' **disciples**. In *Jesus of Nazareth, King of the Jews* (1999), Paula Fredriksen noted that the single most solid fact about Jesus was his **death** under **Pontius Pilate** and contends that Pilate had Jesus executed because other Jews proclaimed Jesus to be the **Messiah**. Amy-Jill Levine in *The Misunderstood Jew* (2006) argued that Jesus dressed like a Jew, lived and taught like a Jew, argued with other Jews, and died like other Jews on a Roman **cross**. These modern Jewish interpretations of Jesus consider him entirely within the context of Judaism, make abundant use of rabbinic sources, insist on his basic fidelity to the Torah and Jewish customs, blame Pilate for his death, regard his **resurrection** as symbolic or spiritual at best, and trace the development of his movement into a separate (and hostile) religion to **Paul** and Hellenism in general.

JEWISHNESS OF JESUS. That Jesus of **Nazareth** was born, lived, and died in the Land of **Israel** in the early part of what we now call the first century CE cannot be doubted. He was a Jewish **teacher**, though of a somewhat unusual kind. He spoke Aramaic, used the methods of the Jewish teachers of his time, and addressed other Jews. The content of his teaching was firmly rooted in Judaism as expressed in the Hebrew Bible and the Jewish tradition. Along with other Jews of his day, Jesus looked forward to the time when **God** would intervene in his people's history and when all creation would acknowledge the sovereignty of God (the **kingdom of God**). However, our increased knowledge about the diversity within Palestinian Judaism in Jesus' time makes it difficult to know precisely what kind of Jew Jesus was. Was he a **Pharisee, Sadducee, Essene**, or (most likely) none of these? He stood closest to the Pharisees. Even though the **Gospels** frequently portray Jesus in conflict with the Pharisees, they do keep inviting him to dinner (Luke 7:36, 14:1) and do seem to share an agenda with him even if they do not always agree with him. Efforts by some German biblical scholars in the Nazi period to deny the Jewishness of Jesus and to portray him as an Aryan persecuted by the Jews represent the triumph of propaganda over history.

JOHN, GOSPEL OF. Independent of and different from the other three **canonical Gospels**, John's Gospel spreads Jesus' public ministry over three years and recounts his several journeys to **Jerusalem**. It also includes a different set of characters: **Nicodemus**, the **Samaritan** woman, the man born blind, **Lazarus**, and the **Beloved Disciple**. It presents Jesus as giving long speeches about his own identity and significance (rather than about the **kingdom of God**). Its basic theological idea is that Jesus is the revealer and the revelation of **God**. This **Gospel** seems to have been the product of a school or circle that took **John the son of Zebedee** as its patron, and was composed for a

Jewish-Christian community on the verge of being expelled from the **synagogue** (see 9:22, 12:42, 16:2) in the late first century CE. It is often divided into two main parts: the Book of **Signs**—Jesus' public ministry (chaps. 1–12); and the Book of Glory—his **farewell discourses**, and **passion-resurrection** (chaps 13–21). It portrays Jesus as the Word/**Wisdom** of God, as existing before the creation of the world, and as divine (1:1–18, 20:28).

JOHN, SON OF ZEBEDEE. A **Galilean fisherman**, the brother of **James**, one of Jesus' first **disciples** (Matt 4:18–22; Mark 1:16–20), a member of the **twelve apostles**, and part of Jesus' inner circle along with **Peter** and James. In tradition he has been identified as the **Beloved Disciple** in **John's Gospel** and the author of **Revelation**, though modern scholars have doubts on both matters. However, many scholars do identify him as the founder or patron of the Johannine school or circle from which John's Gospel and the Letters of John emanated.

JOHN THE BAPTIST. A Jewish religious teacher and **prophet** associated with Jesus. The major sources about John are the four **Gospels** and **Josephus** (*Ant.* 18.116–119). In **Luke's** **infancy narrative**, the births of John and Jesus are closely intertwined, and they seem to be related through **Mary** and **Elizabeth**. According to Luke 1:80, John went off as a young man to the **"wilderness,"** presumably the Judean Desert, where the **Dead Sea Scrolls** were found. John eventually started an independent Jewish religious movement, featuring the symbolic ritual of washing (**baptism**) as a sign of **repentance** in preparation for the coming **kingdom of God** (Matt 3:1–12; Mark 1:4–8; Luke 3:1–20). Jesus became part of John's movement and underwent John's baptism (Matt 3:13–17; Mark 1:9–11; Luke 3:21–22). According to John 1:19–42, some of Jesus' first followers came from John's circle. Despite Jesus' roots in John's movement, all the Gospels emphasize Jesus' superiority to him and portray John as the one who prepared the way for Jesus (Mark 1:2–3). According to Mark 6:14–29, John was executed under **Herod Antipas** because he confronted Herod on account of his irregular **marriage** to Herodias. Josephus, however, suggests that Herod had John killed mainly because he regarded him as a political threat.

JONAH. The **prophet** mentioned in 2 Kgs 14:25 and the major figure in the short OT book that bears his name. He is the subject of the "**sign** of Jonah" mentioned in Matt 16:4 and elaborated in Matt 12:39–41 and Luke 11:29–30, 11:32. Matt 12:40 focuses on the prophet's three-day-and-night stay in the belly of the sea monster as a prophecy of Jesus' **burial** and **resurrection**. **Luke**, however, makes no mention of the resurrection, and takes the sign to be the surprising **repentance** of **sinners** in response to Jesus' preaching.

JOSEPH OF ARIMATHEA. From a small village in the Judean hill country (see 1 Sam 1:1), Joseph was a member of the Jewish council or **Sanhedrin** (Mark 15:43) and the one in whose **tomb** Jesus was **buried** (Matt 27:57–60; Mark 15:43–46; Luke 23:50–53; John 19:38). Joseph may have acted merely to fulfill the law in Deut 21:23 about burying the corpse of an executed person on the day of **death**. However, according to Matt 27:57 and John 19:38, Joseph had already become one of Jesus' **disciples**.

JOSEPH, THE HUSBAND OF MARY. Through the legal paternity of Joseph, Jesus was called the **Son of David**. Joseph's Davidic ancestry was traced by **Matthew** through Jacob back to **Solomon** (1:6, 1:16) and by **Luke** through Eli to Nathan (3:23, 3:31). Jesus' contemporaries regarded Joseph as the legal father of Jesus (Luke 4:22; John 1:45, 6:42), though the **Gospels** insist that Jesus was conceived not by Joseph but by the **Holy Spirit** (Matt 1:18; Luke 1:35). Joseph worked as a **carpenter**, builder, or craftsman (Matt 13:55). He is a major character only in Matthew's **infancy narrative** where he is portrayed as a "just man" who responds to **God**'s directives in **dreams**. Joseph's absence from Jesus' adult life in the Gospels has led to the assumptions that he had died by then and was relatively old when he married **Mary**. The references to Jesus' "**brothers and sisters**" (Matt 12:46–50, 13:55–56; Mark 3:31–35) have often been explained as Joseph's **children** from a previous **marriage** that ended with his wife's death. In later **apocryphal Gospels**, Joseph plays more prominent and often fantastic roles.

JOSEPHUS. A Palestinian Jew born around the time of Jesus' **death**, he was an active participant in the Jewish revolt against the Romans

(66–70 CE), went over to the Roman side, and wrote several books for them: *Jewish War* (an account of the revolt and its causes), *Jewish Antiquities* (a history of **Israel** from earliest times to the revolt), *Life* (his autobiography and self-defense), and *Against Apion* (a response to slanders against the Jewish people). He died near the end of the first century or in the early years of the second century. In his *Antiquities* (18.116–119) he describes **John the Baptist** as a good man who "commanded the Jews to practice virtue, by expressing justice toward one another and piety toward **God,** and to come together to **baptism.**" He claims that John was executed because **Herod Antipas** feared his popularity and regarded him as a political rival. Josephus also mentions briefly the condemnation and death of **James** "the **brother** of Jesus" (*Ant.* 20.200). He also provides the following description of Jesus in *Antiquities* 18.63–64:

> About this time arose Jesus, a wise man, if indeed it be lawful to call him a man. For he was a doer of wonderful deeds, and a **teacher** of men who gladly receive the truth. He drew to himself many both of the Jews and of the **Gentiles.** He was the Christ; and when **Pilate,** on the indictment of the principal men among us, had condemned him to the **cross,** those who had loved him at the first did not cease to do so, for he appeared to them again alive on the third day, the divine **prophets** having foretold these and ten thousand other wonderful things about him. And even to this day the race of Christians, who are named from him, has not died out.

The critical problem is determining how much of this text (if any at all) came directly from Josephus. Several phrases sound like interpolations made by the Christian **scribes** who transmitted his works: "if indeed it be lawful to call him a man," "He was the Christ," "he appeared to them again alive on the third day," and so on. It is not impossible that Josephus mentioned Jesus. But exactly what he wrote is now hard to know.

JUBILEE. The 50th year after a series of seven sabbatical years. The OT legislation pertaining to the Jubilee year appears in Lev 25:8–55. In a Jubilee year, land was to be restored to its original ownership, and **Israelite** debt-slaves were to be freed and allowed to return to their land. It was also to be a year of rest for the land, and so there was to be no sowing, reaping, or harvesting. In association with the sabbatical year there was probably also a general remission of debts. The principle underlying the legislation is that **God** ultimately owns all the land and all the people on it. Whether the legislation was ever actually put into practice is dubious. It seems to have remained a utopian and **eschatological** ideal, which found its way into the book of *Jubilees* and various **Qumran** texts. Some interpreters find an allusion to the Jubilee year in Isa 61:1–2 ("good news to the poor . . . release to captives . . . let the oppressed go free"), which serves as the biblical text for Jesus' inaugural sermon in the **synagogue** at **Nazareth** according to Luke 4:16–21.

JUDAS, GOSPEL OF. A gnostic revelation discourse preserved in a fourth-century Coptic manuscript, which may reflect the Greek *Gospel of Judas* mentioned by Irenaeus in the late second century. Its title comes from the last line ("The **Gospel** of Judas"), and its content suggests that it was intended to be *about* Judas rather than *by* Judas. Most of the document purports to relate dialogues between Jesus and Judas (and other members of the **twelve apostles**). Its first line describes the work as "the secret account of the revelation that Jesus spoke in conversation with **Judas Iscariot** during a week three days before he celebrated **Passover**." It is so infused with gnostic concepts and concerns that it really tells us nothing about the **historical Jesus** or the historical Judas. Rather, it represents Sethian **gnosticism**, a movement that regarded Seth, a son of **Adam** (Gen 4:25), as a **savior** figure. Whether Judas is presented in this work as benevolent (in helping Jesus escape from the confines of the flesh) or malevolent (possessed by a **demon**) depends on how certain words and phrases are translated. Its chief value is as a witness to the diversity within Christianity in the second and third centuries. However, it is hard to know how widespread and influential this kind of gnosticism was at that time.

JUDAS ISCARIOT. The surname, which serves to distinguish him from others named Judas or Jude, has been interpreted in many ways ranging from his putative place of origin (Kerioth) to his having been a terrorist (*sicarius* = "dagger man" in Latin). One of the **twelve apostles**, Judas is often identified as the one who **betrayed** Jesus (Matt 10:4; Mark 3:19; Luke 6:16; John 6:71). In John 12:7

he is called a thief, and in 13:29 he is said to have been the community treasurer. According to all the **Gospels** (Matt 26:14–16; Mark 14:10–11; Luke 22:3–6; John 18:2–3), Judas was an integral part of the plot that led to Jesus' **death**. While the Evangelists indicate that he acted out of greed, modern scholars have suggested other possible motives: forcing Jesus to act as the **Messiah**, initiating a dialogue between Jesus and the Jewish authorities, or confronting the Roman authorities with the Messiah of **Israel. Matthew** and **Luke** agree that Judas died a gruesome death connected with the purchase of a field. According to Matt 27:3–10, Judas **repented**, returned the **money** (30 pieces of silver), and hanged himself out of despair. The **priests** then used the money to buy a field in which foreigners were buried (the Potter's Field). According to Acts 1:18–19, Judas himself purchased a field but died in a terrible fall there, thus making it doubly "a Field of Blood" (*Hakeldama* in Aramaic).

JUDE. (1) One of the **twelve apostles** mentioned in Luke 6:16 and Acts 1:13 as "son of **James.**" He is often identified with **Thaddaeus** (Matt 10:3; Mark 3:18). He is probably the "**Judas** (not Iscariot)" mentioned in John 14:22. (2) One of the "**brothers**" of Jesus (and James) mentioned in Matt 13:55 and Mark 6:3. He is the implied (if not the real) author of the NT letter that bears his name. There he describes himself as "a servant of Jesus Christ and brother of James."

JUDEA. *See* JERUSALEM.

JUDGMENT, LAST. *See* LAST JUDGMENT.

– K –

KÄSEMANN, ERNST (1906–1998). Professor of NT on the Protestant theological faculty at Tübingen. A student of **Rudolf Bultmann**, Käsemann challenged his teacher's skepticism about knowing the historical Jesus and thus initiated the second **quest for the historical Jesus** in the mid-1950s. He emphasized especially the criterion of double dissimilarity: A statement can be ascribed to Jesus with confidence when there are no grounds for deriving the tradition from either Judaism or early Christianity. He viewed Jesus as setting himself above **Moses** and thus shattering the letter of the Law. While describing **apocalyptic** as "the mother of Christian theology," he interpreted Jesus as concerned not so much with the end of the world but rather with calling people to serve **God** and to **love** one another in everyday life.

KEYS OF THE KINGDOM. In Matt 16:19 Jesus promises **Peter** that he will give him "the keys of the **kingdom of heaven**." The motif of the keys is rooted in **Isaiah**'s prophecy to Shebna that he would be replaced by Eliakim as chief steward over the royal household of Judah: "I will place on his shoulder the key of the house of **David**; he shall open, and none shall shut; and he shall shut, and none shall open" (Isa 22:22). Just as Eliakim was to have authority over the comings and goings in the royal palace, so Peter is to have charge over entry into the kingdom of God. Thus Peter appears to be the prime minister and major-domo in the kingdom proclaimed by Jesus.

KING OF THE JEWS. The Roman "outsider" translation of the Jewish "insider" term **"Messiah"** becomes prominent especially in the **Gospels**' accounts of Jesus' condemnation and execution. When the Roman governor **Pontius Pilate** in Mark 15:2 asks Jesus whether he is "the King of the Jews," Jesus refuses to answer. When Pilate asks the crowd to choose between Jesus and **Barabbas** (15:9, 15:12), he uses the **title** "King of the Jews." When the soldiers mock Jesus as if he were a king, they salute him as "King of the Jews" (15:18). And the legal charge against Jesus according to Mark 15:26 is expressed as "King of the Jews." While to Jews it conveyed hopes and visions of a new and better King **David**, to the Romans it meant just another in a long line of Jewish rebels and insurgents who had to be cut off quickly and brutally. The title is equally prominent in **John**'s account of these same events (John 18:33, 18:39, 19:3, 19:14–15, 19:19). For Pilate the repeated use of this title with regard to Jesus conveyed **mockery** of both Jesus and the Jewish people. The irony is that for the Evangelists and their first readers, Jesus was in fact the Messiah/King of the Jews.

KINGDOM OF GOD/HEAVEN. The biblical term used to describe **God**'s rule in the present and future. In keeping with Jewish sensitivities about using the divine name too often, **Matthew** frequently refers to the "kingdom of **heaven**." While the OT kingship **Psalms** (93, 95, 97, 99) affirm that "the **Lord** is king," around Jesus' time the focus had shifted from present to future, and in some Jewish circles there was hope for a spectacular manifestation of God's reign in the near future. That Jesus shared this hope is indicated by his **prayer**, "Thy kingdom come" (Matt 6:10; Luke 11:2). His basic message is summarized in Mark 1:15: "The time is fulfilled, and the kingdom of God is at hand; **repent** and believe in the good news." His many **parables** that explicitly refer to God's kingdom (as in Matt 13) look forward to something amazingly large (mustard bush, huge amounts of bread, great harvest, great catch of **fish**) and valuable (**treasure** in a field, precious **pearl**), thus suggesting that then there will be a clearer and more obvious manifestation of God's kingly rule than there is at present. This manifestation will involve the **resurrection** of the dead, the **Last Judgment**, and rewards and punishments. These parables also indicate that the kingdom is present even if in a small way (seeds, leaven) and deserves total commitment on the part of those who perceive it. *See also* REALIZED ESCHATOLOGY.

KLAUSNER, JOSEPH (1874–1958). Klausner's *Jesus of Nazareth: His Life, Times, and Teaching* (1926) was the first comprehensive study of Jesus written in modern Hebrew by an Israeli/**Zionist** scholar. According to Klausner, Jesus was a Jew from his birth to his last breath. At his **baptism**, Jesus came to believe that he was **Israel**'s hoped-for **Messiah** and became obsessed with the idea. Nevertheless, he remained faithful to the **Torah** and observed the ceremonial laws like a true **Pharisaic** Jew. All his **ethical teachings**, while somewhat extreme and ascetic, were paralleled in various Jewish texts. He went up to **Jerusalem** in the hope of being recognized there. But **Judas**, an intelligent Judean, had come to regard Jesus as a false Messiah and set in motion the events that led to his **death**. Nevertheless, ultimate responsibility for Jesus' death lay with the Roman governor **Pontius Pilate**. Jesus' **tomb** was found empty because **Joseph of Arimathea** had taken his corpse away. The **appearances** of the risen Jesus were only spiritual visions. While critical of Jesus for his failure to attend to the requirements of Jewish national identity, Klausner regarded Jesus as a great teacher of morality and a real artist in his **parables**.

– L –

L TRADITION. The designation of material found only in **Luke's Gospel** that cannot be explained by Luke's dependence on **Mark** or the Sayings Source **Q**. Such material includes the **infancy narrative**, **parables** such as the **Good Samaritan** and the **Prodigal Son**, stories about **Martha and Mary** and about **Zacchaeus**, and the **appearances** of the risen Jesus in Luke 24. The critical historical questions include whether this material represents one or several sources, and how much of it was composed directly by the Evangelist.

LAMB OF GOD. A lamb is a sheep less than one year old. In the OT lambs were offered in various sacrificial rituals and were eaten at **Passover** meals. The term was also used metaphorically to describe the sufferings of innocent persons on behalf of others: the **Suffering** Servant (Isa 53:7), and the prophet **Jeremiah** (Jer 11:10). It is against this background that **John the Baptist** identifies Jesus to his own **disciples**, "Here is the Lamb of God who takes away the sin of the world" (John 1:29; see also 1:36). The link between the lamb motif (rooted in Isa 53:7) and Jesus appears again in Acts 8:32 and 1 Pet 1:19, and is prominent in **Revelation** 5 (the risen Jesus as the Slain Lamb).

LANGUAGES OF JESUS. It is generally assumed by scholars that Jesus spoke Aramaic, a Semitic language closely related to Hebrew. It is relatively easy to translate back into Aramaic some of his sayings as well as the **Lord's Prayer** (Matt 6:9–13; Luke 11:2–4). When the Persians defeated the Babylonians in the sixth century BCE, they used Aramaic as the official language in the western parts of their empire and it soon also became the language of the common people. Among Jews, Hebrew continued as the sacred language of "Scripture" and in some circles as a written and spoken language. With the Greek conquest of the Persian Empire under Alexander the Great (died 323 BCE), the Greek language was used at least in administrative matters and some legal documents. The **Dead Sea Scrolls** confirm the use of the three languages in Palestine—Aramaic, Hebrew, and Greek—in Jesus' time. It is likely that Jesus read the Scriptures in Hebrew, taught in Aramaic, used Greek in certain settings (e.g., talking with **Pontius Pilate**), and was perhaps exposed to some Latin.

LAST JUDGMENT. The idea of a worldwide last judgment, one that will mark the end of human history as we know it and will involve rewards for the **righteous** and punishments for the wicked, developed from the OT theme of "the **day of the Lord.**" The accounts about the Last Judgment in the **Gospels** give a prominent position to the glorious **Son of Man.** The imagery comes from Dan 7:14 where one "like a son of man" is given dominion and glory and kingship." The Gospel writers identified the glorious Son of Man as the risen Jesus and viewed his pivotal role in these future events as part of his second coming. According to Matt 25:31–46, the risen Jesus as the glorious Son of Man (see Matt 16:27, 19:28, 24:30) will serve as the judge of "all the nations." His task is to separate the righteous (the sheep) from the wicked (the goats). The criteria that he will use in judging are deeds of kindness to "the least." Those deeds include feeding the hungry, giving drink to the thirsty, welcoming the stranger, clothing the naked, caring for the sick, and visiting the imprisoned. Those who have done these deeds for "the least" will come to enjoy eternal life with **God** and the Son of Man, while those who neglected them will face eternal condemnation. This judgment scene is an obviously dramatic projection of a future event, and it is not a guarantee that it will happen exactly in this way.

LAST SUPPER/LORD'S SUPPER. The **Synoptic Gospels** present similar accounts of Jesus' Last Supper with his **disciples** in Matt 26:17–35, Mark 14:12–31, and Luke 22:7–38. They agree that the Last Supper was a Passover **meal** (though there is no mention of a **lamb**) at which Jesus prophesied that his disciples would betray and deny him. They go on to describe how Jesus took bread and **wine,** identified them with his body and blood ("This is my body . . . my blood"), and interpreted them in the light of his impending **death** as a **sacrifice** for sins and as establishing a new **covenant.** In **Paul**'s version of the **Lord**'s Supper in 1 Cor 11:23–26, Jesus directs that his disciples should "do this in remembrance of me." The account of Jesus' Last Supper in John 13–17 features Jesus' symbolic action of washing his disciples' feet as well as his prophecies about **betrayal.** In **John**'s **chronology,** Jesus' Last Supper takes place on the evening before the evening that began **Passover,** and he dies when the Passover lambs were being slaughtered in the temple. Most of John's

Last Supper account (chaps. 14–17) is devoted to Jesus' **farewell discourses** in which he outlines how the movement begun by him can carry on without his earthly presence: through faith and **love**, and through the guidance of the **Advocate**/Paraclete/**Holy Spirit**. From the perspective of history, Jesus' Last Supper seems not to have been an official Passover meal but rather (as John suggests) a meal celebrated in the spirit or context of Passover. Christians regard Jesus' Last Supper as the origin of the sacrament of the Eucharist/ Lord's Supper.

LAW OF MOSES. The term refers to the 613 commandments in the first five books of the OT (the Torah or Pentateuch), which have traditionally been ascribed to **Moses**. Jesus appears generally to have observed and respected the Law of Moses ("the Law"). According to Matt 5:17–20, Jesus came "not to observe but to fulfill" the Law and the **prophets**, and promises that those who keep the command- ments and teach others to do so will be called great in the **kingdom of heaven**. Even in the so-called antitheses in Matt 5:21–48, Jesus does not abrogate the biblical commandments but rather challenges his followers to go to their roots and do everything to avoid breaking them. In his debates with the **Pharisees** and **scribes**, Jesus criticizes their interpretations and traditions, but not the Law itself (see Matt 15:1–20; Mark 7:1–21). The parenthetical comment that Jesus "de- clared all foods **clean**" in Mark 7:19 surely came from **Mark**, not Jesus. Otherwise this would not have become the major issue that it became in early Christian circles; see Gal 2 and Acts 15. However, both **John** and **Paul** insisted that participation in Jesus' **death** and **resurrection** rather than observance of the Mosaic Law is what brings about right relationship with **God**, that the revelation that Jesus brings is superior to that granted to Moses, and that Jesus' **teaching** constitutes the divinely authorized interpretation of the Mosaic Law.

LAZARUS. (1) The brother of **Martha and Mary**, who lived in **Bethany** in **Judea**. According to John 11:1–44, Jesus restored him to life after he had been dead for four days. In John 12:1–8 he is pres- ent at the **meal** at which Mary **anointed** Jesus' feet with expensive perfume. The popular interest in Lazarus, according to John 12:9–11, prompted the **chief priests** to want to have Jesus killed. Some modern scholars have identified Lazarus as the **Beloved Disciple**, a prominent figure in **John's Gospel**, though this is far from certain. (2) The poor man in Jesus' parable of the **Rich Man and Lazarus** in Luke 16:19–31 is named Lazarus (meaning "**God** helps"). He is the only character who is given a proper name in any of Jesus' **parables**. Whether there is any connection with the figure bearing the same name in John's Gospel is doubtful.

LEAVEN. *See* YEAST.

LEGION. A Latin military loanword (*legio*) taken over into Greek and Hebrew. It refers to a military unit of about 6,000 men. However, in the NT it is used in a loose and metaphorical sense. In Mark 5:9 the **Gerasene** demoniac is said to be possessed by a **demon** named "Legion; for we are many" (see also Mark 5:15; Luke 8:30). Some interpreters regard this use of "legion" as a not very subtle criticism of the Roman military occupation of the area. According to Matt 26:53, Jesus tells those who were **arresting** him that if he asked, **God** would send him more than 12 legions of **angels** to protect and defend him.

LEPROSY. The biblical terms *sa'arat* (Hebrew) and *lepra* (Greek) are probably not to be equated with modern leprosy (Hansen's disease) but rather seem to refer to a wider variety of skin disorders that at least in antiquity were regarded as communicable and dangerous. The OT legislation surrounding leprosy is treated in detail in Lev 13–14. Those who had such conditions were regarded as "unclean," and those who had physical contact with them were also rendered "unclean." When approached by a leper, however, Jesus in Mark 1:40–45 (Matt 8:1–4; Luke 5:12–16) touches him, heals him immediately and completely, and directs him to follow the legal procedure to have himself declared "**clean**." In Luke 17:11–19 Jesus heals 10 lepers by word alone and without apparent physical contact. When sending out the **twelve apostles**, Jesus instructs them to "cleanse lepers" (Matt 10:8). Simon "the leper" (Mark 14:3), at whose house Jesus dined in **Bethany**, had presumably been healed of his "leprosy," perhaps by Jesus himself.

LETTER TO THE HEBREWS. *See* HEBREWS, LETTER TO THE.

LIGHT. First in the order of creation (Gen 1:1–5), light can refer to the heavenly luminaries (sun, moon, stars), morning or dawn, or the light of a lamp or a **fire**. Throughout the Bible, light is an important **ethical** and theological symbol. In **Matthew's Gospel** Jesus says that the **righteous** are "full of light" (6:22) and should display their light in their good works (5:14–16). In **John's Gospel** the image of light is applied especially to Jesus, who is the "true light" (John 1:4–9) and the "light of the world" (8:12, 9:5, 12:46). His followers will not walk in darkness because they "will have the light of life" (8:12). At the end of his public ministry, Jesus proclaims, "I have come as light into the world, so that everyone who believes in me should not remain in darkness" (12:46). In describing **Judas'** exit from the **Last Supper** in order to carry out his **betrayal** of Jesus, the Evangelist comments, "And it was night" (13:30).

LITERARY CRITICISM. This type of analysis of a **Gospel** text involves investigation of its words and images, characters, plot or structure, literary form, and meaning. With the help of biblical lexicons and concordances, it is possible to situate a word or image (e.g., **covenant**) in the framework of its historical development and thus better to appreciate its meaning in a specific text. Attending to how the characters interact in a story or how a speech unfolds is essential to grasping what the Evangelists wished to communicate. The ancient writers sometimes used forms of logic and discourse patterns (e.g., concentric structures—ABA) that may be foreign to readers today. The Gospels, which are long narratives about Jesus' deeds and words, contain within themselves smaller literary forms such as **parables**, healing stories, hymns, **proverbs**, and so on. Recognizing the literary forms that the writers chose is an indispensable step toward understanding their messages.

LITHOSTRATOS. *See* GABBATHA.

LITTLE ONES. A term used especially by **Matthew** in different contexts with different meanings. In the **Missionary Discourse** "these little ones" in Matt 10:42 seems to refer to the **twelve apostles** being sent out by Jesus. In the Community Discourse "these little ones" in 18:6, 18:10, and 18:14 appears to describe simple members of Jesus' movement who must not be led astray or despised because **God** has a special care for them. In the judgment scene in the **Eschatological Discourse** "the least of these" (25:40, 45) are those who should be the objects of good deeds done by members of "all the nations," who will be judged by the **Son of Man** on the basis of those deeds. Whether here they are Christian missionaries, simple believers, or just persons in need is not clear.

LOGOS. The Greek term meaning "word" was used to describe Jesus in John 1:1–18 as existing before creation and as present at creation (1:1–5) and as having taken human form ("flesh") and having lived among humankind (1:14). The term was used in Stoic philosophy and by Philo to describe the vital force and rational principle that guides and directs the universe. While some scholars find a background for the Johannine usage in the OT prophetic literature ("the word of the **Lord**"), a more likely background is the Jewish personification of **Wisdom** as a feminine figure (Prov 8:22–31; Sir 24:1–22; Wis 7; see also Col 1:15–20 and Heb 1:3 in the NT). While not explicitly mentioned in the body of **John's Gospel**, the designation of Jesus as the Word of God in the prologue expresses that **Gospel**'s major theme: Jesus is the revealer and the revelation of **God**.

LORD. In some contexts in the **Gospels** the term "Lord" (*Kyrios*) can be understood simply as a mark of politeness, the equivalent of "Sir." In the Greek versions of the OT, however, *Kyrios* is often used as the translation of the Hebrew divine name YHWH. In early Christian circles the highly theological connotation of the word was used commonly with regard to Jesus, thus suggesting his divinity. In the earliest NT letter (from around 50 CE), **Paul** refers to Jesus as "the Lord Jesus Christ" (1 Thess 1:1) without feeling the need to explain or defend his choice of words. Indeed "Jesus is Lord" (1 Cor 12:3) was an early Christian expression of faith, and the climax of the early Christian hymn preserved in Phil 2:6–11 is the confession by the entire cosmos that "Jesus Christ is Lord" (2:11). Since the Gospels were written some 20 years or more after Paul's letters, it is likely that where *Kyrios* appears with reference to Jesus, the Evangelists

MACCABEES. The Jewish dynasty founded in the 160s BCE by the **priest** Mattathias, the Hasmonean who ruled **Judea** and environs until the Romans began to exercise more direct control in the late first century BCE. The dynasty takes its name from the nickname of Judas (1 Macc 2:4), which has some connection with the Hebrew word for "hammer." Through the political and military efforts of Mattathias' brothers Jonathan and Simon, they managed to combine the roles of high priest, military leader, and chief politician (1 Macc 14:41–43). The exploits of the first few generations are described in 1 and 2 Maccabees, while the later generations are covered by **Josephus** in his *Jewish War* and *Jewish Antiquities*.

MAGI. Persian and Babylonian scholars and **priests** who were experts in astronomy/astrology and **dream** interpretation. According to Matt 2:1–12, they came to **Jerusalem** on the grounds that they had seen the star of the **King of the Jews** at its rising. What this phenomenon was has long been the subject of scientific speculation (comet, conjunction of planets, etc.), without any definitive solution. The prophecy of Balaam in Num 24:17 ("a star shall come out of Jacob") may be in the background. When the "star" stops over **Bethlehem**, they find the infant Jesus, offer him homage as befits a king, give him precious gifts, and return home without telling **Herod the Great** where the **child** was (2:7–8, 16). The traditional idea of three Magi derived from the number of gifts, not from any number of persons within the text.

MAGNIFICAT. The hymn attributed to **Mary** (but to **Elizabeth** in some ancient manuscripts) in Luke 1:46–55 is traditionally referred to by the first word in its Latin version meaning "magnifies" ("My soul magnifies the **Lord**"). In it, Mary rejoices that she is to be the mother of Jesus and interprets her role in his conception as an instance of how God raises up the lowly and puts down the proud, powerful, and rich, and of how **God** deals mercifully with his people **Israel**. The hymn is full of words and phrases from Hannah's song in 1 Sam 2:1–10.

MALCHUS. According to John 18:10, the name of the servant of the high **priest Caiaphas** whose right ear **Peter** cut off when Jesus was being **arrested**. The name is Nabataean. He is not named in the parallel texts (Matt 26:51; Mark 14:47; Luke 22:50). Luke in 22:51 claims that Jesus then touched the servant's ear and healed him.

MAMMON. The word occurs in Hebrew and Aramaic texts with the meanings "wealth, **money**, property." It derives from the Semitic root *'aman* ("believe, trust"—the origin of "**Amen**"), and refers to "that in which one places trust." In Matt 6:24 Jesus warns that "you cannot serve **God** and Mammon." In Luke 16:9, 16:11 it is specified as "unrighteous Mammon."

MARK, GOSPEL OF. Written around 70 CE probably at **Rome**, this **Gospel** is generally regarded as the earliest complete narrative of Jesus' public ministry. It presents Jesus' activities according to a three-part geographical outline: in **Galilee** and environs (1:1–8:21), on the way from Galilee to **Jerusalem** (8:22–10:52), and in Jerusalem during Holy Week (11:1–16:8). The central theme of all of Jesus' teaching and activity is the **kingdom of God** (1:15). Mark assumes familiarity with the various honorific titles applied to Jesus in early Christian circles: **Messiah**/Christ, **Son of David, Son of Man, Son of God, Lord**, etc. While portraying Jesus as a powerful healer and as a wise and authoritative **teacher**, Mark insists that he is also the **suffering** Messiah, and that his true identity cannot be understood apart from the mystery of the **cross**: "The Son of Man came . . . to give his life as a **ransom** for many" (10:45).

MARK, SECRET GOSPEL OF. Allegedly discovered by biblical scholar Morton Smith at the Mar Saba Monastery near **Jerusalem** in 1958, an otherwise unknown letter ascribed to Clement of Alexandria contains two quotations taken from a supposedly fuller version of **Mark's Gospel**. The longer quotation follows Mark 10:32–34 and tells how Jesus restored a young man to life at the request of his sister at **Bethany**. It sounds like an abbreviated version of the **Lazarus** story in John 11:1–44 until the young man invites Jesus to his home and they engage in what could be interpreted as a homosexual tryst while Jesus was "teaching him the mystery of the **kingdom of God**." The shorter quotation comes after Mark 10:46a and says that Jesus refused to receive the young man's sister and mother as well as his

own mother. While a few scholars regard these texts as really reflecting an early version of Mark's Gospel, many others suspect that they
are the activity of a later forger, perhaps even Smith himself.

MARRIAGE. In Judaism of Jesus' time, **divorce** was allowed on the
basis of Deut 24:1–4. But in Mark 10:2–9, Jesus interprets this **Mosaic** permission for divorce as a concession to the people's hardness
of heart. Instead he appeals to two earlier OT texts from Genesis to
propose that lifelong monogamy was **God**'s original intention: "God
made them male and female" (Gen 1:27); and "For this reason a man
shall leave his father and mother, and be joined to his wife, and the
two shall become one flesh" (Gen 2:24). Then from these two texts
he draws the conclusion that "what God has joined together, let no
one separate." (10:9). That Jesus taught lifelong monogamy as the
positive ideal of marriage is indicated by the many other NT texts
that confirm this **teaching** (1 Cor 7:10–11; Mark 10:10–12; Luke
16:18; Matt 5:32, 19:3–9), though some exceptions are made. Moreover, this restrictive position fits well with his other radical **teachings**
and is highly unusual (if not unique) in the Judaism of his time.

MARTHA AND MARY. The two sisters who, according to Luke
10:38–42, offered hospitality to Jesus "in a certain village" early in
Luke's journey narrative. While Martha busies herself with household tasks, Mary listens to what Jesus has to say and is praised by
him for choosing "the better part." In John 11:1–12:8 the two sisters
are living with their brother **Lazarus** in **Bethany**, near **Jerusalem**.
According to John 11:5, Jesus **"loved"** the three of them. When Jesus
arrives at their home, however, Lazarus has been dead for four days.
Both sisters gently rebuke Jesus: **"Lord,** if you had been here, my
brother would not have died" (John 11:21, 11:32). In response, and
as a foreshadowing of his own **resurrection**, Jesus restores Lazarus
to life. According to John 12:1–8, Martha served the dinner for Jesus,
at which Mary **anointed** his feet with expensive perfume and wiped
them with her hair.

MARY, GOSPEL OF. Related to the **Nag Hammadi** writings in style
and content, this work is one of the tractates in the Berlin **Gnostic**
Codex. The "Mary" in the title is **Mary Magdalene**. After engaging

in dialogue with his **disciples**, the risen Jesus departs and the disciples lament his absence and wonder how they can face the task of proclaiming his **gospel** to the **Gentiles**. Mary reassures them that Jesus' grace will be with them and will protect them. When Mary begins to reveal to them the secret **teachings** she learned from the risen Jesus in a vision, **Peter** expresses disbelief at her report. Levi, however, defends her and reminds them that Jesus "**loved** her more than us." Thus Mary exercises her role as the **apostle** to the apostles. Although this work tells us nothing about the historical figure of Jesus, it gives special prominence to Mary Magdalene and suggests her greater importance in some early Christian circles than even **Mary**, the mother of Jesus.

MARY, MOTHER OF JESUS. In Matt 1:18–25, **Joseph** finds his fiancée Mary to be pregnant and prepares to **divorce** her quietly when he is told in a dream that "the **child** conceived in her is from the **Holy Spirit**." Joseph in turn **marries** her and takes the child Jesus as his own. Along with Joseph and the child Jesus, Mary undergoes the trials and dangers described in Matt 2. Mary is especially prominent in Luke 1–2. There she receives the announcement from the **angel Gabriel** in **Nazareth** that her child will be the **Messiah** and **Son of God** (Luke 1:32, 35), is greeted by **Elizabeth** as "the mother of my **Lord**" (1:43), recites the hymn of praise known as the *Magnificat* (1:46–55), gives birth to Jesus in **Bethlehem** (2:7), is visited by shepherds (2:16), performs the Jewish rites of presentation and purification (2:22–38), returns to Nazareth (2:39–40), and searches for and finds the boy Jesus in the **Jerusalem temple** (2:41–52). Luke's emphasis on Mary as one who hears the word of **God** and acts upon it (see 1:38, 1:45, 2:19, 2:51) prepares for Jesus' own definition of his true **disciples** as those who hear the word of God and do it (8:21, 11:28), and suggests that Mary fits that definition perfectly. According to Acts 1:14, Mary was with Jesus' disciples in **Jerusalem** after his **ascension** and before Pentecost, thus making her the only person with Jesus from the beginning to the end of his earthly life. Mark refers to Mary twice, with reference to the "brothers" of Jesus (3:31–35, 6:3). Whether the **brothers and sisters** were full siblings, stepchildren of Joseph, or cousins has been debated for many centuries. In **John's Gospel**, Mary appears twice—at **Cana** (2:1–11) and at the **cross** (19:25–27), where she is called simply "the mother of Jesus." At the wedding feast in Cana she intercedes with Jesus, who miraculously turns water into **wine**. At the cross she forms a community of compassion with her son Jesus and the **Beloved Disciple**.

MARY MAGDALENE. A faithful follower of Jesus and a prominent witness to his **death** and **resurrection**. Her surname reflects her origin in the village of Magdala, on the western shore of the **Sea of Galilee**. According to Luke 8:2–3, Mary had been the beneficiary of an **exorcism** (presumably by Jesus), and, along with other **women**, provided for him and his companions "out of their resources." There is no reason to identify Mary with the "sinful woman" of Luke 7:36–50. The **Gospels** all agree that Mary Magdalene was present at Jesus' crucifixion and saw him die, that she went to the right **tomb** where she had seen him **buried**, and experienced him as alive again (Matt 28:9–10; John 20:11–18). The risen Jesus' commission to her to tell the other **disciples** that he was alive has led to the traditional description of her as "the **apostle** to the apostles."

MATTHEW, GOSPEL OF. In revising and expanding **Mark's Gospel**, Matthew followed Mark's basic geographical outline and included the many honorific titles of Jesus. But he greatly expanded Jesus' **teaching** by including material from the Sayings Source **Q** and other special traditions (**M**). He presented this material in five great speeches: the **Sermon on the Mount** (chaps. 5–7), the **Missionary Discourse** (10), the **Parables** (13), the Community Discourse (18), and the **Eschatological Discourse** (24–25). Composed around 85–90 CE probably at Antioch in Syria, this **Gospel** represents a Jewish–Christian response to the crisis facing all Jews after 70 CE about how the heritage of **Israel** as **God**'s people might be carried on. Matthew insisted that Jesus was the authoritative interpreter of that tradition, and the one in whom the prophetic promises in the Hebrew Scriptures were being fulfilled. By adding an **infancy narrative** in chapters 1–2, Matthew emphasized the Jewish roots of Jesus, and suggested that even in the events surrounding his birth Jesus was fulfilling Israel's Scriptures.

MEALS. *See* TABLE FELLOWSHIP.

MEIER, JOHN P. (1942–). In his multivolume project entitled *A Marginal Jew: Rethinking the Historical Jesus,* Meier, a Catholic **priest** of the archdiocese of New York and professor of NT at the University of Notre Dame, defined his primary task as history rather than theology. In *The Roots of the Problem and the Person* (1991), he treats sources and methodology and begins the discussion of Jesus' life. In *Mentor, Message, and Miracles* (1994), he deals with **John the Baptist**, Jesus' proclamation of **God's kingdom**, and his **miracles.** In *Companions and Competitors* (2001), he considers Jesus in his relationships with other Jews and situates him in the context of first-century Palestinian Judaism. In *Law and Love* (2009) he discusses Jesus' attitude toward and observance of the **Mosaic Law,** and which (if any) of the **love commands** in the **Gospels** come from Jesus and what were their range and meaning. The fifth and final volume will concern Jesus' **parables,** his self-designations or titles, and what led to his **death.** Central to Meier's undertaking is the application of the **criteria of authenticity** developed by NT scholars in the twentieth century. His five primary criteria are embarrassment (what created difficulty for the early **church**), discontinuity (with regard to Judaism and early Christianity), multiple attestation (material found in several independent traditions), coherence (what best fits with the first three criteria), and rejection and execution (what led to Jesus' death). The secondary (and more dubious) criteria include traces of Aramaic, Palestinian environment, vivid narration, and the supposed tendencies of the developing tradition. Meier's project involves applying these criteria to practically everything in the **Synoptic Gospels** (and occasionally to **John**) and discovering what may (or may not) be attributed with confidence to the **historical Jesus.**

MESSIAH. The term derives from the Hebrew root meaning "**anoint,**" and its Greek equivalent is *Christos.* In NT times the word could refer to a future descendant of **David** who (it was hoped) would restore **Israel** to greatness among the nations and serve as a powerful military leader (see *Psalms of Solomon* 17). Although there was no single, unified version of the Messiah among Jews, the connection with David was central (2 Sam 7:10–14; Ps 2). Other "messianic" OT texts included Gen 49:10, Num 24:17, Isa 11:1, and Jer 23:5–6, 33:14–17. While portraying Jesus as the Messiah, the Evangelists also insisted that his messiahship could only be understood in light of his **death** and **resurrection**. Indeed, Jesus accepts this title only where and when it is seemed most unlikely—at the moment of his condemnation before the Jewish council (Mark 14:61–62). His commands to be silent about his identity as the Messiah throughout **Mark's Gospel** (the so-called **messianic secret**) reinforce that very point. Moreover, the episode about David's son and the interpretation of Ps 110:1 in Mark 12:35–37 suggests that Messiah/Son of David did not adequately express the dignity of Jesus as **Lord**. Nevertheless, Christians very early referred to him as "Jesus Christ" (1 Thess 1:1) as if Messiah/Christ were his surname.

MESSIANIC SECRET. A motif chiefly in **Mark's Gospel** in which Jesus seems deliberately to hide his identity as the **Messiah**. The clearest example is in Mark 8:30, where after **Peter** has confessed Jesus to be the Messiah, Mark adds, "And he [Jesus] sternly ordered them not to tell anyone about him." Other elements in the Markan messianic secret motif are Jesus' injunctions to silence in **miracle** stories, his private instructions to his **disciples**, and his unsuccessful efforts at hiding from the public. Some interpret it as Jesus' effort to prevent a **violent** revolution centered on him, while others view it as Mark's attempt to explain the tension between the early **church**'s belief in Jesus as the Messiah and Jesus' own refusal to identify himself as the Messiah. A better explanation may be that Mark sought to redefine the term "Messiah" in the light of Jesus' **death** and **resurrection**, and so he put off revealing Jesus' true identity as the Messiah until his death (15:39) and resurrection (9:9).

MIRACLES. While today a miracle is frequently defined as an event that is an exception to the laws of nature, the Bible regards miracles more broadly as extraordinary and surprising events ("**signs and wonders**") that lead one to surmise that **God** was at work. In the OT **Moses** and the prophets **Elijah** and **Elisha** perform miracles. And **Israel**'s rescue from slavery at the exodus is considered to be the greatest miracle of all. In the **Synoptic Gospels** Jesus does 17 healings, 6 **exorcisms**, and 8 **nature miracles** (not counting parallel accounts). In the healings and exorcisms there is usually an element of faith on the petitioner's part, and the healing is generally immediate and complete. In the nature miracles there are many symbolic aspects and OT allusions. In **John's Gospel** he performs seven "signs" ranging from turning water into **wine** at **Cana** (John 2:1–11) to raising **Lazarus** from the dead (John 11:1–44). Even Jesus' opponents admit that he worked miracles. Their question concerned by what power— God or **Satan**—he did them. So in Mark 3:22–29 the **scribes** from **Jerusalem** charge that Jesus was possessed by a **demon** and was an instrument of Satan. Jesus responds by showing how illogical their position was, and suggests that it amounts to **blasphemy** against the **Holy Spirit**—the **unforgivable sin**. The key to understanding Jesus' miracles comes in the saying in Luke 11:20: "But if it is by the finger of God that I cast out demons, then the **kingdom of God** has come upon you." In other words, they are signs of the presence of God's kingdom in Jesus' person and ministry, and thus anticipations or pointers to the fullness of God's kingdom yet to come. While there are some parallels between Jesus' miracles and those done by Jewish **Galilean** charismatics like Hanina ben Dosa and Honi the Circle-drawer, Jesus generally acts on his own authority and power and so transcends the roles of petitioner and intermediary.

MISSIONARY DISCOURSE. In Jesus' time both in Palestine and all over the Greco-Roman world, religions and philosophies were spread by traveling missionaries. In each of the **Synoptic Gospels**, Jesus sends out his **disciples** to carry on and extend his mission of proclaiming **God's kingdom** in word and deed: Mark 6:6b–13; Matt 10:5–42; and Luke 9:1–6, 10:1–12. Jesus' instructions to them emphasize the importance of focusing on the mission of witnessing to **God**'s kingdom in its present and future aspects. He insists that they adopt a very simple lifestyle and accept whatever lodging they receive from local people. He also warns them to expect opposition, rejection, and persecution. Jesus' missionary discourses provided his disciples with concrete instructions for carrying out their task, and those who might encounter them with a checklist to help them distinguish authentic missionaries from imposters or charlatans.

MOCKERY. In the **passion narratives** Jesus is mocked first by members of the Jewish council or **Sanhedrin** (Mark 14:65; Matt 26:67–68; Luke 22:63–64), who are said to have spit on him, struck him, blindfolded him, and taunted him with the challenge to prophesy. While to the perpetrators this was mockery, to the Evangelists and their first readers the mockers were ironically correct in identifying Jesus as a **prophet**. Likewise, after **Pilate** sentenced Jesus to die, his soldiers engaged in mocking Jesus as a king or even an emperor (Mark 15:16–20; Matt 27:27–31; John 19:2–3). They dressed Jesus in a purple (or scarlet) robe, put a **crown of thorns** on him, placed a reed in his right hand like a scepter, knelt before him, and greeted him with "Hail, **King of the Jews**." Again those who mock Jesus are ironically correct: Jesus really is the King of the Jews. Finally when Jesus hangs on the **cross** (Mark 15:27–32; Matt 27:37–44; Luke 23:35–43), he is mocked by passers-by, **chief priests**, and even those dying with him. They too ironically identify Jesus as the **Messiah**, King of the Jews, and **Son of God**.

MONEY. According to Matt 20:2, 20:9, a day's work was valued at a denarius. The coin handed to Jesus in the dispute about paying taxes to Caesar (Matt 22:19; Mark 12:15; Luke 20:24) was most likely a denarius bearing the emperor's image and an inscription honoring him as in some way divine. Large transactions involved the **talent** (Matt 18:24, 25:14–30) or the mina (Luke 19:13–25). Smaller denominations included the chalkos, lepton, assarion, and quadrans. The temple tax (Matt 17:24–27) amounted to a didrachma, which was half a shekel; the Greek stater in the **fish**'s mouth equaled four drachmas, enough to pay for both Jesus and **Peter**. While necessarily involved in the use of money and relying on others for material support (Luke 8:3), Jesus warned against becoming enslaved to money: "You cannot serve **God** and wealth/**Mammon**" (Matt 6:24; Luke 16:13). Luke criticized the **Pharisees** as "lovers of money" (16:14). Jesus sent his **disciples** out without money (Mark 6:8 parr.). His apparent frustration with the commercialization of the **Jerusalem temple** and especially the activities of the moneychangers there led to his prophetic action in "**cleansing**" the temple (Mark 11:15–19).

MOSES. The great liberator and lawgiver of ancient **Israel** is generally referred to in the **Gospels** with respect as the one responsible for promulgating the Torah and the specific laws within it. In Matt 2 there are several parallels between the infancies of Jesus and Moses as he is portrayed in Exod 1–2. In the **Sermon on the Mount** (Matt 5–7), Jesus appears as the authoritative interpreter of the **Law of Moses**, especially in 5:17–48. At the **transfiguration** of Jesus, Moses and **Elijah** represent the Law and the **Prophets** (Matt 17:3–4; Mark 9:4–5; Luke 9:30, 9:33), and serve as witnesses to the glory of Jesus.

MOTHER OF JESUS. *See* MARY, MOTHER OF JESUS.

MOUNT OF OLIVES. Also known as Olivet, this is a ridge running north–south, to the east of **Jerusalem**. Its soil is relatively fertile, and olive trees have been cultivated on it for many centuries. **Gethsemane**, which means "oil press," was on it or near it. According to Zech 14:4, the Mount of Olives is where God will appear and defeat **Israel**'s enemies forever and the **kingdom of God** will appear. This is where Jesus begins his triumphal entry into Jerusalem (Matt 21:1–9; Mark 11:1–10; Luke 19:29–38), delivers his final (**eschatological**) **discourse** (Matt 24:3; Mark 13:3), **prays** before his **arrest** (Matt 26:30; Mark 14:26; Luke 22:39; John 18:1), and **ascends** into **heaven** (Luke 24:50; Acts 1:12).

MUSTARD SEED, PARABLE OF (MARK 4:30–32; MATT 13:31–32; LUKE 13:18–19). This short **parable** illustrates key aspects of Jesus' understanding of the **kingdom of God**: Its small beginning will issue in a great harvest; something is happening in the present; and the process is mysterious, suggesting divine guidance. Similar points are made in its companion parable of the **Seed Growing Secretly** (Mark 4:26–29).

MYTH. In general, a myth is a story or narrative that expresses the basic values and customs of a culture or a people. With regard to the **Gospels** the most famous proponent of the "mythical" approach was David Friedrich Strauss (1808–1874) in his *The Life of Jesus Critically Examined*. Strauss sought to find a middle way between supernaturalism and rationalism interpreting the Gospels. Whereas the supernaturalists took all the Gospel stories literally, the rationalists explained them away. Strauss conceived of the category of "evangelical mythus" as more adequate to what he regarded as the nature of the Gospels. He defined the category as "a narrative relating directly or indirectly to Jesus, which may be considered not as the expression of a fact, but as the product of an idea of his earliest followers" (p. 86). In this approach, the Gospel stories about Jesus were understood as primarily vehicles for early Christians to communicate general truths. Almost a hundred years later, **Rudolf Bultmann** proposed the project of "demythologization," which involved identifying those truths and translating them into the categories of existentialist philosophy.

– N –

NAG HAMMADI GOSPELS. In late 1945 there were discovered in Egypt 12 codices (books) containing 52 treatises written in Coptic, a late form of Egyptian using Greek letters of the alphabet. The books seem to have been part of the library of a Christian monastery and were produced in the mid-fourth century CE. Among the treatises were several works with the title "**Gospel.**" Here the term was meant more in its original sense of "good news" than in the acquired sense of a narrative about Jesus' life and **teachings**. The *Gospel of Truth* is a gnostic meditation on the knowledge imparted by the Word of God from the **Father** and the joy and wholeness it brings to its recipients. The *Gospel of Thomas* is a collection of 114 sayings attributed to Jesus, many of which are given a gnostic interpretation. The *Gospel of Philip* is a rambling discourse on various topics, and is distinctive for its gnostic interpretations of sacraments. The *Gospel of the Egyptians* (not the same as the **apocryphal** Jewish-Christian Gospel quoted by some **Church** Fathers) describes the gnostic **savior** figure Seth in terms analogous to what the NT says about Jesus. Related to these Nag Hammadi Gospels are the *Gospel of Mary* (which features **Mary Magdalene** as the teacher of the **apostles**) and the *Gospel of Judas* (which describes **Judas'** role in Jesus' last days), since both are gnostic in orientation. **Gnosticism** was a philosophy or worldview that prized spiritual knowledge as the highest good, and these Gospels were part of the Christian appropriation of this approach. They were composed in Greek in the second and third centuries, and then translated into Coptic. Their Coptic versions were preserved by monks in Egypt. The Nag Hammadi codices seem to have been hidden away in the 360s CE until their recovery in the mid-twentieth century. While fascinating in their own right and important for their contributions to the history of philosophy and of early Christianity, they tell us little or nothing about the historical figure of Jesus. The possible exception is the *Gospel of Thomas*, which may contain some early versions of Jesus' sayings when they are stripped of their gnostic overlay.

NAME OF JESUS. *See* JESUS, NAME OF.

NARRATIVE CRITICISM. As a form of **literary criticism**, narrative criticism pays special attention to a **Gospel** text as it now stands before us, that is, to the "text in front of us," rather than to what may be behind the text or what we might want the text to say to us. It focuses on the narrator and the implied reader and their points of view, as well as the characters in the text, the plot, the time and place, and so on.

NATHANAEL. The **disciple** introduced to Jesus by **Philip** in John 1:45–51. While initially skeptical due to Jesus' apparent origin in **Nazareth**, Nathanael quickly comes to regard him as "**Son of God**" and "King of **Israel**" (1:49). According to John 21:2, Nathanael was from **Cana** in **Galilee**. He has sometimes been identified with Bartholomew in the Synoptic lists of the **twelve apostles** (Matt 10:3; Mark 3:18; Luke 6:14).

NATURE MIRACLES. While most of Jesus' **miracles** are healings and **exorcisms**, several of them more directly involve the suspension of the laws of nature. They include his stilling a storm (Mark 4:35–41; Matt 8:23–27; Luke 8:22–25), feeding 5,000 persons (Mark 6:35–44; Matt 14:15–21; Luke 9:12–17) and feeding 4,000 persons (Mark 8:1–10; Matt 15:32–39), walking on water (Mark 6:45–52; Matt 14:22–33; John 6:16–121), getting **money** to pay the temple tax (Matt 17:24–27), changing water into **wine** (John 2:1–11), cursing and withering the **fig tree** (Mark 11:12–14, 11:20–21; Matt 21:18–20), and bringing about a miraculous catch of **fish** (Luke 5:1–11; John 21:1–14). These stories are full of OT echoes and allusions, and have obvious symbolic and theological significance. They give the impression of having been told and retold in early Christian circles, to the point that historians find it difficult to isolate what might have been their factual core (if any).

NAZARETH. A village in central **Galilee**, south of Sepphoris. The comment attributed to **Nathanael** in John 1:46 ("Can anything good come from Nazareth?") suggests its obscurity and lack of importance. According to Luke 2:4, Nazareth was the home of **Joseph** and **Mary**. Nazareth was regarded as Jesus' hometown (Matt 13:54; Mark 6:1; Luke 4:16) before he set off on his public ministry. He is often called a "Nazarene" (Mark 1:24, 10:46; John 18:5, 18:7), and his followers were known as "Nazarenes" (Acts 24:5). The **Gospels** agree that Jesus in his ministry had little success in Nazareth (Matt 13:54–58; Mark 6:1–6; Luke 4:16–30).

NAZIRITE. According to Num 6:1–21, men or **women** might consecrate themselves to **God** as nazirites for a specific period with a special vow. During this time, they were to abstain from **wine**, let their hair grow, and avoid contact with corpses. The accounts of the births of Samson (Judg 13:4–14) and Samuel (1 Sam 1:11) suggest that an infant might be consecrated as a nazirite to God. In Luke 1:15, **John the Baptist** is described in nazirite terms ("he must never drink wine or strong drink"). The designation of Jesus as a "Nazorean" in Matt 2:23 may also be associated with his status as a nazirite. According to Acts 18:18 and 21:20–26, **Paul** participated in the rituals connected with closing a period of observing a nazirite vow.

NET, PARABLE OF THE FISH (MATT 13:47–50). The companion to the parable of the **Wheat and the Weeds** (Matt 13:24–30, 13:36–43), it uses the process of **fishermen** sorting out the catch from their net to illustrate some aspects of the **kingdom of God**. It envisions a final judgment when the **righteous** and the wicked will be separated and treated justly in terms of rewards and punishments, and counsels patience and tolerance in the present with regard to the mixed reception of Jesus' proclamation of **God**'s kingdom. *See also* LAST JUDGMENT.

NICODEMUS. A **Pharisee** and a Jewish leader who according to John 3:1–10 visited Jesus by night and engaged him in dialogue. His misunderstanding of Jesus' **teaching** about the need to be born "from above" as being born "again" leads into a monologue in 3:11–21 that summarizes the great themes of Johannine theology. According to John 7:50–51, Nicodemus tries to convince the other Jewish leaders to give Jesus a fair hearing. And from John 19:39 we find that Nicodemus assisted **Joseph of Arimathea** in seeing to the **burial of Jesus**. The implication may be that he too had become a **disciple** of Jesus.

NICODEMUS, GOSPEL OF. The two major parts of this work, *Acts of Pilate* and *Christ's Descent into Hell*, are generally dated to the fifth or sixth century. The first part purports to rely on an account by **Nicodemus** (see John 3:1–10, 7:50–51, 19:39) about events surrounding Jesus' **death** and **resurrection**, with a rather favorable attitude toward **Pilate** and a very negative portrayal of the Jewish leaders. It expands greatly on the canonical **passion** accounts and reads like a modern novel. The second part considers the effects of Christ's descent into Sheol/**Hades** (see 1 Pet 3:19, 4:6) on those who had been imprisoned there and its impact on **Satan** and Hades as the now-defeated opponents of Christ. While interesting and entertaining, this work, like most of the **apocryphal Gospels**, tells us more about the time when it was written than about Jesus as he lived and died in first-century Palestine.

NINEVEH, NINEVITES. The ancient capital of the Assyrian Empire and its inhabitants. They appear in the **Gospels** only in Matt 12:41 and Luke 11:30, 11:32, as part of the "**sign** of **Jonah**" passages. In the OT book of Jonah, these hated enemies of **Israel** repent in response to the **prophet**'s preaching. In the NT they compare favorably to Jesus' contemporaries in Israel who refuse to **repent** in response to his preaching of **God's kingdom**.

NOAH AND THE FLOOD, PARABLE OF (MATT 24:37–39; LUKE 17:26–27). Just as the great flood (see Gen 6–7) came upon Noah's **generation** suddenly and disrupted normal human existence, so will the (second) coming of the **Son of Man** be sudden and disruptive. This point is underlined with a similar **parable** about Lot's generation in Luke 17:28–30 and several short parables (two men in a field, two **women** at the mill, the thief in the night) in Matt 24:40–44 and Luke 17:31–35 (and 12:39–40).

NUNC DIMITTIS. The short hymn about the infant Jesus attributed to the old man **Simeon** in the **Jerusalem temple** according to Luke 2:29–32 is often referred by the opening words in its Latin version, meaning "Now you may dismiss." Drawing on phrases chiefly from Isa 40–55, the hymn identifies the infant Jesus as the **salvation** (Isa 40:5) to be seen by all peoples (Isa 52:10), the **light** to the **Gentiles** (Isa 42:6, 49:6), and the glory of **Israel** (Isa 46:13).

– O –

OATHS AND SWEARING. In Matt 5:33–37, Jesus quotes Lev 19:12 (see also Exod 20:16; Deut 5:20) about not swearing false oaths and acknowledges the obligation to fulfill one's vows to **God**. Then he forbids swearing by various substitutes for the divine name— **heaven**, earth, or **Jerusalem**—that had developed in some circles in Judaism. He concludes that if you wish to avoid swearing falsely, avoid swearing oaths at all, and be content with merely saying, "Yes, yes" and "No, no." The same **teaching** appears in Jas 5:12, without its being attributed directly to Jesus. The prohibition of oaths fits well with Jesus' other radical teachings and was unusual (if not unique) in the Judaism of his time.

ORAL LAW. In **rabbinic literature** the Torah (or Law) consists not only of the first five books of the written Bible but also of the traditions and customs related to biblical and other teachings integrated into the whole complex of Judaism. The assumption is that on Mount Sinai **God** delivered to **Moses** some traditions orally rather than in writing, and these have been faithfully transmitted orally among Jews for many generations (see Mishnah *Abot* 1:1). According to **Josephus**, "the **Pharisees** have passed on to the people certain regulations handed down by former **generations** and not recorded in the **Laws of Moses**" (*Ant.* 13.297). This view explains why the debates between Jesus and the Pharisees were often so hostile, since Jesus seems to have devalued the Pharisees' reliance on **oral traditions** (see Mark 7:1–23; Matt 15:1–20).

ORAL TRADITION. The **Gospels** originated in what was primarily an oral culture. Rather than writing books, the earliest Christians handed down their memories of and traditions about Jesus in small oral units, many of which eventually made their way into the four **canonical Gospels**. The devices of keywords, repetitions, and chiastic and concentric structures (e.g., Mark 9:42–50) bear witness to the underlying process of oral transmission of materials about Jesus. Even when the **Gospels** appeared in written narrative forms, they were most likely read or recited orally in communal settings, and so most early Christians would have heard (rather than read) these texts. For historians, the prominence of oral transmission as the earliest vehicle for information about Jesus raises questions about the accuracy, extent, and authenticity of the material.

– P –

PALM SUNDAY, ENTRY INTO JERUSALEM ON. The designation derives from **John**'s account of Jesus' entry into **Jerusalem** and the **crowd**'s action in taking "branches of palm trees" and going out to meet him. But palm branches would be better suited to the feasts of Tabernacles (Lev 23:39–43) and Hanukkah (1 Macc 13:51; 2 Macc 10:7). The terms used in Matt 21:8 and Mark 11:8 are not so specific, and **Luke** omits any mention. More important than the variety of branches is the event that took place on Palm Sunday—the "triumphal" entry of Jesus into Jerusalem: Matt 21:1–9, Mark 11:1–10, Luke 19:28–40, and John 12:12–19. The event was undoubtedly a symbolic action or **prophetic** demonstration, and full of **messianic** overtones. The king rides on a **donkey** (Zech 9:9) and comes from the **Mount of Olives** (Zech 14:4), and the crowd celebrates the coming of **David**'s **kingdom** (Ps 118:26). Coming at **Passover**, the action of Jesus would have alarmed both the Roman officials and the Jewish leadership, who would have regarded Jesus as another in a long line of Jewish religious-political troublemakers. It is historically very likely that Jesus inaugurated his ministry in Jerusalem in a provocative way like this. It surely contributed to his **arrest** and **death**. But how many people witnessed it, and what effect it had on the general population of the city, we do not know.

PAPYRUS EGERTON 2. The fragments from this papyrus codex are dated to around 150 CE. The first leaf reports on a hostile confrontation between Jesus and some **scribes** in Johannine language, and goes on to describe Jesus healing a **leper** as in Mark 1:40–44. The second leaf first narrates a confrontation between Jesus and some opponents about giving kings their due (see Mark 12:13–17), and then has Jesus enact one of his "seed" **parables** and so produces a marvelous harvest (see Mark 4:1–34). The papyrus is important for its very early dating and as a witness to the practice of drawing on (**oral** or written?) materials found in various **canonical Gospels**. Whether it provides any additional valuable historical information about Jesus is doubtful.

PARABLES. Derived from the Greek verb *paraballo* ("place beside"), a parable suggests an analogy between one thing and another. The Hebrew equivalent term *mashal* has a wider scope, including **proverbs**, riddles, puzzles, examples, etc. The classic definition (from **C. H. Dodd**) is that a parable is a narrative taken from nature or everyday life about an interesting and unusual case that points to another level (the **kingdom of God**) and teases the listener/reader into active thinking. In the **Synoptic Gospels** Jesus frequently uses parables to illustrate his understanding of the kingdom of **God**, which was the central theme of his **teaching** and activity. Many parables begin with phrases such as "the kingdom of God is like." There are collections of Jesus' parables in Matt 13, Mark 4, and Luke 8. Other parables are prominent in Matt 24–25 and throughout Luke 9–19. It is generally assumed that in the parables we can hear the voice of Jesus, if not always his exact words. Many of them reflect everyday life in **Galilee** in Jesus' time, where agriculture and **fishing** were major economic enterprises. Since Jesus understood that bringing about the fullness of the kingdom is to be God's task in the future ("Thy kingdom come"), analogies with his hearers' everyday lives (parables) were an appropriate vehicle for his teachings about it. Throughout history, Jesus' parables have often been interpreted as allegories in which each element was identified with someone or something else. The result was frequently an obscuring of the more basic point about the kingdom of God and related matters. Modern parable scholarship, following C. H. Dodd and **Joachim Jeremias**, has restored the parables to their original setting in Jesus' proclamation of God's kingdom. It has also enlivened appreciation of Jesus' skill as a storyteller and of the elements of mystery and challenge inherent in his parables. Entries on the most important individual **Gospel** parables are provided throughout this volume.

PARACLETE. *See* ADVOCATE.

PARADISE. Based on an Old Persian word, "paradise" originally referred to a royal park with trees and streams. In the Greek translation of the OT, *paradeisos* was used to describe the Garden of Eden in Gen 2–3. Then in Jewish **apocalyptic** writings the term was used to describe the future abode of the **righteous (heaven)**. This sense underlies Jesus' promise to the "good thief" in Luke 24:43, "Today you will be with me in paradise." Thus even on the **cross** Jesus continues his ministry of compassion to marginal persons.

PAROUSIA. The Greek word *parousia* means "presence, arrival, advent," and is used in the NT and Christian theology to refer to belief in the second coming of the risen Jesus after his **resurrection** and **ascension**. Early Christians looked forward to the second coming of Jesus as a pivotal moment in the fulfillment of their hopes for eternal life in the **kingdom of God**. They devised a short **prayer** in Aramaic, *Maranatha*, which means "Our **Lord**, come." This prayer appears in Aramaic in 1 Cor 16:22 and in Greek in Rev 22:20. The use of Aramaic, which was the language of Jesus and his first followers, suggests that the prayer originated very early in the history of Christianity. Its occurrence at the end of two NT books, among other prayers and greetings, indicates that it was well known and widely accepted. The earliest complete document in the NT, **Paul**'s First Letter to the Thessalonians, shows that belief in Jesus' second coming was part of Christian faith from earliest times. Paul regarded the Thessalonians as a source of hope for himself "before our Lord

Jesus at his coming" (2:19). In his scenario for the end of this age and the **Last Judgment,** Paul assigned a prominent role to the risen Jesus and envisioned eternal life as being with him forever (4:13–18). He also warned that the **day of the Lord** will come "like a thief in the night" (5:2), that is, suddenly and when least expected.

PASSION NARRATIVES. The accounts of Jesus' passion and **death** in the four **Gospels**—Matt 26–27, Mark 14–15, Luke 22–23, and John 18–19—agree on many basic matters. They tell us that Jesus was **betrayed** by **Judas**, was **arrested**, underwent two hearings or **trials**, was sentenced to die by crucifixion, died on a **cross**, and was **buried** outside the walls of **Jerusalem**. **Mark**'s passion narrative seems to be the earliest written source. However, large blocks of it may well have existed before Mark wrote his Gospel around 70 CE. **Matthew** and **Luke** independently used Mark's narrative as a source and included material from other traditions as well. While agreeing on many points with the others, **John**'s passion narrative represents a separate tradition. None of the Evangelists set out to write a detailed chronicle of the events leading up to Jesus' death, though each provides some reliable historical facts. But their primary interest was in the theological significance of Jesus' death: as a **sacrifice** for us and for our sins (Mark), in accord with **God**'s will revealed in the Scriptures (Matthew), as an example of fidelity to God and to his own principles (Luke), and as part of his work in revealing God and returning in glory to his **Father** (John).

PASSION PREDICTIONS. At three points in his journey to **Jerusalem** according to **Mark** (8:31, 9:31, 10:33–34), Jesus prophesied in some detail about his coming **passion**, **death**, and **resurrection**. These sayings appear also in Matt 16:21, 17:22–23, and 20:18, as well as in Luke 9:22, 9:44, and 18:31–32. In each case Jesus refers to himself as the "**Son of Man**." The link between the Son of Man and **suffering** is not made elsewhere in the Jewish tradition. While the focus of these statements is Jesus' passion and death, each prediction ends with a prophecy of his resurrection. At each point the **disciples** fail to understand, and Jesus has to correct them and provide further instruction. The third passion prediction is so detailed that it has been described as the "program" for the **passion narrative**. This observation raises the historical question about the extent to which these passion-resurrection predictions were mainly prophecies after the fact (*vaticinia ex eventu*). That Jesus had strong forebodings of the fate that awaited him in Jerusalem is very likely. The critical issue is whether he spoke about it with such clarity and in such detail.

PASSOVER. The **festival** celebrating **God**'s deliverance of **Israel** from slavery in Egypt; it was originally an agricultural festival and was observed over an eight-day period. The extensive description of Passover in Exod 12–13 presents it primarily as a household or family celebration at which a lamb is slaughtered, cooked, and eaten. In Deut 16:1–8 and later texts, however, Passover became a pilgrimage feast (to **Jerusalem** and its temple) and the lamb was understood to be primarily a **sacrifice** offered to **God**. In the **Synoptic Gospels**, chiefly on the basis of Mark 14:12–16, Jesus' **Last Supper** is assumed to be an official Passover meal celebrated at the beginning of the eight-day festival, though there is no mention of the lamb or any other distinctive foods or rituals pertaining to Passover. **John**, however, links Jesus' death with the slaughter of the Passover sacrifices in the **Jerusalem temple** (John 13:1, 19:14, 19:31, 19:42), before the official start of the festival ("the day of preparation"). Thus Jesus dies as "the **Lamb of God**" (John 1:29, 19:36), the perfect sacrifice offered to God. The connection between Jesus' **death** and Passover was already made by **Paul** in 1 Cor 5:7–8.

PAUL. The letters of Paul are the earliest complete documents (from the 50s CE) in the New Testament. Paul focused especially on Jesus' **death** and **resurrection**. His interest lay not in the details of those events but rather in their significance for believers and their theological implications. Paul was convinced that Jesus had made possible a new and better way of relating to **God**. From this conviction he developed theological terms such as justification, redemption, reconciliation, **salvation**, sanctification, and so on. He showed little interest in the events of Jesus' public ministry or in his **teachings**. However, he did cite Jesus' prohibition of **divorce** in 1 Cor 7:10–11, though he immediately allowed an exception to it. And he quoted Jesus' words at the **Last Supper** in 1 Cor 11:24–25.

PEARL, PARABLE OF THE (MATT 13:45–46). Paired with the parable of the **Hidden Treasure**, this short parable stresses the extraordinarily great value of the **kingdom of God** and the single-minded response it deserves. The importance of the search is highlighted.

PERRIN, NORMAN (1920–1976). In *Rediscovering the Teaching of Jesus* (1967), Perrin, then teaching at the University of Chicago, sought to establish what may be known with reasonable certainty about the **teaching** of Jesus. In doing so he made abundant use of comparative material from **rabbinic** and other Jewish sources (after the pattern of his teacher, **Joachim Jeremias**), while incorporating the **form-critical** and **hermeneutical** perspectives of **Rudolph Bultmann**. The basic tools that Perrin used were the criteria for detecting historical material underlying the **Gospel** texts: dissimilarity, coherence, and multiple attestation. And he applied these criteria to passages that held the best promise of recovering the teachings of Jesus: the **parables**, the **kingdom of God** texts, and the **Lord's Prayer**.

PETER. A **Galilean fisherman** named Simon, son of Jona, whom Jesus nicknamed "Peter" (meaning "**Rocky**"), presumably in reference to some character trait of his (Mark 3:16; John 1:42). According to John 1:44, he and his brother **Andrew** were from Bethsaida. Jesus called them to be among his first **disciples** while they were working as fishermen in **Capernaum** (Mark 1:16–18). They became part of the **twelve apostles**, and Peter along with **James** and **John** formed the inner circle among them. Peter correctly identified Jesus as the **Messiah** (Mark 8:29) but was rebuked by him for refusing to accept Jesus' prophecy of his **suffering** and **death** (8:32). He was also one of the witnesses to Jesus' **transfiguration** (Mark 9:2–8). While Peter served as the spokesman for the 12 and is always named first among them, he is nonetheless portrayed by **Matthew** as an example of "little faith." All the Gospels agree in their **passion narratives** (Matt 26:69–75; Mark 14:66–72; Luke 22:54–62; John 18:15–18) that Peter denied even knowing Jesus. This was not the kind of story that early Christians would have made up about one of their heroes, and so it must have some historical basis. Nevertheless, after his experience of the risen Jesus, Peter became the archetype of the forgiven sinner (John 21:15–19) and was transformed into a fearless preacher of the **gospel** of Jesus (Acts 1–12).

PETER, GOSPEL OF. The extant section of this late second-century CE work purportedly written by Simon **Peter** begins with the **trial of Jesus** before **Pilate**, narrates the events surrounding Jesus' **death** and **resurrection**, and breaks off before the risen Jesus' **appearance** to Peter and other **disciples** in **Galilee**. Most of the material clearly depends on the four **canonical Gospels**, though it is presented with anti-Jewish and early **gnostic** tendencies. What is unique is its description of Jesus' resurrection in which two huge men (**angels?**) descend from **heaven** and assist Jesus out of the **tomb** with "a **cross** following him." Then another man comes down, enters the tomb, and delivers the message to **Mary Magdalene** and the other **women** that Jesus "is risen and gone." Whether this episode reflects an early tradition or is simply the product of one writer's imagination is debated among scholars.

PHARISEES. The Pharisees were an observant and influential group of Jews prominent in **Israel** from the second century BCE to the first century CE. Their name most likely derives from the Hebrew word *perushim* ("separated ones"). At some points in their history they appear to have been a strong social-political movement having influence over both rulers and the common people, while at other times they seem to have been more like a religious sect or even a Hellenistic philosophical school promoting a distinctive way of Jewish life. According to the Mishnah, their chief interests were eating in a state of ritual **purity**, tithing and agricultural offerings, making rules about raising crops, observing the **Sabbath** and other Jewish **festivals**, and clarifying **marriage** laws. According to **Josephus**, they insisted on free will, the **resurrection of the dead**, and divine judgment resulting in rewards and punishments. In comparison with other contemporary Jewish movements (**Sadducees, Essenes,** etc.) they seem to have been more innovative and progressive in adapting the precepts of the **Torah** to the changing circumstances and demands of their age. The **Gospels** present them as the chief opponents of Jesus, emphasizing careful observance of the Law and the traditions surrounding it, seeking popular respect and influence, and sharing common **meals** (perhaps in their view replicating the temple cult in ordinary homes). Of all the Jewish groups in his time, Jesus seems to have been closest to the Pharisees, sharing at least a theological agenda with them, and agreeing with them on belief in the resurrection of the dead and on some Sabbath observances. He is frequently invited to the houses of Pharisees and shares meals with them. The vigorous criticisms of the Pharisees (and **scribes**) in Matt 23 probably reflect the formative role of the Pharisees in the renewal of Judaism after the destruction of **Jerusalem** and its **temple** in 70 CE. **Paul** was a Pharisee before his experience of the risen Jesus on the Damascus Road (Phil 3:5; Acts 23:6).

PHILIP. A follower of Jesus, who is always listed fifth among the **twelve apostles** (Matt 10:3; Mark 3:18; Luke 6:14; Acts 1:13). In **John's Gospel**, Philip is one of Jesus' first **disciples** and is said to be from Bethsaida (1:43–44; see 12:21), serves as foil to Jesus in two passages (6:5–7, 14:8–11), and acts as the intermediary for some Greeks who wish to see Jesus (12:20–21). The evangelist Philip who is prominent in Acts 8 (see also 6:5 and 21:8) may be the same person as the **apostle** Philip.

PHILIP, GOSPEL OF. Attributed to **Philip** the **apostle**, this Coptic **gnostic** text found at **Nag Hammadi** is a collection of statements about various topics, including the sacraments. It is notable for attributing human **suffering** and death to the separation of the sexes with the sin of **Adam** and Eve, and for defining Christ's mission as repairing that separation and uniting the two sexes and so giving life again to those who had died because of the separation. Not a narrative **gospel** like the four **canonical Gospels**, the work was probably written in Greek by a Valentinian gnostic in the second half of the third century, perhaps in Syria. It tells us nothing about Jesus as a historical figure.

PHYLACTERIES. In Matt 23:5, Jesus illustrates the religious ostentation of the **scribes** and **Pharisees** by charging that "they make their phylacteries broad." A phylactery in this context is a small leather case strapped to the forehead and arm during **prayer**. Several OT passages (Exod 13:1–16; Deut 6:4–9, 11:13–22) speak of having a sign, a memorial, and frontlets between the eyes and on the arm while in prayer. **Rabbinic** practice took these passages literally and enclosed miniature copies of these texts in cases called *tefillin* ("prayers"). The term "phylactery" suggests that they were also regarded as protections or amulets.

PILATE, PONTIUS. The Roman governor or prefect of **Judea** from 26 to 36 CE, under whom Jesus was executed. While **Josephus** and Philo describe him as obstinate, cruel, and corrupt, the **Gospel passion narratives** portray him as weak and vacillating, at least in the case of Jesus. He becomes a major figure when the Jewish leaders hand Jesus over to his jurisdiction (Matt 27; Mark 15; Luke 23; John 18:28–19:38). According to John 18:31, Jews at this time could not administer capital punishment. While initially reluctant to act in Jesus' case, he eventually gives into the **crowd**'s pressure (incited by the **chief priests** and **scribes**) on him. While the Evangelists tend to blame the Jewish leaders for Jesus' execution, from a legal perspective Pilate had the major responsibility. The mode of Jesus' execution (crucifixion) and the official charge on the **cross** ("**King of the Jews**") confirm the primary Roman responsibility.

POOR, POVERTY. In the Bible the "poor" may lack material goods, honor, and/or power. In the **Gospels** Jesus and his **disciples** embrace material poverty in the service of their mission to proclaim **God**'s kingdom. Jesus regards the poor as especially close to God: "Blessed are you who are poor, for yours is the **kingdom of God**" (Luke 6:20). He also declares that excessive concern for wealth can be an obstacle to approaching God and entering God's kingdom, while voluntary poverty for the sake of the kingdom will be rewarded abundantly in this age and the age to come (Mark 10:23–31). Jesus also challenges his followers to share their material goods in the present time, especially in the **parable of the Rich Man and Lazarus** in Luke 16:19–31. The message of that story is that the present is the appropriate time to share with the poor before it is too late and the "great chasm" will be fixed between **heaven** and **Hades**.

POUNDS, PARABLE OF THE (LUKE 19:11–27). The content of this **parable** is close to that of the parable of the **Talents** in Matt

25:14–30, which recommends bold, decisive, and fruitful action in preparation for the **final judgment** accompanying the full coming of **God's kingdom** and the glorious **Son of Man**. In **Luke**'s version, the context is Jesus' final journey to **Jerusalem**, and it serves to correct the impression that his entry into the city will mark the final establishment of **God**'s kingdom. Many scholars find in Luke 19:12–15 an allusion to one of **Herod**'s embassies to the Roman emperor to seek official approval for his reign in Palestine.

PRAETORIUM. Originally the Latin designation for the tent of the praetor (or general) in a military camp, the term came to designate the headquarters of a Roman prefect or governor. According to Mark 15:16, Matt 27:27, and John 18:28, 18:33, and 19:9, the praetorium was where Jesus was interrogated by **Pontius Pilate**. In this case, the praetorium seems to have been located in **Jerusalem**—either at the Fortress Antonia north of the **temple** area, or (more likely) at **Herod the Great**'s palace at the western edge of the city.

PRAYER. Prayer involves raising the mind and heart to **God** and its expression in words. In the Bible the two basic forms of prayer are petition and praise. According to **Luke**, Jesus prayed at the most important moments in his ministry, and in his **teaching** he encouraged persistence in prayers of petition (see Luke 11:1–13, 18:1–14). The **Lord's Prayer** ("Our Father") is represented in Matt 6:9–13 and Luke 11:2–4 as Jesus' own prayer for the full coming of **God's kingdom**. In **Gethsemane** Jesus schools himself in prayer to accept the **cup** of **suffering**, and on the **cross** he recites lament **psalms** (Mark 15:34; Matt 27:46; Luke 23:46). Luke's account of Jesus' infancy features the hymns of praise known as the *Magnificat*, the *Benedictus*, and the *Nunc Dimittis*. Other early Christian hymns about Jesus can be found in Phil 2:6–11, Col 1:15–20, and John 1:1–18.

PRE-EXISTENCE. According to the early Christian hymn preserved in Col 1:15–20, Jesus was "the firstborn of all creation" and "before all things." Likewise in John 1:1–18 Jesus as the Word of **God** was "in the beginning with God," and "all things came into being through him." In John 8:58, Jesus declares "before **Abraham** was, I am." The NT claims about Jesus' pre-existence echo the descriptions of personified **Wisdom** in Prov 8:22–31 ("the Lord created me at the beginning of his work") and Sir 24:3–22 ("I came forth from the mouth of the Most High").

PRIEST. In the OT, priests came from the tribe of Levi (Deut 10:9, 33:8–11) and traced their ancestry to Aaron (Exod 28:1). Only the author of **Hebrews** describes Jesus as a priest, though he recognized that Jesus belonged to the tribe of Judah and so could not qualify or function as a priest on earth (see 7:14). Nevertheless, because he regarded Jesus' **death** as the perfect **sacrifice** for sins and believed that Jesus offered himself willingly, he reasoned that Jesus should be considered as the great high priest. And so he developed the idea of an older and better priesthood associated with Melchizedek (Gen 14:18–20; Ps 110:4) and assigned Jesus to that priesthood. Much of Hebrews is devoted to showing the inadequacy of the Levitical priesthood and the superiority of the priesthood of Jesus.

PRODIGAL SON, PARABLE OF THE (LUKE 15:11–32). This parable is the third in the series of **parables** in Luke 15 about a lost sheep, a lost coin, and a lost son. They are directed to **Pharisees** and **scribes** who grumble about Jesus' ministry to marginal persons such as "**tax collectors** and **sinners**." The two short parables establish the basic dynamic: Something important has been lost, a search is made, what was lost is found, and so there is great rejoicing. Thus Jesus defends his special concern for spiritually "lost" persons. In the long parable in Luke 15:11–32, a younger son demands his share of his inheritance from his father, goes off and squanders the **money**, and finds himself feeding pigs (a particularly degrading occupation for Jews). When he resolves to return home and begs his father's forgiveness, the father not only accepts his apology but even runs out to meet him, embraces him, and arranges a great celebration to mark his return. Whereas the younger son was prodigal in the negative sense of being wasteful with material possessions, the father is prodigal in the positive sense of being extravagantly merciful and forgiving. Whether the older son eventually accepted his father's explanation ("we had to celebrate") or remained adamant in refusing to join in the rejoicing is left open, thus challenging the Pharisees and scribes to appreciate the positive effects of Jesus' ministry to the spiritually lost and to respond properly.

PRONOUNCEMENT STORIES. *See CHREIA.*

PROPHET. A person who is inspired and commissioned to speak on **God**'s behalf and to proclaim God's will. The message of the prophet often concerns the future. In the OT **Isaiah, Jeremiah,** and Ezekiel are the most prominent prophets. In the **Gospels, John the Baptist** is called a prophet (Matt 14:5, 21:26; Mark 11:32; Luke 1:76). In some circles Jesus was regarded as one of the ancient prophets who had come back to life (Matt 16:14; Mark 8:28; Luke 9:8, 9:19). He was also acclaimed as a prophet because of his extraordinary knowledge and his ability to work **miracles** (John 4:19, 9:17). His lack of acceptance in some circumstances is explained by the **proverb** that prophets are generally not honored in their home areas (Matt 13:57; Mark 6:4; Luke 4:24; John 4:44). To his contemporaries, Jesus looked and acted like a prophet. His authoritative manner of **teaching**, use of symbolic actions, and focus on the future coming of **God's kingdom** led them to conclude that "a great prophet has arisen among us" (Luke 7:16; see also John 6:14, 7:40). Early Christians understood Jesus to be the prophet like **Moses** promised in Deut 18:15, 18:19 (Acts 3:22–26, 7:37).

PROSELYTES. Derived from the Greek verb meaning "come over," the term refers to those who became attracted and converted to Jewish religious practice. There is much controversy over whether Judaism in Jesus' time was a missionary or proselytizing religion. Jesus' saying in Matt 23:15 suggests that the **scribes** and **Pharisees** did engage in making converts. But Jesus takes a very negative attitude toward the kind of Judaism they were promoting and the results that they achieved: "For you cross sea and land to make a single convert, and you make the new convert twice as much a **child** of hell as you yourselves." In Acts there is some evidence pertaining to "God-fearers" who associated themselves with the **synagogue** but did not convert fully to Judaism coming over into the early Christian movement. Such persons probably constituted a large proportion of the **Gentiles** who became early Christians. This would explain why and how **Paul** and other NT writers could assume in their readers a basic familiarity with the Jewish Scriptures and with Jewish beliefs and customs.

PROSTITUTES. Women who engage in sexual relations for hire. In **Matthew**'s **genealogy of Jesus** (Matt 1:1–17) two of the female figures, Tamar (Gen 38) and Rahab (Judg 2), can be described as having acted as prostitutes. According to Matt 21:32, **John the Baptist** (and Jesus) had great success with "**tax collectors** and prostitutes." In Luke 15:30, the elder son accuses the **prodigal son** of having devoured his inheritance "with prostitutes." In Luke 7:36–50, the woman who had been "a **sinner**" is presumed to have been a prostitute. However, her sins are declared forgiven, and she expresses her appreciation for Jesus by **anointing** his feet. The proximity of this passage to the report about **Mary Magdalene** in Luke 8:2–3 ("from whom seven **demons** had gone out") led to the (most likely incorrect) conclusion that she had been a prostitute and that she was the sinful woman of Luke 7:36–50.

PROVERBS. *See* APHORISMS.

PSALMS. The collection of 150 hymns, laments, thanksgivings, and so forth that were composed originally (for the most part) and used in connection with rituals conducted in the **Jerusalem temple** and were eventually gathered into the biblical book of Psalms. Along with the books of **Isaiah** and Deuteronomy, the Psalms exercised great influence on early Christians, who interpreted them as having been fulfilled in Jesus. The "**messianic**" Psalms 2 and 110 attracted special interest (see **Hebrews** in particular), and the interpretation of Ps 110:1 is the topic of Jesus' own statement in Mark 12:35–37 (Matt 22:41–45; Luke 20:41–44). According to Mark 15:34 and Matt 27:46, the last words of Jesus were the first words of Psalm 22: "My **God**, my God, why have you forsaken me?" To understand these words one must read the entire psalm, which alternates between laments and expressions of trust in God, and issues in the vindication of the sufferer. In Luke 23:46 the last words of Jesus ("**Father**, into your hand I commend my spirit") echo Psalm 31:6, another lament psalm. Again, it is necessary to read the whole psalm to grasp how early Christians interpreted the **death** and **resurrection** of Jesus.

PURITY. See CLEAN AND UNCLEAN.

– Q –

Q. The collection of Jesus' sayings thought to have been used independently by **Matthew** and **Luke** in their revised and expanded versions of **Mark** is designated by the letter Q, deriving from the German word *Quelle* (meaning "source"). The Q source is a hypothesis based on comparison of texts in the **Synoptic Gospels**: Q is where Matthew and Luke coincide, and Mark has nothing or something very different. The Q source is considered to have existed in Greek perhaps around 50 CE as an anthology of Jesus' sayings (like parts of Proverbs, Sirach, and the *Gospel of Thomas*) and without **infancy** or **passion narratives**.

QUEST FOR THE HISTORICAL JESUS. The phrase refers to the attempt to recover the facts about Jesus by using the tools of modern historiographical research. The historical Jesus is really the historians' Jesus, that is, the Jesus reconstructed out of literary fragments by historians. The early history of the quest was brilliantly described by **Albert Schweitzer** in the early 1900s. In the late eighteenth century, **H. S. Reimarus** sought to peel away the ecclesiastical wrappings in the **Gospels** to get back to the simple historical figure of Jesus. During the nineteenth century, liberal German Protestant scholars took a rationalist approach to the Gospel **miracles** and explained most of them away. D. F. Strauss proposed **myth** as an approach to the Gospels as a middle way between the supernaturalism of the **churches** and the rationalism of the Enlightenment critics. Schweitzer focused on Jewish **eschatology** as the proper setting for Jesus' life and his **teaching** about the **kingdom of God**. During the twentieth century, the major developments in the quest included the distinction between the Jesus of history and the Christ of faith, the Gospel **parables** as a privileged entry point into Jesus' own teachings about God's kingdom, the development of **criteria of authentication** for determining what Jesus said and did, and the increasing interest in locating Jesus within Judaism. Scholars today show special interest in Jesus as an eschatological **prophet** and a **wisdom** teacher. The **canonical Gospels** assume a continuity between earthly Jesus and the risen Christ. Indeed, the object of orthodox Christian faith is not and never has been the historians' Jesus but rather the earthly and risen Jesus, the one who says, "I died, and behold I am alive forever" (Rev 1:19).

QUIRINIUS. According to Luke 2:1–2, the reason why Jesus was born in **Bethlehem** was that the Roman emperor Augustus ordered all his subjects ("all the world") to return to their hometowns and be registered in a **census** "while Quirinius was governor of Syria." That is how **Joseph** and **Mary** found themselves in Bethlehem rather than **Nazareth**. However, **Luke**'s statements cause some historical problems. There is no independent evidence that Augustus (emperor from 27 BCE to 14 CE) ever ordered such a comprehensive census. Moreover, the governor of Syria in the last years of **Herod the Great** (who died in 4 BCE) when Jesus was born (see Luke 1:5) was named Saturninus. Quirinius was his assistant, and he himself became governor of Syria only in 6 CE. According to **Josephus** (*Ant.* 18.1), Quirinius did conduct a census but it was only in 6 CE (see Acts 5:37). So there seems to be a discrepancy of 10 years between Herod's death and the census of Quirinius (Luke 2:1–2). Perhaps the best solution is that Luke got confused. He had a tradition that placed Jesus' birth under Herod and at the time of a census, and the census that he knew best was the one under Quirinius (Acts 5:37).

QUMRAN. Khirbet Qumran, 14 km (8.5 mi.) south of **Jericho**, overlooking the northwest shore of the Dead Sea. It was the principal site where the **Dead Sea Scrolls** were discovered in 1947. In Jesus' time it was inhabited by a Jewish religious movement (probably **Essenes**), with whom **John the Baptist** may have had some association (Luke 1:80).

– R –

RABBI. A term of respect, derived from the Aramaic/Hebrew word *rab*, meaning "great." Only after 70 CE did it become formally connected to the Jewish teachers who underwent some kind of rabbinic "ordination." In **Mark's Gospel**, Jesus' **disciples** address him as

"Rabbi" (9:5, 11:21, 14:45), whereas in **John's Gospel** both insiders and outsiders call Jesus "Rabbi" (1:39, 1:50, 3:2, 3:26, 4:31, 6:25, 9:2, 11:8). **Luke** avoids the term, perhaps because his largely **Gentile** audience may not have understood or appreciated the Semitic term. In **Matthew's Gospel** only **Judas** calls Jesus "Rabbi" (26:25, 26:49), in very ironic situations as his **betrayal** unfolds. And Jesus in 23:7–8 warns his disciples not to be called "Rabbi." These negative uses very likely reflect the tension existing between the Matthean community and the early or formative phase of the rabbinic movement after 70 CE.

RABBINIC LITERATURE. The earliest written collection of rabbinic teachings is the Mishnah, put into shape in Palestine around 200 CE. Its teachings are arranged in tractates that in turn make up its six Orders: Seeds, Torts, **Festivals, Women, Purities,** and Holy Things. Teachings not included in the Mishnah are gathered in the Tosefta ("Additions"), which is like the Mishnah in structure and date. The Talmuds comment on, update, and expand the Mishnah. The **Jerusalem** or Palestinian Talmud was edited around 400 CE, and the Babylonian Talmud was put into form around 500 CE and has been the more authoritative guide to Jewish life. The **Targums** are Aramaic paraphrases or expansions of the Hebrew Bible that adapt the biblical text to more refined theological views and add popular traditions of interpretation. The Midrashim are anthologies of comments on the Hebrew Scriptures. Some are arranged like modern verse-by-verse biblical commentaries, while others are collections of homilies. The Hekhalot literature contains Jewish mystical writings. Attempts at using the rabbinic writings as historical sources for understanding Jesus run into some serious critical questions. How much (if any) of the rabbinic tradition goes back to Jesus' time or before 70 CE? How much continuity was there between the **Pharisaic** and rabbinic movements? How representative and authoritative was rabbinic Judaism in its own time?

RABBINIC TRADITIONS ABOUT JESUS. The few references to Jesus in the Talmuds and Midrash sound like parodies or garbled reports on features in the **Gospels.** They claim that Jesus was born illegitimately, was rejected by Jewish **rabbis,** had five **disciples,**

practiced magic, abrogated the **Law of Moses**, falsely claimed to be the **Son of God**, and was hanged on the eve of **Passover** for sorcery. These traditions were collected into a work known as the *Toledot Yeshu* ("The History of Jesus"), probably in the ninth or tenth century CE. Their historical value consists only in their witness to how some Jewish teachers interpreted and dealt with Christian traditions and beliefs about Jesus.

RAISINGS OF THE DEAD. The most spectacular **miracles** attributed to Jesus in the **Gospels** are his restoring several dead persons to life: Jairus' daughter (Matt 9:18–26), the son of the widow of Nain (Luke 7:11–17), and **Lazarus** (John 11:1–44). In the case of Jairus' daughter, only **Matthew** explicitly states that she had died (9:18; cf. Mark 5:23; Luke 8:42). His noting that the girl "arose" (9:25; see Mark 5:41–42; Luke 8:54) suggests a connection with Jesus' own **resurrection**. That the son of the widow of Nain was really dead is clear from his mother and the **crowd** accompanying his bier (Luke 7:12). Here Jesus' directive to him ("Young man, I say to you, rise!" 7:14) points forward to Jesus' own resurrection. The longest and most elaborate account of Jesus raising a dead person concerns Lazarus in John 11:1–44. That Lazarus was really dead is emphasized by his having been already four days in his **tomb** (11:17). Jesus' dialogues with Lazarus' sisters, **Martha and Mary,** revolve around his claim to be "the resurrection and the life" (11:25). His success in restoring Lazarus to life is the seventh and last "**sign**" in the series of seven signs in John 2–12. Historians often explain away these stories as originally healings that have been transformed into raisings of the dead, or they regard them simply as theological products of early Christian imagination. In the Gospels, however, they are taken very seriously as anticipations of Jesus' own resurrection and are mentioned among the "deeds of the **Messiah**" listed as accomplished by Jesus in his response to **John the Baptist**'s emissaries ("the dead are raised," Matt 11:5; Luke 7:22).

RANSOM SAYING. According to Mark 10:45 (and Matt 20:28), Jesus prophesied that as the **Son of Man** he came "to give his life as a ransom for many." The Greek term *lytron* ("ransom") refers to the price for buying the freedom of a captive or a slave. For a theological use of the term, see 4 Macc 17:21 where the martyrdoms of the mother and her seven sons (see 2 Macc 7) are interpreted as an atoning **sacrifice** and a ransom: "the tyrant was punished, and the homeland purified—they having become, as it were, a ransom for the sin of our nation." The related Greek word *apolytrosis* ("redemption") appears frequently in the NT letters to describe the saving effects of Jesus' **death** and **resurrection** (see Rom 3:24, 8:23; 1 Cor 1:30; Eph 1:7, 1:14, 4:30; Heb 9:15, 11:35).

RATZINGER, JOSEPH (POPE BENEDICT XVI). Born in 1927, Ratzinger was for many years a German university theology professor before serving as archbishop of Munich (1977–1982) and prefect of the Roman Congregation of the Doctrine of the Faith (1981–2005). He was elected bishop of **Rome** (pope) in April 2005. By training and occupation a systematic theologian, Ratzinger had a longstanding interest in biblical interpretation and in the **quest for the historical Jesus**. In his book *Jesus of Nazareth*, vol. 1 (2007), he contends that the Jesus of the **Gospels** is the Jesus we know and expresses skepticism about various attempts to reconstruct the "real" Jesus behind the Gospels. For him the primary data for Christian theology are the words and deeds of Jesus as they are remembered in the NT. He regards this Jesus as the key to a Christian understanding of the OT, and his divinity as proclaimed in **John's Gospel** (1:1, 20:28) as the necessary presupposition for reading the Gospels with the eyes of faith.

REALIZED ESCHATOLOGY. While the fullness of **God**'s kingdom remains in the future, Jesus also emphasized the present or inaugurated dimension of God's reign. Thus in Luke 11:20 (see Matt 12:28) he explains his **exorcisms** in terms of the anticipation of God's kingdom in his own ministry: "But if it is by the finger of God that I cast out **demons**, then the **kingdom of God** has come upon you." Likewise in Luke 17:21 he affirms that "the kingdom of God is among you." And in Matt 11:12 the kingdom is enough of a present reality to have suffered **violence** from the time of **John the Baptist** to Jesus. The most dramatic **sign** of the presence of God's kingdom is the **resurrection of Jesus**. Resurrection was understood to be a collective event to take place at the end of human history. That a single person (Jesus) should be granted eternal life in its fullness (resurrection) before the other end-time events have taken place means that the fullness of God's kingdom is already in the process of coming.

REDACTION CRITICISM. Applied to the **Gospels** and the historical study of Jesus, redaction (or, editorial) criticism investigates how the Evangelists used their sources about Jesus to address the concerns of their original readers in the late first century CE. The child of **form criticism** and **source criticism**, redaction criticism proceeds from the realization that the Evangelists' choice of material, the order in which they placed what they had collected, and the alterations they made in the traditional material were determined to some extent by their own theological outlooks and the needs of their readers. Whereas form criticism and source criticism are mainly concerned with the pre-Gospel stage of the documents, redaction criticism deals with the final product of the Gospel and what the individual Evangelist has done in producing it.

REIMARUS, HERMANN SAMUEL (1694–1768). Professor of oriental languages at Hamburg, Reimarus initiated the modern **quest for the historical Jesus** through his work on the aims of Jesus and his **disciples**. According to him, Jesus believed that the **kingdom** of the **Messiah** was about to be brought in according to the earthly and political expectations of the **apocalyptically** oriented Jews of his time. Jesus thought that by sending out his disciples people would flock to him and proclaim him as the Messiah and then the kingdom would come (see Matt 10:23). When that failed to occur, Jesus went to **Jerusalem** where he expected to be recognized as the Messiah. But the people there refused to do so, and Jesus was **arrested** and put to **death**. After his surprising death, his loyal followers fell back on the figure of the **Son of Man** in Dan 7:13–14 and awaited the **Parousia** or second coming of Jesus. In Reimarus' view, Jesus was a failed Jewish visionary, and Christianity was founded on his mistake and that of his followers.

RENAN, ERNEST (1823–1892). In *La vie de Jésus* (1863), Renan took **John's Gospel** as his basic source and used his literary skills to portray Jesus as a charming **teacher** who went about **Galilee** offering forgiveness to all who **loved** him. However, when he went to **Jerusalem** Jesus became a revolutionary and a wonder-worker/magician, and interpreted the **kingdom of God** in terms of Jewish **apocalyptic**. That change set the stage for his tragedy. At his last **Passover**, Jesus met persecution and martyrdom through the jealousy between **Judas** and John. Though a best-seller in his day, Renan's life of Jesus has generally been dismissed as more a romantic novel than a work of historical scholarship.

REPENTANCE. In the OT, repentance for humans involves turning away (*shub*) from sin to **righteousness**. In the NT, the Greek term *metanoia* envisions a change of mind (*nous*) and thus a change in behavior. According to Mark 1:15 (Matt 4:17), Jesus began his public ministry with a call to repent in the face of the coming **kingdom of God** and the divine judgment associated with it. In this way he was following **John**, who appeared "proclaiming a **baptism** of repentance for the **forgiveness of sins**" (Mark 1:4). In Mark 6:12, Jesus sends out his **disciples** on a mission in order that the people might repent. And in Luke 24:47 the risen Jesus relates his **death** and **resurrection** to the proclamation of "repentance and forgiveness of sins" to all nations.

RESURRECTION OF JESUS. The early Christians claimed that Jesus was restored to life after his **death** on the **cross** and that he was experienced as alive again by various followers in a series of **appearances** (1 Cor 15:3–8). They also claimed that on Easter Sunday morning his **tomb** was found empty (Mark 16:1–8 parr.). Their explanation was that Jesus had truly been **raised from the dead**. The **Gospels** contain accounts of his appearances in **Jerusalem** and environs (Matt 28:9–10; Luke 24:13–53; John 20:11–29) as well as in **Galilee** (Matt 28:16–20; John 21:1–23). Mark 16:9–20 is generally regarded as a second-century summary of the appearances found in the other Gospels. These accounts display some tension between the material and the spiritual dimensions of Jesus' resurrected existence. The remarkable change that came over Jesus' followers—from being deserters and deniers to being fearless preachers of Jesus' resurrection—is often viewed as the best proof of the power of Jesus' resurrection and the new age that it inaugurated.

RESURRECTION OF THE DEAD. The belief that the dead will be brought back to life, body and soul, to face the **Last Judgment** and to receive the appropriate rewards and punishments. In the early parts of the OT the dead were expected to live on in Sheol, a dark and gloomy place (see Psalm 88). In Dan 12:2–3, however, the hope is that the wise and **righteous** will arise to eternal happiness and shine like stars. In 2 Macc 7, there are strong statements about bodily resurrection in the dialogues between the wicked king and the seven sons and their mother. In the **Wisdom** of **Solomon** 3:1–9 there is a mixture of immortality of the soul and resurrection of the body. In Jesus' time the **Pharisees** were the major proponents of belief in resurrection of the dead and postmortem judgment according to one's deeds (Luke 14:14). According to Mark 12:18–27 (Matt 22:23–33; Luke 20:27–40), Jesus sided with the Pharisees against the **Sadducees**. In that debate with the Sadducees, Jesus finds a precedent in the **Torah** for belief in resurrection (Exod 3:6, 3:15–16) and insists that resurrected life is not the same as earthly life.

REVELATION, BOOK OF. Written in the late first century CE on the island of Patmos, the book of Revelation (or the **Apocalypse**) is primarily concerned with the risen Jesus. The catalyst for **John**'s apocalyptic scenarios was his vision of the risen Jesus described in Rev 1:9–20. Then after conveying the risen Jesus' reports on the seven **churches** (2:1–3:22), John describes the risen Jesus as the "slain **Lamb**" who alone in the **heavenly** court was found worthy to open the sealed book about the future (chaps. 4–5). The various scenarios that follow—seven seals, seven trumpets, and seven bowls—lead into visions of the destruction of Babylon (**Rome**) and the emergence of the New **Jerusalem**. In 12:4–5, John describes in truncated fashion the birth of the **Messiah**, the threat that he and his mother faced, and his exaltation to the heavenly realm. In 19:11–16 he depicts the **eschatological** intervention of the risen Jesus as the divine warrior, and gives him the title "King of kings and **Lord** of lords." And in 22:16 the risen Jesus identifies himself as "the root and descendant of **David**, the bright morning star."

REVENGE. The goal of the OT law of retaliation—"an eye for an eye" (Exod 21:24; Lev 21:20; Deut 19:21)—was to keep revenge within boundaries and to avoid the escalation of **violence**. In Matt 5:38–42 Jesus quotes that OT **teaching** and presents an even greater challenge: "Do not resist with **evil**" (not "an evildoer" as in the NRSV). Then he gives several extreme examples of not retaliating for evil with evil, and thus breaking the cycle of violence. These examples involve turning the other cheek, giving up your shirt too, going the extra mile, and giving indiscriminately to beggars. Jesus' strategy of nonviolent resistance was practiced effectively by Gandhi and Martin Luther King Jr. in the twentieth century.

RICH MAN AND LAZARUS, PARABLE OF THE (LUKE 16:19–31). Part of Jesus' instructions about the responsible use of material goods in Luke 16, this **parable** is a warning to the rich to share what they possess with the **poor** now, before it is too late to do so. It contrasts a rich man who customarily wears fine clothes and dines very well and a poor man named **Lazarus** who is a beggar. At death, however, their situations are reversed. When the rich man begs for mercy in his **suffering**, **Abraham** tells him that "between you and us a great chasm has been fixed." When he asks that a messenger be sent to his five brothers, Abraham tells him that "they have **Moses** and the **prophets**." The message is that the obligation of the rich to share their possessions with the poor is clear from the Hebrew Scriptures. The point: Share your goods with the poor in the present time.

RIGHTEOUSNESS. Upright behavior that meets divine and human standards. While accepting and living up to the basic ideals of Jewish piety, Jesus viewed himself as sent especially to minister to **sinners** rather than the righteous (Mark 2:17), presumably to help make them righteous in the proper **way**. He viewed himself and **John the Baptist** as messengers who "justified" **God's wisdom** (Luke 7:35; Matt 11:19). In the parable of the **tax collector** and the **Pharisee** (Luke 18:9–14), it is the tax collector who goes home "justified." Jesus seems to have opposed attempts at self-justification (Luke 10:29, 16:15). In **Matthew's Gospel**, Jesus calls for righteous living (5:10, 5:20, 6:1) and seems to regard righteousness as an **eschatological** gift like the **kingdom of God** (5:6, 6:33). This latter usage set the stage for **Paul's** profound theological development of the theme with respect to God's righteousness (**covenant** fidelity), its definitive manifestation in Jesus, and human righteousness (justification by faith).

ROCK. The rocky soil of the Land of **Israel** provided the background for the metaphorical uses of the many biblical "rock" images that emphasize stability and security. Near the end of the **Sermon on the Mount** in Matt 7:24–27, Jesus urges his hearers to build their house on rock, that is, on the wise **teaching** contained in the sermon. In Matt 16:18, Jesus promises that his **church** will be built on the "rock" (**Peter** means "Rocky"), and that the power of **evil** will not prevail against it. In 1 Pet 2:6–8, Jesus is described as the rejected stone who became the **cornerstone**/capstone in **God**'s true temple (Ps 118:22; see Isa 8:14, 28:16). In 1 Cor 10:4 Jesus is the rock who is the source of living water for God's people (see Num 20:7–8; John 4:13–14, 7:37–39).

ROME. In the second century BCE the **Maccabees**, having thrown off the yoke of the Seleucids in Syria and threatened by the Ptolemies in Egypt, made overtures toward an alliance with the Romans (see 1 Macc 8). This treaty gave the Judeans a foreign protector and the Romans a foothold in the eastern Mediterranean. In the mid 60s of the first century BCE, the Roman general Pompey was called into Judea to settle a dispute over the Jewish high priesthood, and in 4 CE the Romans replaced Herod Archelaus with a Roman governor or prefect. **Pontius Pilate** was the Roman governor of Judea from 26 to 36 CE. He had his headquarters in **Caesarea Maritima** and visited **Jerusalem** frequently during pilgrimage feasts, which could turn into occasions for insurgencies. When Jesus came to Jerusalem in 30 CE or so, he probably appeared to Pilate like another in the long line of Jewish religious-political troublemakers. Jesus' "triumphal entry" and his "**cleansing**" of the temple confirmed both Pilate and the local Jewish leaders in their suspicions that Jesus was indeed a dangerous person. The Roman policy was to react to such figures quickly and brutally, so as to discourage others who might be planning a rebellion. Thus Jesus suffered and died "under Pontius Pilate," the Roman governor of Judea.

– S –

SABBATH. Derived from the Hebrew word for "cease, stop, rest," the term "Sabbath" refers to the Jewish observance of the seventh day of the week (Saturday) as a day of rest and religious observance by Jews. According to Gen 2:3, the Sabbath was part of the very structure of **God's** creation. In the two versions of the **Decalogue**, the Sabbath commandment appears in different theological contexts: the creation in Exod 20:11, and the exodus in Deut 5:15. In Jesus' time the chief topic of controversy among Jews was what constituted "work" on the Sabbath day of rest. The **Gospels** portray Jesus as generally observant and respectful of the Sabbath commandment, but as critical of the **Pharisees'** traditions and having the personal authority to do what stricter observers might not allow (see Matt 12:1–14; Mark 2:23–3:6; Luke 13:10–17; John 5:1–18, 7:19–24).

SACKCLOTH AND ASHES. According to Matt 11:21 and Luke 10:13, if Jesus' **miracles** done in Chorazin and Bethsaida (**Galilean** towns in which Jesus had ministered) had been done in **Tyre and Sidon** (ancient pagan enemies of **Israel** in southern Lebanon), the latter cities would have repented "in sackcloth and ashes." Sackcloth was dark-colored material made of goat or camel hair. Wearing such an uncomfortable garment would have symbolized mourning and/or **repentance.** Heaping ashes on one's head would also have signified mourning and/or repentance in the face of possible catastrophe. In other words, those wicked cities of the past would have responded more positively than Jesus' fellow Galileans did to the significance of his miracles as anticipatory signs of **God's kingdom** and would have undertaken the repentance that it demanded (Mark 1:15).

SACRIFICE. In ancient **Israel** sacrifices were an integral part of religious life. While in early times (before **Solomon**) sacrifices were offered at various shrines, eventually the **Jerusalem temple** became the only place where they could be offered. The sacrifices included burnt offerings (holocausts), peace offerings, and purificatory or expiatory offerings. These were interpreted variously as gifts to **God,** ways of initiating or confirming relationships with God, or making **atonement** for sins. The latter purpose was at the heart of the rituals for the Day of Atonement described in Lev 16. In early Christian circles, the **death of Jesus** was interpreted as a sacrifice for sins: "Christ died for our sins in accordance with the Scriptures" (1 Cor 15:3); and "through the redemption that is in Christ Jesus, whom God put forward as a sacrifice of atonement by his **blood**, effective through faith" (Rom 3:24–25). Both passages are generally regarded as very early summaries of Christian belief. The **letter to the Hebrews** (especially 4:14–10:18) describes Jesus' death as the "perfect" (in the sense of effective) sacrifice for sins (in contrast to those repeatedly offered by Jewish **priests**) and as offered willingly by Jesus the great high priest.

SADDUCEES. The Sadducees were a Jewish religious and political movement in Palestine from the second century BCE to the first century CE. Their name may derive from the Hebrew word *saddikim* ("**righteous** ones") or from Zadok who was the high priest under King **David** (1 Kgs 1:26). In the sources roughly contemporary with Jesus, the term sometimes describes a conservative group of **priests** and their supporters (**Dead Sea Scrolls**), and sometimes refers to an aristocratic and Hellenizing priestly group in **Jerusalem**. **Josephus** says that the Sadducees denied the immortality of the soul, attributed all human activity to free will, and rejected traditions not contained in the **Torah**. In the **Gospels** they are sometimes allied with the **Pharisees** as opponents of Jesus (Matt 3:7, 16:6; Mark 12:18). In Acts they are active at the **Jerusalem temple** (4:1, 5:17, 23:6) and are said to reject beliefs in **angels** and spirits and in the **resurrection** (23:8).

SALOME. A woman follower of Jesus who witnessed the **death of Jesus** (Mark 15:40) and found his **tomb** empty on Easter Sunday (Mark 16:1). She is not to be confused with the Salome (not named in the NT) who danced at **Herod Antipas'** birthday banquet and was instrumental in the gruesome execution of **John the Baptist** (Mark 6:17–29).

SALVATION. The verb "save" in the **Gospels** can refer to rescue from danger, to heal, or to help someone experience divine salvation. It is sometimes difficult to determine which meaning is intended, as in those cases where Jesus says, "Your faith has saved you." In Matt 1:21 the **name of Jesus** is interpreted to mean, "he will save his people from their sins," while in Luke 2:30 **Simeon** identifies the infant Jesus as the embodiment of the saving power of **God**. In Luke 19:10, Jesus defines his own mission as bringing salvation: "For the **Son of Man** came to seek out and save the lost." Likewise in John 3:16–17, God is said to have sent his **Son** "in order that the world might be saved through him." And the climax of Jesus' encounter with the **Samaritans** is their confession, "This is truly the **Savior** of the world" (John 4:42). In the Gospels salvation is closely connected with Jesus and his mission. In its most comprehensive sense it involves entering the **kingdom of God** and enjoying eternal life. While its fullness may be future, it can be experienced in the present through encounter with Jesus, especially in his power to heal and **forgive sins**.

SAMARIA, SAMARITANS. Samaria refers to the district in the Holy Land between **Galilee** to the north and Judea to the south. Its capital city was called Samaria/Sebaste, and it included Shechem and Mount Gerizim. In ancient **Israel**, Samaritans were simply those who lived in the district of Samaria (2 Kgs 17:29). In later Jewish history and in Jesus' time, the term described an ethnic-religious movement independent of and at odds with the **Jerusalem temple** and its Judean authorities. The cultic center for the Samaritans was at Mount Gerizim, at present-day Nablus. In Matt 10:5, Samaritans are equated with **Gentiles**, and Jesus and his followers observe the Galilean-Judean custom by avoiding Samaritan territory on their journey up to **Jerusalem** (Luke 9:51–56). The surprising feature of Jesus' **parable** in Luke 10:25–37 is that the good neighbor turns out to be a Samaritan. Likewise, it is surprising that the only healed **leper** who comes back to thank Jesus in Luke 17:11–19 is a Samaritan. Jesus' willingness to converse with a Samaritan woman in John 4 is also presented as shocking.

SANDERS, E. P. (1937–). Professor emeritus of NT at Duke University, Sanders in *Jesus and Judaism* (1985) sought to interpret Jesus entirely within Judaism, that is, as a first-century Jew who must be explained wholly within his historical Jewish context. He argued that Jesus saw himself as **God's** last messenger before the establishment of his **kingdom**. Crucial, according to Sanders, was Jesus' prophetic demonstration at the **Jerusalem temple** (Mark 11:15–19). Jesus expected that the temple system would soon be destroyed and that God would bring about a new age and a new temple (see Mark 14:57–58). In categorizing Jesus, Sanders prefers the term "**eschatological** charismatic." Because Jesus' actions and **teachings** about God's coming kingdom threatened both the Jewish leaders in Jerusalem and the Roman officials, he was **arrested**, tried, and executed under **Pontius Pilate**. Since the **disciples** were not arrested, however, it appears that Pilate did not regard Jesus as much of a real threat.

SANHEDRIN. In the **Gospels** and elsewhere, the Greek word *synedrion* is used for both judicial courts in general (Matt 5:22, 10:17; Mark 13:9) and the supreme judicial and legislative Jewish court in **Jerusalem** presided over by the high **priest** (Matt 26:59; Mark 14:55). Mark 14:55–65 (followed in Matt 26:57–68 and Luke 22:66–71) gives the impression that Jesus was put on **trial** before the high council in Jerusalem and sentenced to **death** by it. John 18:12–14, 18:19–24, however, seems to envision a series of preliminary investigations before the high priests Annas and **Caiaphas**, and then an official trial before the Roman governor **Pontius Pilate**.

SATAN. Derived from the Hebrew word for "adversary," in Job 1–2 and Zech 3, Satan is still a member of the heavenly court and serves as the prosecuting attorney, whereas in the **Gospels** and in other Jewish writings of their time he appears as the enemy of **God** and Jesus and of those who belong to them. In the **temptation** narratives (Matt 4:1–11; Luke 4:1–13), Satan (or, the devil) tests Jesus' fidelity to his call as **Son of God** by promising physical comfort, celebrity, and political power "if you will fall down and worship me" (Matt 4:9). At each point Jesus refuses in words taken from Deut 6–8, thus showing what kind of Son of God he is. In the debates over the source of Jesus' power as a healer and **exorcist**, Satan appears as the source of **evil** and as Jesus' rival (Matt 12:26; Mark 3:23, 3:26; Luke 11:18). When **Peter** rejects the idea of the **suffering Messiah**, Jesus rebukes him as a "Satan" (Matt 16:23; Mark 8:38). According to Luke 22:3 and John 13:27, Satan entered into **Judas Iscariot** at the beginning of the **passion narrative**.

SAVIOR. A divine title (Luke 1:47) and used also with regard to Roman emperors, the term "Savior" is applied to Jesus sparingly in the **Gospels** but more frequently in the Pastoral Epistles and other later NT writings. According to Matt 1:21, Jesus—in keeping with his name—came into the world to "save his people from their sins." In Luke 2:11 the **angel** describes the newborn **child** to the shepherds as the "Savior, which is the **Messiah**, the **Lord**," thus echoing titles given to the emperor and suggesting Jesus' superiority even to the emperor. As a result of their encounter with Jesus, the **Samaritans** declare that Jesus "is truly the Savior of the world" (John 4:42).

SCANDAL. In the **Gospels** a scandal is an action or circumstance that leads another to act contrary to the proper course of conduct or set of beliefs. It is thus a trap or stumbling block (the basic meaning of the Greek word *skandalon*) along someone's way and can refer to temptation to sin or enticement to apostasy. In Matt 18:6–9 the verb "scandalize" and its related noun appear six times. When **Peter** tries to dissuade Jesus from taking the **way** of the **cross**, Jesus in Matt 16:23 refers to him as a *skandalon*. For other references to scandal in Matthew, see 5:29–30, 11:6, 15:12, 17:27, 24:10, and 26:31–32.

SCHÜSSLER FIORENZA, ELISABETH (1938–). In her groundbreaking work *In Memory of Her: A Feminist Theological Reconstruction of Christian Origins* (1983), she described the movement begun by Jesus as a "discipleship of equals" in which **women** were welcomed and assumed key roles, to the point that in the new family of Jesus there were no "fathers" in the sense of males who exercised patriarchal authority. In her view, Jesus is best understood as a "woman identified man" who broke down barriers between men and women (which were then built up again by the early **church**).

SCHWEITZER, ALBERT (1875–1965). Theologian, philosopher, musician, and physician, who was awarded the Nobel Prize in 1953 for his humanitarian medical work in Africa. His 1906 German book, *Von Reimarus zu Wrede* (English, 1910, entitled *The Quest of the Historical Jesus*), analyzed attempts by many scholars to uncover the "real" Jesus from the late 1700s to his own time. For each scholar he provided background information, described the author's method and results, and offered a critical analysis of his efforts. After initially describing the critical investigation of Jesus' life as "the greatest achievement of German theology," his conclusion was that "there is nothing more negative than the result of the critical study of the life of Jesus." Schweitzer himself seems to have regarded Jesus as a failed visionary. According to him, Jesus believed that the **Son of Man** and **God's kingdom** were going to come in his own day, and so he instructed his **disciples** as he sent them forth on their mission that "you will not have gone through all the towns of **Israel** before the Son of Man comes" (Matt 10:23). When the mission failed to produce the kingdom, Jesus then imagined that his own **death** would compel the coming of the kingdom. But Jesus found himself crushed by "the wheel of the world." Schweitzer concluded that it is not Jesus as historically known but Jesus as spiritually risen who is significant for our time and can help it.

SCOURGING. According to Mark 15:15 (Matt 27:26; Luke 23:16; John 19:1), Jesus was flogged or scourged with whips before he was handed over by **Pilate** to be crucified. The whips may well have had pieces of bone attached to the cords, so as to pierce the skin and inflict even more terrible pain. Though sometimes used as a punishment by itself (Matt 10:17, 23:34; Acts 5:40, 22:19; 2 Cor 11:24–25), in Jesus' case the purpose of the scourging seems to have been to weaken or soften him up for **death** by crucifixion. Scourging is mentioned explicitly in one of Jesus' **passion predictions** (Mark 10:34; Matt 20:19; Luke 18:33).

SCRIBES. In ancient **Israel**, scribes were those who composed and wrote out legal and other documents. This task demanded literacy and knowledge of the **Torah** (since that was the law, at least in most Jewish circles). By 200 BCE the scribes in Israel seemed also to have functioned as religious intellectuals and were educated broadly in **wisdom** schools such as that of Ben Sira in **Jerusalem**. In the NT they often appear alongside the **Pharisees**, elders, and **chief priests**. The references to the "scribes of the Pharisees" (Mark 2:16; Acts 23:9) suggest that they could belong to other Jewish parties also. The scribes in the NT generally side with the opponents of Jesus (but see Mark 12:28–34) and are paired with the Pharisees as the object of Jesus' vigorous denunciation of **hypocrisy** in Matt 23. Their emphasis on knowledge of the Torah and on study contributed to the revival of Judaism after 70 CE.

SEA OF GALILEE. See GALILEE, SEA OF.

SEED GROWING SECRETLY, PARABLE OF THE (MARK 4:26–29). This short **parable** illustrates several aspects of Jesus' understanding of **God's kingdom**: Its small beginning will issue in a great harvest; something is happening in the present; and the process is mysterious, suggesting divine guidance. Similar points are made in its companion parable of the **Mustard Seed** (Mark 4:30–32).

SEPTUAGINT. The term meaning "seventy" is used for Greek translations of the Hebrew Scriptures, produced from the third to the first century BCE, mainly in Alexandria in Egypt. The name derives from the tradition in the *Letter of Aristeas* that 70 (or 72) Jewish elders translated the Hebrew **Torah** into Greek. The Septuagint is important as a witness to developments in the textual history of the OT, to the beliefs and ideas of Greek-speaking Jews, and to what became the Bible of the early **church**. Some fragments of the OT in Greek were found among the **Qumran** scrolls. While it is unlikely that Jesus himself used the Bible in Greek, some of the material attributed to him in the **Gospels** (e.g., Mark 12:1–12, 12:35–37) supposes the use of a Greek version either by the Evangelist or a later **scribe**.

SERMON ON THE MOUNT. The summary of Jesus' teachings in Matt 5–7 takes the form of a **wisdom** instruction and includes material from the Sayings Source **Q** (see Luke 6:20–49), **Mark**, and traditions special to the Evangelist **Matthew** (**M**). It appears early in Matthew's narrative of Jesus' public life and is the first of five large discourses by Jesus. In Matthew's theological geography, the mountain is a place for divine revelation (see Exod 19). The audience for the sermon includes both the **disciples** (5:1) and the **crowds** (7:28). After an introduction (5:3–16) featuring a series of **beatitudes** and images for Jesus' followers (salt, city on a hill, **light**), Jesus in 5:17–20 urges them to practice a better **righteousness** than that of the **scribes** and **Pharisees**. The first major part (5:21–48) is a series of six antitheses ("you have heard . . . but I say to you") in which Jesus quotes an OT passage and challenges his hearers to go deeper than mere literal observance on matters such as murder, adultery, **divorce**, **oaths**, retaliation, and dealing with enemies. Next in 6:1–18 he stresses performing acts of piety (**almsgiving, prayer, fasting**) to worship **God** rather than merely to gain a public reputation for holiness. Then in 6:19–7:12 Jesus provides wise advice on a variety of topics: **treasures**, eyes, masters, anxiety, judgments, dogs and pigs, prayer, and the **Golden Rule**. The admonitions concluding the sermon (7:13–27) emphasize the importance of putting these **teachings** into practice. While the Sermon on the Mount seems to have been constructed by Matthew out of traditional materials, most scholars maintain that behind these traditions it is possible to hear the voice of Jesus and to come into contact with many of his most characteristic teachings.

SERMON ON THE PLAIN. The summary of Jesus' **ethical** teachings, largely derived from the Sayings Source **Q**, and preserved in Luke 6:20–49. In **Luke**'s theological geography, the plain or level place is where Jesus meets and instructs the **crowds**. With the four **beatitudes** (6:20–23) at the beginning of the sermon, Jesus declares blessed or fortunate the **poor**, hungry, weeping, and persecuted. Then in 6:24–26 he declares unhappy or even cursed the rich, full, laughing, and famous. In the core of the sermon (6:27–38), Jesus teaches about **love** of enemies, offers four extreme cases of what that might mean, and gives as reasons for doing so the **Golden Rule** (treat others as you wish them to treat you) and the imitation of **God**'s example in **loving** all creatures (even those who are hostile to him). In 6:39–49, Jesus concludes by warning against **hypocrites** and false teachers, insisting that good persons do good deeds, and urging his followers to build their lives on the solid foundation of his **teachings**.

SERVANT OF GOD. Four passages in **Isaiah** 40–55 (42:1–9, 49:1–13, 50:4–11, 52:13–53:12) refer to a mysterious figure known as the Servant of God. Whether in the sixth century BCE he was understood to be an individual among the exiles in Babylon or a collective figure for **Israel** has been debated for centuries. Early Christians, however, were convinced that Jesus was the Servant of God, and this identification runs throughout the **Gospels**: Jesus as the **light** to the nations (Isa 42:6, 49:6; cf. Luke 2:32), as God's beloved **Son** (Isa 42:1; cf. Mark 1:11, 9:7 parr.), as the **Lamb of God** (Isa 53:7, 53:12; cf. John 1:29), and as the one who bore our infirmities (Isa 53:4; cf. Matt 8:17), gave his life as a **ransom** for many (Isa 53:10–12; cf. Mark 10:45), and was reckoned with transgressors (Isa 53:9; cf. Luke 22:37). The identification of Jesus as the **Suffering** Servant is made explicit in Acts 8:32–35 and 1 Pet 2:21–25. It is likely that Jesus related the sufferings he faced with those attributed to the Servant of God in Isa 40–55.

SERVANT PARABLES. Several of Jesus' **parables** illustrate proper attitudes in the face of the coming **kingdom of God** and the **Son of Man**'s return with reference to relationships between servants (or slaves) and their master. Servants left in charge of a household should always be vigilant, since they do not know the exact time of their master's arrival (Mark 13:33–37; Matt 24:45–51; Luke 12:41–48). The parable of the Unforgiving Servant (Matt 18:23–35) suggests that those who receive forgiveness from **God** must be willing to extend forgiveness to others. The parables of the **Talents** (Matt 25:14–30) and the **Pounds** (Luke 19:12–27) demand that those who await the coming of God's kingdom must be diligent in the present. And the parable of the Worthless Servant (Luke 17:7–10) is a reminder that humans are the servants and God is the master.

SHEEP AND GOATS, PARABLE OF THE (MATT 25:31–46). In this judgment scene, the **Son of Man** presides, and rewards some and condemns others. Those who are judged are "all the nations," and they are judged on the basis of their acts of mercy and kindness to "the least." The **parable** assumes a mystical identification between the least and the glorious Son of Man. Those who show mercy (the sheep) to the needy will enter eternal life, while those who fail to do so (the goats) will be condemned to eternal punishment. *See also* LITTLE ONES.

SHROUD. The linen cloth in which the corpse of Jesus was wrapped by **Joseph of Arimathea**. We are probably to imagine a large linen

cloth like a bed sheet. In the **Synoptic Gospels** the Greek term is
sindon (Matt 27:59; Mark 15:46; Luke 23:53), while in John it is
othonia ("cloth wrappings"). According to John 20:1–10, the risen
Jesus left behind his **burial** clothes in the **tomb** neatly. In some
circles the burial cloth of Jesus has been identified as the Shroud of
Turin, though there has been a long and vigorous debate among both
historians and scientists about its antiquity and authenticity. If it is
ancient and authentic, then it provides a "snapshot" of Jesus' body
and vivid proof of the physical **sufferings** that he underwent during
his **passion** and **death**.

SIGNS. The term "signs" (*semeia* in Greek) is used to describe Jesus'
miracles in **John's Gospel**. The seven "signs" include Jesus changing water into **wine** (John 2:1–12), his healing the official's son
(4:43–54), healing a paralyzed man (5:1–16), feeding 5,000 persons
(6:1–15), walking on the water (6:16–25), healing a man born blind
(9:1–7), and raising **Lazarus** from the dead (11:1–44). The signs
point to Jesus as the revealer and revelation of **God**. Several of them
provide Jesus with the occasion to deliver a substantial discourse
about his identity as the **Son of God** and his relationship to God as
his **Father**.

SIMEON. The righteous and devout elderly man who, according to
Luke 2:25–35, encountered the infant Jesus in the **Jerusalem temple**
and recognized him as the **Messiah** through the guidance of the
Holy Spirit. In the song known from its first two Latin words as
Nunc Dimittis (Luke 2:29–32), he describes Jesus as the fulfillment
of **Israel**'s hopes in the language of Isa 40–55 and prophesies that
Jesus and those around him (especially his mother) will endure much
suffering.

SIMON OF CYRENE. According to Mark 15:21, Matt 27:32, and
Luke 23:26, Simon of Cyrene was compelled to carry the **cross** of Jesus. Roman soldiers had the right to force subject civilians to perform
such tasks for them (see Matt 5:41). Cyrene was the capital of Cyre-
naica, part of modern Libya. Simon was very likely a Jew who either
had settled in Judea or was there on pilgrimage. The note that he was
"coming in from the country" suggests that he was going to **Jeru-**

salem to celebrate **Passover** and that the place of Jesus' crucifixion was near a road. There is no indication that he had known Jesus beforehand. The designation of him as "the **father** of Alexander and Rufus" is sometimes taken to mean that **Mark**'s readers (at **Rome?**) may have known his sons as fellow Christians (see Rom 16:13).

SIMON THE CANANAEAN/ZEALOT. One of the **twelve apostles** listed in Matt 10:4, Mark 3:18, Luke 6:15, and Acts 1:13. Whereas **Mark** and **Matthew** refer to him as the "Cananaean" (suggesting that he came from **Cana** or Canaan), Luke in two lists calls him "the **Zealot**" (which may suggest his membership in a Jewish insurgent movement). The epithets probably represent two different translations or interpretations of the same Hebrew or Aramaic word *qanah*, meaning "be zealous/jealous."

SINLESSNESS OF JESUS. The clearest NT statement about Jesus' sinlessness appears in Heb 4:15 where the author describes Jesus' ability to sympathize with human weakness despite having remained sinless: "we have one [a high **priest**] who in every respect has been tested as we are, yet without sin." Likewise, in treating the **sufferings** of Jesus the author of 1 Pet in 2:22 links Jesus to the Suffering Servant of Isa 53 by writing: "He committed no sin, and no deceit was found in his mouth." The dialogue between **John the Baptist** and Jesus in Matt 3:14–15 suggests some discomfort that Jesus should have undergone a **baptism** associated with **repentance** and the **forgiveness of sins**. **Paul**'s assertion that **God** made Jesus "to be sin who knew no sin" (2 Cor 5:21) affirms the sinlessness of Jesus and interprets his **death** as a "sin" offering so that "we might become the **righteousness** of God."

SINNERS. Those whose behavior or activity did not accord with the prevailing moral and religious standards. In the **Gospels** the term applies primarily to those who did not observe the **Law of Moses** in detail and were therefore shunned by the more observant (Mark 2:15–16; Matt 9:10–13, 11:19; Luke 5:30, 7:34, 15:1–2, etc.). They are often mentioned alongside "**tax collectors**," suggesting that those whose occupations made it impossible for them to observe the Mosaic Law and/or rendered them "**unclean**" (herding pigs, tanning,

prostitution, etc.) might also be classified as "sinners." In Mark 2:17, Jesus claims that he came to call sinners and presumably to bring spiritual healing to them. His associations with such persons led the **scribes** and **Pharisees** (and probably many others) to doubt Jesus' authenticity as a religious **teacher** and forced Jesus to defend his own behavior (as in Luke 15:1–32).

SLAUGHTER OF THE INNOCENTS. The episode described in Matt 2:16–18, according to which **Herod the Great** ordered that all male **children** born in and around **Bethlehem** should be put to death. While there is no other ancient historical evidence for this event, it is at least consistent with Herod's ruthlessness in defending his royal prerogatives. The apparent motive for Herod's action was to destroy any possible rivals for his claim to be **"King of the Jews,"** and its model was Pharaoh's desire to kill all the Hebrew male children in **Moses'** time according to Exod 1:15–22. Since Herod died in March–April of 4 BCE, it has become customary to date Jesus' birth approximately two years before (that is, 7 or 6 BCE). According to Gen 35:19, Rachel died in the vicinity of Bethlehem. Whereas in Jer 31:16–17, Rachel is told to stop weeping because her children were coming back from exile, in Matt 2:18 the quotation is used to associate the slaughter of the innocent children with Rachel's weeping.

SOCIOLOGICAL APPROACH. As defined and applied by **Gerd Theissen** in *Sociology of Early Palestinian Christianity* (1978), this approach involves the description of typical social attitudes and behaviors within the Jesus movement and the analysis of its interactions with Jewish society in Palestine. It classifies Jesus and his first followers as wandering charismatics, going from place to place and depending on sympathizers in local communities. It also considers the influence of the broader society on the Jesus movement with regard to its spatial rootlessness, rural ambivalence toward **Jerusalem**, nominal theocracy, and radical approach to cultural norms.

SODOM AND GOMORRAH. Two cities near the Dead Sea, notorious for their inhospitality and sexual depravity, and destroyed because of it (Gen 19). In the **Gospels** (Matt 10:15, 11:23–24; Luke

10:12, 17:29), they appear as examples of sinful places that deserve punishment for their sins and serve as warnings to those who fail to accept Jesus and his proclamation of **God's kingdom** and the divine judgment that will accompany it.

SOLOMON. Son of David and Bathsheba, one of the first kings in ancient **Israel**, who was most famous for his building projects (including the **Jerusalem temple**) and his **wisdom**. In Matt 1:6–7 he is listed among the ancestors of Jesus. He also serves as a point of comparison for Jesus regarding his glory (Matt 6:29; Luke 12:27) and wisdom (Matt 12:42; Luke 11:31). John 10:23 mentions Solomon's "portico" as part of the **Jerusalem** temple complex and the site of Jesus' confrontation with "the Jews" at the feast of Dedication/Hanukkah.

SON OF GOD. In the OT the title can refer to the king in particular or **Israel** in general. In later Jewish writings, **angels** are called "sons of God," and the **suffering** just person can also be a "son of God" (Wis 2:16–18). The title was also adopted independently by Roman emperors. In the NT Jesus is the Son of God. In **Mark** the **voice from heaven** identifies Jesus as the Son of God at his **baptism** and **transfiguration** (1:11, 9:7), and even **demons** recognize him as such (3:11, 5:7). The **Gentile centurion** overseeing Jesus' execution is moved to confess him to be the Son of God (15:39). In **Matthew** the **disciples** acknowledge Jesus to be the Son of God (14:33), and **Peter** identifies him as "the Son of the living God" (16:16). In **Luke**'s **infancy narrative** the angel **Gabriel** promises that Jesus will be called "Son of the Most High" (1:32) and "Son of God" (1:35). The title "Son of God" is especially prominent in **John's Gospel** where it is said that the **Father** and the Son are one (10:30), and that the Father sent the Son into the world (3:17, 5:23, 10:36) and gave him all things (3:35, 5:22, 5:26). Jesus is the object of confessions of faith as the Son of God (1:34, 1:49, 11:27), and those who believe in him as the Son of God will have eternal life (3:16, 3:36, 5:21, 6:40). The Johannine Evangelist claims that he wrote his **Gospel** so that others may believe (or come to believe) that Jesus is "the Son of God" (20:31).

SON OF MAN. A title used frequently by Jesus in the **Gospels** and reflecting idioms in Hebrew (*ben 'adam*) and Aramaic (*bar 'enash*). Its OT backgrounds include humans as descended from **Adam**, the divine address to Ezekiel as "son of man," and the heavenly figure who is "one like a son of man" (an **angel**?) in Dan 7:13–14 and *1 Enoch* 37–71. In the Gospels, Jesus often uses "Son of Man" to refer to himself in the context of his earthly ministry to **forgive sins** (Mark 2:10), as **lord** of the **Sabbath** (Mark 2:28), as having nowhere to lay his head (Matt 8:20), and so on. He also employs it in his **predictions** about his **passion**, **death**, and **resurrection** (Mark 8:31, 9:31, 10:33–34). And it appears in prophecies about his future coming of the Son of Man in judgment (Mark 8:38, 14:62; Matt 16:27–28, 19:28; Luke 17:22, 17:24, 17:26, 17:30, 21:36). In **John's Gospel** the title describes Jesus as the man from **heaven** (John 1:51, 3:13, 6:62) and appears in connection with the idea of Jesus' death as an exaltation (3:14, 12:23, 12:34, 13:31).

SONS OF THUNDER. The nickname given to **James** and **John**, the sons of **Zebedee**, in Mark 3:17. The Greek phrase supposedly renders "**Boanerges**," which is not an exact transliteration of the Hebrew *bene regesh*. It is not clear why James and John were given this name. Was it something about their character (hot-headed?), their politics (insurgents?), family history, or something else?

SOURCE CRITICISM. Applied to the **Gospels** and the historical study of Jesus, source criticism seeks to establish the presence of preexisting material about Jesus that has been incorporated into the present form of the documents. Its major concerns are determining the presence of a source, the meaning of the source, and how the source has been used. In the Gospels the most obvious uses of literary sources are the many quotations of Old Testament texts, many of which are prefaced by comments such as "As it is written in the **prophet Isaiah**" (Mark 1:2). As the earliest Evangelist writing around the year 70 CE, **Mark** may well have had access to sources containing a series of controversy stories (in 2:1–3:6), a collection of "seed" **parables** (in 4:1–34), a cycle of **miracle** stories (in 4:35–5:47), and a **passion narrative** (in 14:1–16:8). In their revised and expanded versions of Mark, **Matthew** and **Luke** made use independently of a collection of sayings attributed to Jesus and now designated as **Q**, as well as traditions unique to their Gospels and now designated as **M** and **L** materials, respectively. In the preface to his Gospel (1:1–4), Luke acknowledges having done careful research on the various sources about Jesus that were available to him. **John** seems to have incorporated a collection of seven miracle stories ("**signs**") in chapters 1–12, some material now included in Jesus' **farewell discourse** in John 14–17, and a passion narrative somewhat different from the one in Mark.

SOWER, PARABLE OF (MARK 4:3–9; MATT 13:3–9; LUKE 8:5–8). The **parable** describes three unsuccessful sowings, and one remarkably successful one. It suggests that Jesus' followers need not be discouraged by the apparent rejection of his preaching about **God's kingdom** in some circles, and that the small beginnings represented by his ministry will eventually usher in a huge harvest. The problem is not with the seeds (the good news of God's kingdom) or the sower (Jesus) but rather with the soils (the recipients). The homiletic interpretation in Mark 4:13–20 makes explicit what prevents positive receptions of Jesus' message and at the same time holds out hope for a superabundant harvest.

STAR OF BETHLEHEM. The astral phenomenon that accompanied Jesus' birth according to Matt 2:2, 2:7, 2:9, and 2:10. The idea that unusual astral events might accompany the birth or death of a great figure was widely accepted in antiquity. The nature of the astral phenomenon reported by the **Magi** at Jesus' birth as a "star" has been variously interpreted as a new star (supernova), a comet, or a conjunction of the planets Jupiter and Saturn in 7 BCE. The expression "at its rising" in Matt 2:2 fits better with the supernova or comet explanations. However, the "star" motif in Matt 2:1–12 probably owes more to Num 24:17 ("a star shall come forth out of Jacob") than to any specific astral phenomenon.

STRAUSS, DAVID FRIEDRICH. *See* MYTH.

SUFFERING. In the OT there is a general assumption that wise and **righteous** persons will prosper, while wicked and foolish persons will suffer. However, this law of retribution is subjected to rigorous scrutiny in the book of Job. Almost a third of the 150 psalms are classified as laments, in which suffering persons try to deal with their sufferings and retain their trust in **God**. In Jesus' time there was a tendency to defer God's justice and retribution to the **Last Judgment**. In the NT Jesus summarizes and personifies the OT approaches to suffering. In his **teaching** he both upholds and questions the law of retribution. While his miraculous healings are **signs** of the presence of **God's kingdom**, he repeatedly warns his **disciples** to expect suffering. Like Job, he struggles in **Gethsemane** to accept the suffering he faces (Mark 14:32–42). At the hour of his **death** he recites the lament of the righteous sufferer (Psalm 22). He dies on the **cross** "for us" and "for our sins," and so he fulfills his mission to "give his life as a **ransom** for many" (Mark 10:45). He undergoes a martyr's death while showing his fidelity to his own teachings about **love** of enemies, concern for marginal persons, and trust in God (Luke 23:32–49). His **resurrection** is the most decisive event yet in the coming of God's kingdom. Because he has been tested through suffering, Jesus is able to "sympathize with our weakness" (Heb 4:15) as the great high **priest**.

SYNAGOGUE. The place of assembly and worship for Jewish communities in **Israel** and the Diaspora. While some have traced the origins of the synagogue back to the exile (sixth century BCE), the earliest physical evidence comes from the first century BCE. The **Gospels** agree that Jesus taught in synagogues. According to **Mark**, Jesus performed his first healing/**exorcism** in the synagogue at **Capernaum** (Mark 1:21–28), and healed a man with a withered hand in a synagogue on a **Sabbath** (3:1–6). However, once Jesus is rejected in the synagogue at **Nazareth** (6:1–6), he does not enter a synagogue again and the word appears in hostile contexts (12:39, 13:9). **Matthew** speaks ominously of "their synagogues" (Matt 4:23, 9:35, 10:17, 12:9, 13:54), thus reflecting the situation of his own community in conflict with the local synagogue near the end of the first century CE. **Luke** in 4:16–30 shifts the rejection of Jesus in the Nazareth synagogue to the beginning of Jesus' public activity and uses the incident as the occasion to introduce many of the major themes to be developed in the rest of his narrative. While **John** notes that Jesus taught in synagogues (John 6:59, 18:20), Jesus warns that his followers will be put out of the synagogue (16:2; see also 9:22, 12:42).

SYNOPTIC GOSPELS. The word "synoptic" means "sharing a common vision" and/or "seeing at a glance." The **Gospels** attributed to **Matthew**, **Mark**, and **Luke** provide a common view of Jesus' public ministry that differs from **John's Gospel**. A "synopsis" of the Gospels presents these texts in parallel (usually vertical) columns, thus allowing the user to see the common features and differences at a glance. The first three Gospels present a common view of Jesus' public ministry: association with **John the Baptist**, gathering **disciples** and instructing them, ministry of teaching and healing in **Galilee**, one journey to **Jerusalem**, brief activity in Jerusalem, **passion (arrest, trials, suffering, death)**, and empty **tomb**. They portray Jesus as a wise **teacher** and powerful healer, and use the same titles for him (**Son of Man**, **Son of David**, **Messiah**, **Son of God**, **Lord**, etc.). At some points the verbal similarities between two or three Gospels are so great that they cannot be explained merely as due to coincidence or to **oral tradition** and can only be explained by direct borrowing.

SYNOPTIC PROBLEM. This "problem" concerns the relationships among the **Gospels** of **Matthew**, **Mark**, and **Luke**. Some episodes or sayings appear in all three Gospels; some are in two; and some are in only one. The many similarities in wording and content indicate that there is some organic relationship at the level of written sources. Augustine thought that Matthew was the first Gospel, Mark was a poor copy, and Luke used both Gospels in writing his own. In the late eighteenth century, **J. J. Griesbach** modified Augustine's theory: Matthew came first, Luke was second, and Mark is a combination of the two. The most widely held explanation today is the two-source theory. According to it, Mark was the first complete Gospel (about 70 CE). When Matthew and Luke set out independently to revise and expand Mark (around 85–90 CE), they both used independently a collection of sayings attributed to Jesus known now as "**Q**" (from the German word *Quelle* meaning "source") and to special traditions (**M** for Matthew, and **L** for Luke). While there are some minor problems with this theory and more complicated explanations have been proposed, most biblical scholars today work on the basis of the two-source theory.

SYROPHOENICIAN WOMAN. The **Gentile** ("Greek") woman from the region of **Tyre** (in Phoenicia in antiquity) in the Roman province of Syria. According to Mark 7:24–30, she begs Jesus to free her little daughter from possession by an **evil** spirit. Though initially rebuffed and even insulted by Jesus, her faith and persistence win him over and he heals the girl at a distance. This is the only argument in the **Gospels** in which Jesus seems to be bested—and this by a Gentile woman! In Matt 15:21–28 she is described as a "Canaanite," one of the indigenous pagan inhabitants of the area.

– T –

TABLE FELLOWSHIP. Jesus' practice of sharing meals with all kinds of persons (known as open commensality) is among the most certain facts known about him. This practice is mentioned in various sources and in various contexts (e.g., Mark 2:15–17; Luke 15:1–2, 19:1–10). From Luke 7:34 and Matt 11:19 it is clear that as a result Jesus was accused of being "a glutton and a drunkard, a friend of **tax collectors** and **sinners**." His **feeding miracles** of 5,000 persons occur in all four **Gospels** (Mark 6:30–44; Matt 14:13–21; Luke 9:11–17; John 6:5–13), and in Mark 8:1–9 and Matt 15:32–39 he feeds 4,000 persons. Jesus seems to have intended these meals as symbolic demonstrations or enacted **parables** for what he envisioned the **kingdom of God** will be like: "Many will come from east and west and will eat with **Abraham** and Isaac and Jacob in the kingdom of **heaven**" (Matt 8:11; Luke 13:29). Jesus' **Last Supper** with his disciples (Mark 14:22–25 parr.) and the risen Jesus' meals with his followers (Luke 24:13–35, 24:36–49; John 21:9–14) should be interpreted in this context.

TALENTS, PARABLE OF THE (MATT 25:14–30). The setting is the decision by a rich man to distribute large sums of **money** ("talents") to three servants while he goes away on a journey. Whereas those servants who are given five and two talents double the amounts, the **servant** given only one talent buries it and has nothing to show for it in the final accounting. Whereas the master on his return praises and rewards the first two servants, he condemns the third servant as wicked and lazy. Thus the parable recommends bold, decisive, and fruitful action in preparation for the final judgment that will be part of the future coming of **God's kingdom** and of the glorious **Son of Man**. See the related parable of the **Pounds** in Luke 19:11–27. *See also* LAST JUDGMENT.

TALITHA CUM. An Aramaic phrase meaning "Little girl, arise" that occurs in Mark 5:41, in the account of Jesus restoring Jairus' daughter to life. While it may well reflect the words of Jesus, in its present context in the Greek **Gospel** of **Mark** it seems to function as something like a "magic word."

TARGUMS. Aramaic translations and paraphrases of the books of the Hebrew Bible. They were probably used in Jewish communities where Aramaic was the primary language and Hebrew had become a sacred or liturgical language. While some trace them back to the time of Ezra, the earliest physical evidence comes from fragments of Targums of Leviticus and Job that were discovered among the **Qumran** scrolls, which indicate that Targumic activity was carried out in Jesus' time. However, the manuscripts of the classic **rabbinic** Targums—*Onqelos, Neofiti,* and *Pseudo-Jonathan* for the Pentateuch; *Jonathan* for the Former and Latter **Prophets**; and various Targums for the Writings—are from a later time. In these Targums there are many interesting parallels to sayings of Jesus and other aspects of the NT. The critical historical problem for using them in research on Jesus and the NT is their relatively late date. While some scholars regard the rabbinic Targums as rich resources for Jewish popular exegesis, theology, and piety in Jesus' time, others look upon their use as imposing the views of a later rabbinic period on the Judaism of Jesus and his time.

TAX COLLECTORS. In Jesus' time the Romans had imposed on the Jews and other subject peoples a system of "tax-farming." The government auctioned off contracts to wealthy persons who paid the Romans directly and then collected mainly through intermediaries (such as toll collectors) as much as they needed (and usually much more) to cover their investment. Thus those involved in the system were suspected of dishonesty (for overcharging) and collaboration with the Romans (lack of patriotism). Jesus' willingness to eat with tax collectors (Mark 2:15–16), to include the tax collector Levi/**Matthew** among his **twelve apostles** (Matt 10:3; Luke 5:27), and to befriend them (Matt 11:19; Luke 5:30, 7:34) drew vigorous objections from the **scribes** and **Pharisees** (Luke 15:1–2). On the historical level there is every reason to believe that their suspicions that Jesus kept "bad company" were warranted. While in some cases Jesus refers to tax collectors in a denigrating way (Matt 5:46, 18:17), he does portray a tax collector as a model of genuine **prayer** and piety (Luke 18:9–14) and invites himself to the house of **Zacchaeus**, a chief tax collector who was rich (Luke 19:1–10), with the claim that "today **salvation** has come to this house."

TEACHER, JESUS AS. In all four **Gospels** Jesus is addressed as "teacher" (*didaskalos* in Greek), and in several cases he refers to himself as a teacher (e.g., Mark 14:14; Matt 10:24–25; Luke 6:40). In Matt 23:10 he designates himself as the only teacher: "you have one instructor, the **Messiah**." The settings for his teaching include debates with opponents (**scribes, Pharisees, Sadducees**, etc.), Jews at services in **synagogues**, outdoor proclamations to the **crowds**, and instructions for the inner circles of his followers (the **twelve apostles**, other **disciples**). In teaching he used **parables** and parabolic actions, various **wisdom** forms (**aphorisms**, proverbs, admonitions, etc.), interpretations of Scripture, **apocalyptic** warnings, and so on. The primary topics of his teachings were the **kingdom of God** and how to enter it (**Synoptic Gospels**) and his own role within **God**'s plan (**John**). His teachings first circulated in oral form, were eventually committed to writing, and were included in the Gospels (with some adaptations). *See also* ORAL TRADITION.

TEMPLE, CLEANSING OF. The second symbolic action/prophetic demonstration after Jesus' "triumphal" entry on **Palm Sunday**. The **Synoptic Gospels** (Matt 21:12–13; Mark 11:15–17; Luke 19:45–46) place it at the beginning of Jesus' activity in **Jerusalem** during Holy

Week. However, the account of this (or a similar) event appears very early in **John's Gospel** (2:14–16). In the Synoptic account, Jesus disrupts the buying and selling of animals for **sacrifices**, and defends his action by words taken from Isa 56:7 ("My house shall be called a house for **prayer** for all the nations") and Jer 7:11 ("but you have made it a den for robbers"). This provocative action undoubtedly won Jesus the enmity of the **chief priests** and **scribes** for his disrupting the peace of the **temple**, and contributed to his **arrest** and condemnation. Indeed at the hearing or **trial** before the Jewish leaders, one of the charges made against Jesus was that he claimed that he would destroy the temple and build another (Mark 14:58). What exactly Jesus intended by his temple action, however, is not entirely clear. Was he seeking a simple reform of the temple practice? Or was he declaring the end of the temple (or even of Judaism as a whole) as the place of **God**'s presence? Or was it something in between? In John 2:17–21, John interprets Jesus' action and statement about destroying the temple as pointing toward his own **resurrection**. This interpretation fits well with John's understanding of Jesus himself as the privileged locus of God's presence in the world and thus as the substitute for the temple.

TEMPLE IN JERUSALEM. In Jesus' time the **Jerusalem** temple was the complex of buildings and structures on Mount **Zion** that was being rebuilt and expanded as part of the many building projects initiated by **Herod the Great**. According to Luke 2:41–52, Jesus as a boy visited the temple complex and engaged in dialogue with the teachers there. However, during his adult ministry Jesus displays a somewhat negative attitude to the temple. On arriving in Jerusalem he carries out the symbolic action of "**cleansing**" the temple (Mark 11:15–17 parr.). In the Synoptic **Apocalypse** (Mark 13:2–3 parr.) he prophesies the destruction of the temple. And several different sources attribute to Jesus a saying about the destruction and rebuilding of the temple (Mark 14:57–58, 15:29–30; Matt 26:61, 27:40; John 2:18–22; Acts 6:14). Despite the Evangelists' denials and reinterpretations, there must have been some historical basis to this attribution. These passages suggest both Jesus' dissatisfaction with the state of the Jerusalem temple and his conviction that the **kingdom of God** was far more central and important in Jewish life.

TEMPTATION OF JESUS. A better description of this episode in Jesus' life might be "the testing of God's Son," since the point seems to be to establish at the beginning of Jesus' public ministry what kind of **Son of God** he really is. According to the short version in Mark 1:12–13, the **Holy Spirit** "drives" Jesus into the **wilderness** (probably the **Judean** Desert) where he spends 40 days (following the examples of **Moses** in Deut 9:18 and **Elijah** in 1 Kgs 19:8), is tested by **Satan** (the Adversary), lives in harmony with wild beasts, and is served by **angels** (see 1 Kgs 19:5–7). In the longer and more elaborate versions in Matt 4:1–11 and Luke 4:1–13 (perhaps from the Sayings Source **Q**), Jesus is tested by the Devil and is tempted to turn stones into bread, to make a spectacular show in the temple area, and to rule over all the kingdoms of the world. At each stage Jesus proves his fidelity to his heavenly **Father** by quoting a passage from Deut 6–8 (8:3, 6:16, 6:13). Where ancient **Israel** in the wilderness failed in its testing, Jesus proves himself to be the faithful Son of God. **Luke**'s order of the places of the tests—wilderness, mountain, and temple—fits well with his special interest in the **Jerusalem temple**. Some scholars have suggested that the various "temptations" may be issues with which Jesus dealt with throughout his public life (desire for physical pleasure, celebrity, and power), and that the biblical accounts represent an imaginative portrayal or dramatization of his longstanding and recurrent experiences.

TEN MAIDENS, PARABLE OF THE (MATT 25:1–13). The setting of the **parable** is the delayed return home of the **bridegroom** and the bridal party from the household of the bride's father where the **marriage** contract had been negotiated and signed. The ten maidens were expected to welcome the bride into the groom's household. By taking sufficient oil for their lamps, the five wise maidens prepared for the possibility of the bridal party's delay, whereas the five foolish maidens failed to do so and found themselves shut out of the groom's household. The message is one of constant vigilance in the face of the coming **kingdom of God**, even if it seems delayed: "Keep awake therefore, for you do not know on what day your **Lord** is coming" (Matt 24:42).

TEXTUAL CRITICISM. Although there are fragments of **Gospel** texts from the second and third centuries, the earliest substantially complete Greek manuscripts of the four Gospels date from the fourth and fifth centuries. Since we no longer have direct access to the manuscripts written by the original authors (autographs), textual criticism seeks to identify the errors and changes that may have entered into the manuscript traditions, and to get as close as possible to the original form of the text. The original reading must be consistent with the style and content of the documents being studied as well as coherent with the rules of grammar and good sense. The rejected variants may have been unconscious errors (e.g., omitting words or phrases, confusing similar letters, including marginal comments) or deliberate changes (e.g., wrongly "correcting" grammar or style, harmonizing with parallel texts, removing potentially "offensive" material).

THADDAEUS. One of the **twelve apostles** mentioned in Matt 10:3 and Mark 3:18. In Luke 6:16 and Acts 1:13 his place is occupied by "**Judas** [son, or brother] of **James**." In Christian tradition the two have become fused as "Jude Thaddaeus."

THEISSEN, GERD (1943–). Professor of NT at the University of Heidelberg, Theissen has long been concerned with methodological issues in interpreting and applying the NT. His major contributions to modern Jesus research have been in introducing sociological, literary, and religious studies perspectives into the quest. He has given special attention to what the so-called **authenticating criteria** can (and cannot) tell us about Jesus. In his *Sociology of Early Palestinian Christianity* (1978), Theissen described Jesus and his first followers as wandering charismatics and focused especially on their social attitudes and behaviors, as well as their interactions with Jewish society. In *The Shadow of the Galilean* (1987) he provided a **narrative critical** analysis of Jesus from the various viewpoints of mainly fictional characters who (like modern scholars) had not met Jesus directly but were trying to understand and classify him on the basis of what they had heard about him. In *The Historical Jesus: A Comprehensive Guide* (1998), Theissen (with Annette Merz) sought to present the results of modern research on the **historical Jesus** in an objective and comprehensive manner.

THEOPHILUS. The person to whom **Luke's Gospel** and the Acts of the **Apostles** are addressed and dedicated. Whether Theophilus was a real historical person (perhaps Luke's literary patron) or a symbolic figure (a very serious Christian) is disputed. In Luke 1:1–4 he is called "most excellent Theophilus," perhaps suggesting someone of high rank. Luke defines his goal as helping Theophilus (and all his readers) to gain greater certitude about "the things which you have been instructed." The mention of Theophilus in Acts 1:1 indicates that both the author and the addressee were the same as in Luke's Gospel, and that Acts is the second volume in Luke's two-volume work.

THOMAS. One of the **twelve apostles**, mentioned in the various lists (Matt 10:3; Mark 3:18; Luke 6:15; Acts 1:13). In John 11:16 and 21:2 he is called "the twin," and in John 14:5 he asks Jesus where he is going when he departs from his **disciples**. In John 20:24–29, Thomas is absent for the **appearance** of the risen Jesus on Easter afternoon and expresses skepticism about reports that Jesus was alive again. A week later, however, he is present for another appearance of the risen Jesus and is so impressed that he confesses Jesus to be "my **Lord** and my **God**" (20:28), which is the most exalted confession of Jesus in all the **Gospels**.

THOMAS, GOSPEL OF. An anthology of 114 short sayings attributed to Jesus, this work exists in its most complete form in the Coptic version found at **Nag Hammadi**. Fragments of the Greek original were discovered at Oxyrhynchus in Egypt in the late 1800s and dated to around 200 CE. The sayings are prefaced by the sentence, "These are the secret sayings which the living Jesus spoke and which Didymos Judas Thomas wrote down." Since the words "Didymos" and "Thomas" both mean "twin" in Greek and Aramaic, respectively, the reference must be to **Thomas** the **apostle** who in John 11:17 and 20:24 is called "the twin." In form and content, *Gospel of Thomas* is a **wisdom** book, somewhat like Proverbs and Sirach. Saying 1 promises that "whoever finds the interpretation of these sayings will not taste death." Saying 3 insists that "the kingdom is inside of you," and that when you come to know yourselves you will realize that you are "the sons of the living **father**." In this work, the **kingdom of God** is very much a present reality, and there is no interest in the future **apocalyptic eschatology** found in the **canonical Gospels**. Many of the sayings have parallels in the canonical Gospels. While some scholars contend that they depend on the canonical versions, others argue that beneath the **gnostic** editorial overlay it is possible to find independent and even earlier forms of Jesus' sayings.

THOMAS, INFANCY GOSPEL OF. A collection of tales about the exploits of Jesus as a **child** from ages 5 to 12, which circulated in many forms and languages and was attributed to "Thomas the Israelite." Intended to show Jesus' miraculous powers even as a boy, to readers today much of the work seems to portray the child Jesus as willful, undisciplined, and even dangerous. He does work on the **Sabbath**, kills off playmates, and frightens his teachers. However, he also restores the dead to life, heals, brings about a miraculous harvest, helps Joseph in his **carpentry**, and exhibits mystical knowledge. The people around him eventually admit that this child is "either a god or an **angel** of **God**." The cycle of stories ends with a retelling of Luke 2:41–51 in which the 12-year-old Jesus silences the elders and teachers of the **Law of Moses** by his brilliance. This work and those related to it purport to fill in the gaps between the story of Jesus' birth in Luke 2:1–40 and the finding of him in the **temple** in 2:41–51. The basic message is that the miraculous powers that Jesus displayed as an adult were already present even in his **childhood**.

TITLE ON THE CROSS. All four Evangelists agree that the title defining the legal charge against Jesus that **Pontius Pilate** had affixed to the **cross** involved the title "**King of the Jews**." Their wordings, however, are slightly different: "This is Jesus, the King of the Jews" (Matt 27:37); "The King of the Jews" (Mark 15:26); "This is the King of the Jews" (Luke 23:38); and "Jesus of **Nazareth**, the King of the Jews" (John 19:19). According to John 19:20, it was written in three languages: Hebrew (Aramaic?), Latin, and Greek. The charge was based on the Roman perception of Jesus as a potential political insurgent. From the Christian perspective, the title was ironically correct but had a meaning much different from what Pilate intended.

TOMB OF JESUS. According to all the **Gospels** (Matt 27:57–61; Mark 15:42–47; Luke 23:50–56; John 19:38–32), the tomb where Jesus was **buried** belonged to **Joseph of Arimathea**. They also agree that Joseph took charge of Jesus' corpse, and the **women disciples** at the **cross** saw where Jesus was buried. The "tomb" would have been outside the city walls of **Jerusalem**, since burial within the city would have occasioned ritual defilement. The tomb would have taken the shape of a burial cave and was probably intended as a family tomb. The corpse would have been taken from the site of execution (**Calvary**) and stretched out on a platform hewn out of the limestone rock. The expectation was that the flesh would decay over the course of a year or so, and the bones would be gathered and placed in a stone container called an ossuary ("bone box"). The traditional site of Jesus' tomb is now enclosed in the Church of Holy Sepulcher in Jerusalem.

TORAH. *See* LAW OF MOSES.

TRANSFIGURATION. The event described in Mark 9:2–9, Matt 17:1–8, and Luke 9:28–36, as well as 2 Pet 1:16–18, in which **Peter**, **James**, and **John** accompany Jesus to a mountaintop (traditionally identified as Mount Tabor) and witness his transformation (*metamorphosis* in Greek) into a figure of extraordinary brilliance. When **Moses** and **Elijah** appear as representatives of the **Law** and the **Prophets**, Peter suggests prolonging the experience by constructing three booths for them. Then a **voice from heaven** declares Jesus to be "my Son, the Beloved" (Mark 9:7; see 1:11). Suddenly the experience is over, and Jesus and his **disciples** come down and continue their journey to **Jerusalem**. The event is presented as a preview or anticipation of the glory that Jesus will enjoy after his **resurrection**. While the episode appears in the **Gospels** as an event during Jesus' public ministry, some scholars have suggested that an **appearance** of the risen Jesus has been retrojected into his earthly career. Others regard it as an **apocalyptic** vision (see Matt 17:9) as in Rev 1:12–20. Whatever its origin may have been, the Evangelists portrayed it as the manifestation of the true identity and glory of Jesus.

TREASURE, PARABLE OF THE HIDDEN (MATT 13:44). Paired with the parable of the **Pearl**, this short parable emphasizes the extraordinary value of the **kingdom of God** and the total commitment it should elicit. The elements of surprise and joy are highlighted.

TRIAL OF JESUS. The **Synoptic Gospels** present similar accounts of two trials or hearings that Jesus underwent before his condemnation and execution. The first was at the high **priest**'s house, and the second was before the Roman governor/prefect, **Pontius Pilate**. According to Mark 14:57–62, Jesus was accused before the Jewish council of saying that he would destroy the **Jerusalem temple** and of encouraging people to identify him as the **Messiah** and **Son of God**. The first charge is rejected as false (though it probably had some truth to it). But Jesus embraces the second charge and adds that he is also the **Son of Man**. In response, the high priest judges this claim to be **blasphemy**, and the whole council condemns him to **death**. The next morning the Jewish officials hand Jesus over to Pilate, who tries to interrogate Jesus without much success. But giving into the **crowd** stirred up by the **chief priests**, Pilate agrees to have Jesus executed by crucifixion. In **John**'s account there is first a preliminary hearing before Annas (18:12–14) and then an interrogation (18:19–24). Annas then sends Jesus to his son-in-law, the high priest **Caiaphas**, who in turn sends him to Pilate. John's lengthy account of Jesus' trial before Pilate in 18:28–19:16 is elaborately structured, with scenes alternating between outside and inside, and with Pilate's dialogues alternating between the crowd and Jesus. Since according to John 18:31, Jews at that time could not inflict capital punishment, they had to convince Pilate to condemn Jesus to death. Amid the literary artistry and many ironies, it becomes clear that the issue for Pilate was the perception that many people held Jesus to be the Messiah of Jewish expectation, that is, the **King of the Jews**. That would make Jesus a political threat not only to the Roman Empire but also a danger to the relatively peaceful collaboration he had developed with the Jewish political-religious leaders. All the Evangelists tend to emphasize the initiative of the Jewish leaders in having Jesus condemned and executed. However, on the historical level it appears that the ultimate legal responsibility lay with Pilate. This is suggested by the historical situation of the time (see John 18:31), the mode of execution (crucifixion), and the charge ("King of the Jews"). It is fair to say that Pontius Pilate, with the encouragement of and cooperation from some Jewish leaders in **Jerusalem**, was ultimately responsible for Jesus' death.

TRIBULATION, GREAT. The expression comes from Dan 12:1: "There shall be a time of anguish, such as has never occurred since nations first came into existence." In that context the great tribulation is the climax of an overview of ancient Near Eastern history from the Persian kings to Antiochus IV Epiphanes (175–164 BCE). The result will be the **resurrection** and vindication of the wise and **righteous** faithful in **Israel**. However, in Jesus' **eschatological discourse** (Matt 24:21; Mark 13:19) the "tribulation" refers to some dramatic and climactic event before the coming of the glorious **Son of Man** and the **Last Judgment**.

TRINITY. The distinctive Christian understanding of **God** as three persons—**Father**, Son, and **Holy Spirit**—in one God. It is neither modalism (God appeared in three ways or modes) nor tritheism (there are three gods). While not explicit in the **Gospels**, this doctrine has its roots in them. The divinity of Jesus is stated in John 1:1 and 20:28 (see also Matt 16:16), and the divinity of the Holy Spirit is suggested in the **Advocate**/Paraclete passages in John 14:16–26, 15:26, and 16:12–15. The three persons come together in the accounts of Jesus' **baptism** (Mark 1:9–11 parr.), when the Spirit descends on Jesus and the Father declares him to be his beloved Son. The three persons are sometimes named together in what seem to have been early Christian formulas of faith (e.g., Matt 28:19; 2 Cor 13:13; 1 Pet 1:2). Patristic theologians and **church** councils sought to clarify how there can be three persons in one God, and how Jesus can be both human and divine. The key text in these deliberations was often the prologue to **John's Gospel** (1:1–18).

TWELVE APOSTLES. The inner circle of Jesus' **disciples** whom he called to be **apostles**. The lists of the 12 (Matt 10:2–4; Mark 3:16–19; Luke 6:14–16; Acts 1:13) agree as to the number, though there are some discrepancies regarding the names near the end of the lists. The number 12 obviously evokes the 12 tribes of **Israel**, and suggests that Jesus considered his group as a remnant within Israel and an instrument for the renewal of the people of **God**. Jesus promises the 12 that when the **Son of Man** comes they will sit "on twelve thrones, judging the twelve tribes of Israel" (Matt 19:28; Luke 22:30). The choice of Matthias in Acts 1:15–26 to replace

Judas after his **death** attests to the importance attributed to the 12 in the Jesus movement.

TWO SERVANTS, PARABLE OF THE (MATT 24:45–51; LUKE 12:41–46). This **parable** conveys a message of uncertainty about precisely when the **Son of Man** will come and the need for constant vigilance in the meantime. These themes are developed also in the parables of the **Ten Maidens** and the **Talents** that follow. When the master does come, the faithful and wise servant who will be found doing what he should be doing will be amply rewarded. By contrast the wicked servant who is found abusing his office and his fellow servants will be severely punished.

TWO-SOURCE THEORY. *See* SYNOPTIC PROBLEM.

TYRE AND SIDON. Two Phoenician cities on the Mediterranean coast in southern Lebanon that are specially prominent in the OT. In Jesus' time these two cities designated the pagan region northwest of Jewish territory (Matt 11:22). According to Matt 15:21 and Mark 7:24, Jesus "went away to the district of Tyre and Sidon" and encountered a **Syrophoenician/Canaanite woman** who was pleading for her possessed daughter's healing. Whether Jesus actually entered that region or merely went in their direction is not clear (see Matt 10:5, 15:24).

– U –

UNFORGIVABLE SIN. The idea of an unforgivable or eternal sin (Mark 3:28–30; Matt 12:31–32) appears in the context of Jesus' debate with **scribes** from **Jerusalem** who accuse him of being possessed by **Beelzebul** and casting out **demons** by the ruler of demons (**Satan**). After showing how illogical their position is, Jesus declares as **blasphemous** and unforgivable their ascribing Jesus' power to demons and Satan rather than to the **Holy Spirit**. In Luke 12:10 the saying about an unforgivable sin is applied to those who deny the **Son of Man** (Jesus) before others.

UNJUST STEWARD. *See* DISHONEST MANAGER.

– V –

VEIL OF THE TEMPLE. In the Synoptic **passion narratives**, the veil or curtain of the temple sanctuary is torn apart either in response to Jesus' **death** (Matt 27:51; Mark 15:38) or just before it (Luke 23:45). The reference is most likely to the inner curtain in front of the Holy of Holies (see Exod 26:31–35, 40:21). Its tearing seems to be an ominous **sign** for the **Jerusalem temple** and the worship conducted there. Although its precise historical significance is difficult to discern, in the context of the NT it suggests that through Jesus' death on the **cross God** has opened up a new way of relating with humankind in place of the Jerusalem temple (see Heb 10:19–20).

VERMES, GEZA (1924–). In *Jesus the Jew: A Historian's Reading of the Gospels* (1974) and many subsequent books on Jesus, Vermes placed Jesus squarely in the context of first-century **Galilean** Judaism. Describing Jesus as a Galilean *hasid* ("pious one"), he sought to capture Jesus' identity as a charismatic **teacher**, healer, and **miracle** worker. According to Vermes, Jesus' career paralleled that of Hanina Ben Dosa, a younger Galilean contemporary known from **rabbinic** sources as a powerful healer, miracle worker, and teacher. In popular imagination Jesus seemed to be a **prophet** after the pattern of **Elijah** and **Elisha**. However, Jesus' lack of *halakhic* training got him into trouble with the **Pharisees**, and his Galilean origin made him suspect to the authorities in **Jerusalem** who regarded Galilee as a hotbed of nationalistic ferment. According to Vermes, Jesus becoming an object of worship (as happened in Christianity) would have filled him with stupefaction, **anger**, and grief.

VINEYARD, PARABLE OF THE (MARK 12:1–12; MATT 21:33–46; LUKE 20:9–19). This long **parable** places Jesus' ministry to **Israel** (the vineyard as in Isa 5:1–7) as the culmination of its mistreatment of the **prophets** sent by **God** and identifies him as the rejected stone/**rock** of Ps 118:22–23. However, its target in all three **Gospels** is not Israel as a whole but its religious and political leaders. While the nucleus may go back to Jesus, its language (use of the Greek Bible) and theology (Jesus' public claim to be the **Son**

of God) indicate an elaborate process of interpretation within the early **church**.

VIOLENCE. *See* WAR AND VIOLENCE.

VIRGINAL CONCEPTION (VIRGIN BIRTH). The doctrine based on Matt 1:18–25 and Luke 1:26–38 that Jesus was conceived in **Mary** by the **Holy Spirit**, without her having been impregnated by **Joseph**, her husband. According to Matt 1:18, Mary was found to be "with child from the Holy Spirit" before having lived with Joseph. Just when Joseph plans to divorce her, an **angel** appears in a **dream** and tells him that this **child** is from the Holy Spirit. The Evangelist then in 1:22–23 interprets the virginal conception of Jesus as the fulfillment of Isa 7:14: "Look, the virgin shall conceive and bear a son, and they shall name him **Emmanuel**." The quotation uses the Greek word *parthenos* (which can mean "virgin") to translate the Hebrew *'almah* ("young woman"), following the practice of the **Septuagint**. In Luke 1:26–38, the angel **Gabriel** appears to Mary and announces that she will become the mother of Jesus. When she protests that she is a virgin, she is told that "the Holy Spirit will come upon you" (1:35). These are only two NT texts that refer explicitly to the virginal conception of Jesus. That Mary was a virgin before and after the conception of Jesus is strongly defended in *Protevangelium of James*, though Matt 1:25 ("he [Joseph] had no marital relations with her until she had borne a son") does not necessarily imply Mary's perpetual virginity. The doctrine of the Immaculate Conception refers not to the virginal conception of Jesus but rather to the belief that Mary was born without original sin and thus was a fitting instrument to bear the **Son of God**.

VOICE FROM HEAVEN. In the accounts of Jesus' **baptism** (Matt 3:13–17; Mark 1:9–11; Luke 3:21–22), the voice from heaven appears as third in the series of **signs** (after the opening of the **heavens** and the **dove**-like descent of the **Holy Spirit**) that a new era of communication between heaven and earth has begun. It also occurs in the accounts of Jesus' **transfiguration** (Matt 17:5; Mark 9:7; Luke 9:35). In both episodes the voice identifies Jesus as the **Son of God**.

The heavenly voice may have some connection with the **rabbinic** motif of the *bat qôl* ("daughter of a voice"), that is, an echo of a word uttered in heaven.

– W –

WAR AND VIOLENCE. Jesus lived in the Roman Empire as part of a subject people, **Israel**. According to **Luke's infancy narrative**, Jesus' birth held out the promise of peace on earth (2:14), and throughout the **Gospels** there are hints of tensions with the Roman Empire and the claims made about its emperors. Nevertheless, Jesus embraced neither militarism nor pacifism. Rather, he preached the way of nonviolent resistance (Matt 5:38–48; Luke 6:27–36), much like the approaches taken by Gandhi and Martin Luther King Jr. in the twentieth century (which they based largely on the teaching and example of Jesus). While two of his **disciples** (**Judas Iscariot** and **Simon the Cananaean**) may once have had revolutionary connections, there is no evidence that Jesus did or that he encouraged others to do so. However, his proclamation of the **kingdom of God** was (correctly) perceived as such a threat to **Herod**'s kingdom and to the Roman Empire that Jesus was **arrested**, condemned, and executed as another dangerous Jewish **messianic** pretender ("the **King of the Jews**"). His directive to his disciples to buy swords in Luke 22:35–38 is best interpreted ironically as "gallows humor" and their actual use is overruled by him in 22:49–53.

WAY. The word *hodos* in Greek can refer to a road or a journey. In both Testaments, the "way" is used symbolically to describe conduct in accord with **God**'s will (Deut 10:1–13) or following God's leadership (Ps 23:4; Isa 40:3, 43:16–19). The "two ways" involving the choice between good and **evil** conduct is a common theme (Ps 1; Matt 7:13–14). The **Synoptic Gospels** present Jesus' way or journey from northern **Galilee** to **Jerusalem** (Mark 8:22–10:52; Matt 16:13–20:34; Luke 9:51–19:44) as the occasion for him to **teach** about himself (**Christology**) and what it means to follow him (**discipleship**). This journey, of course, will issue in Jesus' **passion**, **death**, and **resurrection**. Having been healed from blindness by Jesus, **Bartimaeus**

"followed him on the way" (Mark 10:52). According to Acts, "the way" served as a designation of the Christian community (9:2, 24:14) or the Christian message (19:9, 19:23, 22:4, 24:22).

WEDDING GARMENT, PARABLE OF THE (MATT 22:11–14). Attached to the Matthean version of the **parable** of the **Great Supper** in 22:1–10, there is a short, probably once independent, parable in 22:11–14 about a man who enters the wedding hall without a wedding garment. When confronted by the king regarding his inappropriate attire, the man offers no explanation and so is ejected by force. The parable concerns the divine judgment, and its point is that merely gaining access to **God's kingdom** is no guarantee of staying in it. Rather, appropriate conduct is required.

WEISS, JOHANNES (1863–1914). Professor at Marburg, Weiss in his 1892 essay on Jesus' preaching concerning the **kingdom of God** contended that Jesus regarded the kingdom as totally future and otherworldly. His role was to proclaim and await it, not to establish it. According to Weiss, Jesus viewed himself as the **Messiah** and his **death** as the **ransom** or price for the kingdom's coming. The kingdom he expected was completely transcendent and had nothing to do with politics. In Weiss's opinion, Jesus offered a personalized and relatively restrained version of the **apocalyptic** ideas expressed more graphically in other Jewish writings of the time. Nevertheless, attention to those apocalyptic writings offers the proper historical background for interpreting Jesus and his preaching.

WHEAT AND WEEDS, PARABLE OF (MATT 13:24–30, 13:36–43). The companion to the **parable** of the **Net** (Matt 13:47–50), it concerns the proper attitude to the mixed reception of Jesus' proclamation of **God's kingdom**. It recommends patience and tolerance in the present, out of confidence that at the **Last Judgment God** will justly reward the **righteous** (the Wheat) and punish the wicked (the Weeds).

WIDOW. In the biblical context, a "widow" seems most often to be understood in its strict sense as a woman whose husband and father-in-law had died and had no sons to support her. Thus she was among the neediest and most defenseless of persons in society. **Luke** portrays the widow **Anna** as a model of dependence on **God** (2:36–38), describes Jesus as restoring to life the son of the widow of Nain (7:11–17), holds up a stubborn widow as a model of persistence in **prayer** (18:1–8), and presents a widow as a model of generosity (21:1–4; see Mark 12:41–44). In the early **church**, widows were the object of communal generosity (Acts 6:1), and there eventually emerged an "order" of widows (1 Tim 5:13–16). **James** included in his definition of true religion "caring for orphans and widows" (Jas 1:27).

WILDERNESS. The NT Greek term *eremos* refers to an isolated and generally uninhabited place, though it covers a fairly wide range of locales. In the OT the desert or wilderness can be used positively as the place of **God**'s saving action or negatively as the place of rebellion and testing. **John the Baptist** goes to the desert area as a young man (Luke 1:80) and launches his ministry there, thus recalling the imagery of Isa 40 ("a voice crying in the wilderness," Mark 1:2–8 parr.). Jesus underwent testing in the wilderness before beginning his public activity (Mark 1:12–13; Matt 4:1–11; Luke 4:1–13). Jesus retreats to the wilderness to **pray** (Mark 1:35) and to relax (Mark 6:31) but ends up feeding large **crowds** there (Mark 6:30–44 parr.). According to John 11:54, Jesus retreated to the wilderness before he went to **Jerusalem** for the last time.

WINE. In Palestine in Jesus' time wine was produced from the vineyards as the grapes ripened in late summer and early fall. Wine was processed and consumed in the Mediterranean world from Neolithic times onward, and in the OT (Deut 7:13, 11:14) wine was regarded as one of **God**'s gifts in return for obeying God's commandments. In John 2:1–11, Jesus is said to have supplied exceptionally fine wine miraculously transformed from water for the wedding feast at **Cana**. Some have interpreted this story as a response to the cult of Dionysus making inroads into the more Hellenized parts of Palestine. The **cup** that Jesus shared at the **Last Supper** (Matt 26:27–29; Mark 14:23–25; Luke 22:17–18) would have contained wine, whether the supper was an official **Passover** meal (where several cups of wine would be drunk) or simply a **meal** in the spirit of the Passover season.

WISDOM. To his contemporaries, Jesus would have looked like both a wise **teacher** (sage) and a **prophet**. He made extensive use of the literary forms that wisdom teachers used—proverbs, admonitions, **aphorisms**, **parables**, etc.—to proclaim the coming **kingdom of God** and to provide guidance on how to prepare for its coming and enter it. Many of the topics he treated were also treated by the wisdom teachers of his time: **money** matters, social relations, family obligations, proper speech, and so on. The **Sermon on the Mount** (Matt 5–7) and the **Sermon on the Plain** (Luke 6:20–49) are best understood as wisdom instructions, as in Prov 1–9 and 22–24 and in Sirach. In some early Christian circles, Jesus was celebrated as the Wisdom of God, that is, the incarnation and personification of divine wisdom (Col 1:15–20; Heb 1:3; John 1:1–18). For OT anticipations, see Prov 8:22–31, Wis 7, and Sir 24. **Paul** insisted that the wisdom of Jesus (which he regarded as the wisdom of **God**) can be understood only with reference to the mystery of the **cross** (1 Cor 1:18–2:16).

WOES. Emotional expressions of displeasure or pain ("Alas, Ah"), found especially in the OT **prophets** (Amos 5:18–20, 6:1–7; Isa 5:8–24, 10:1–3, etc.). The prophetic denunciations beginning with "woe" are usually addressed to people with power or influence. Then comes a description of their **evil** actions along with an announcement of a judgment against them. The goal behind these prophetic denunciations was to warn people not to follow such leaders. This literary form was well suited for Jesus' denunciations of the **scribes** and **Pharisees** in Luke 11:37–52 and Matt 23:13–36. **Luke** in 6:24–26 includes a series of four "woes" to balance and highlight the four **beatitudes** in Luke 6:20–23. They warn the rich, full, laughing, and famous that their fortunes will be reversed when **God's kingdom** comes.

WOMAN TAKEN IN ADULTERY. The woman who is accused of adultery in John 7:53–8:11. In the **temple** area, some **scribes** and **Pharisees** bring her to Jesus. The penalty could be death by stoning. When Jesus challenges her accusers to throw the first stone only if they are without sin, they walk away and leave Jesus and the woman alone. He tells her to go away (thus demonstrating **God**'s mercy) and counsels her not to sin again (thus demonstrating God's justice). The passage is not present in the early manuscripts of **John's Gospel**, and it moves around in the later manuscripts. In language and content it sounds more like **Luke** than John.

WOMEN. One form of feminist biblical interpretation gives particular attention to the (often overlooked) prominence of women in the **canonical Gospels**: **Elizabeth**, **Mary**, and **Anna** in the Lukan **infancy narrative**; the women who accompany and support Jesus and the **twelve apostles** (Luke 8:1–3); the many women who are healed and forgiven by Jesus; the **Samaritan** woman in John 4; the faithful women onlookers at the **cross** of Jesus; the women discoverers of the empty **tomb**; and the women recipients of **appearances** of the risen Jesus. **Mary Magdalene** is especially prominent and serves as "the **apostle** to the apostles," while in Luke-Acts, **Mary**, the mother of Jesus, is portrayed as the ideal **disciple** who hears the word of God and acts upon it. **Elisabeth Schüssler Fiorenza** in *In Memory of Her* (1983) has argued that underlying these **Gospel** accounts is Jesus' own vision of his followers as constituting a "discipleship of equals." Other scholars, however, contend that while Jesus and his early movement may have been relatively open to women's participation, they were thoroughly immersed in the patriarchal and hierarchical culture of the ancient Mediterranean world that kept women "in their place."

WREDE, WILLIAM (1859–1906). Professor at Breslau, Wrede is most famous for his 1901 work, *The Messianic Secret in the Gospels*. As German Protestant scholars came to regard Mark as the earliest **Gospel**, they began to use it as their primary source for reconstructing the life of Jesus. Wrede called attention to one of the more puzzling features in **Mark's Gospel** — Jesus' repeated warnings not to divulge his identity as the **Messiah** (Mark 1:25, 1:34, 1:44, 3:12, 5:43, 7:36, 8:30, etc.). Wrede argued that the one responsible for the **messianic secret** motif was not the **historical Jesus** but the Evangelist, and that the messiahship of Jesus in the Gospels was the product of the early **church**'s theological imagination. Wrede's attitude to Mark's Gospel as a historical source for Jesus' life and **teaching** is best described as "thoroughgoing skepticism," and as merely the literary product of early Christianity (much as **Bruno Bauer** had done before him).

WRIGHT, NICHOLAS THOMAS (1948–). Anglican bishop of Durham, United Kingdom, Wright in his *Jesus and the Victory of God* (1996) interpreted Jesus as an **eschatological prophet** who proclaimed the **kingdom of God** by rooting it in ancient **Israel**'s story. The basic elements of that story were the return from exile, the defeat of **evil** and the rescue of **God**'s people, and the return of the God of Israel to Mount **Zion**. He argued that Jesus was seen and saw himself as a prophet after the pattern of **Elijah**. All his actions and **teachings** were in the service of the restoration and renewal of Israel as God's people. According to Wright, Jesus believed that he was Israel's **Messiah**, the one through whom God was to restore the fortunes of Israel. As such, Jesus embodied Israel's story: the exile is over; Jesus' going to **Jerusalem** symbolized God's return to Zion; and Jesus' **death** and **resurrection** won the victory over **evil**. For Wright, the **resurrection of Jesus** (understood in a realistic, rather than merely spiritual or symbolic, way) is the key to understanding Jesus and the movement he started.

– Y –

YEAST, PARABLE OF THE (MATT 13:33; LUKE 13:20–21). Here yeast (or leaven) is a life-giving force (cf. Matt 16:6; 1 Cor 5:6–8) that when added to flour causes it to expand and produce a large amount of bread. Likewise, the apparently small beginnings of **God's kingdom** in Jesus' ministry will yield great results. For yeast/leaven as a negative and corrupting force, see Jesus' warning in Mark 8:14: "beware of the yeast of the **Pharisees** and the yeast of **Herod**."

– Z –

ZACCHAEUS. The chief **tax collector** of **Jericho**, who according to Luke 19:1–10 climbed a tree to catch a glimpse of Jesus passing by. On observing him, Jesus invited himself to Zacchaeus' house. Since tax collectors were suspected of disloyalty and dishonesty, Jesus' friendliness toward Zacchaeus caused some bystanders to grumble. The use of the present tense in Luke 19:8 (literally "I give . . . I pay back") leaves ambiguous whether Zacchaeus should be understood as a **repentant sinner** who vows to mend his **evil** ways, or as an honest and even generous victim of prejudice because of his occupation and wealth.

ZEALOTS. The name given to a Jewish insurgency movement that arose mainly during the time of the Jewish revolt in 66–73 CE and is described by **Josephus** in book 4 of his *Jewish War*. One of the **twelve apostles** of Jesus is named "**Simon the Cananaean**" in Matt 10:4 and Mark 3:18 but "Simon the Zealot" in Luke 6:15 and Acts 1:13. The Hebrew verb *qanah* can mean "be zealous/jealous," and so "zealot" with regard to Simon may simply be a reference to his religious zeal rather than his identity as a militaristic revolutionary. In **John**'s account of Jesus' **cleansing** of the **Jerusalem temple**, his action is defended in John 2:17 on the grounds of Ps 69:9[10], "Zeal for your house will consume me." It is very doubtful that either Jesus or **Simon** belonged to the Zealot Party in an early manifestation or anything like it.

ZEBEDEE. A Galilean **fisherman**, the father of **James** and **John**, who were two of Jesus' first followers and members of the inner circle among the **twelve apostles**. That Zebedee had **nets** and a **boat** as well as hired men according to Mark 1:19–20 indicates that he was a commercial **fisherman** and was perhaps even relatively wealthy. Zebedee is otherwise referred to in the NT with regard to his two sons (Matt 10:2, 27:56; Mark 3:17, 10:35; Luke 5:10; John 21:2). According to Matt 20:20, Zebedee's wife asked Jesus for places of prominence in his **kingdom** on behalf of her sons.

ZECHARIAH. (1) The OT prophet, whose book is the 11th among the 12 Minor **Prophets**. His book is usually divided into two parts: chapters 1–8, from Zechariah between 520 and 518 BCE; and chapters 9–14 from the mid-fifth century and collected in Zechariah's name. Quotations from and allusions to his book are frequent and prominent throughout the **Synoptic Gospels**, especially **Matthew**. The obscurity of the second part of the book made it a rich source of prophetic fulfillments in Jesus' life and teachings. (2) The father of **John the Baptist**, from the priestly order of Abijah, married to

Elizabeth who was also from a priestly family (Luke 1:5–25). While serving in the **Jerusalem temple**, Zechariah is told by the angel **Gabriel** that his elderly wife Elizabeth was to bear an extraordinary **child (John)**. Because he did not believe the **angel**'s words, he was struck mute. According to Luke 1:57–80, Zechariah agreed with Elizabeth that her newborn son should be named John, and then he was able to speak again. In his hymn of praise known as the *Benedictus* (Luke 1:68–79), Zechariah praises **God** not only for the gift of his son John but also (and especially) for Jesus as the fulfillment of God's promises to **Israel**. (3) The "blood of Zechariah son of Berachiah" is mentioned in Matt 23:35 (and Luke 11:51). This may refer to the OT prophet Zechariah son of Barachiah, Zechariah son of Jehoida in 2 Chr 24:20–22, or Zechariah son of Bareis (**Josephus**, *War* 4:334–344)—or some combination of the three.

ZION. A hill in **Jerusalem**, the traditional site of the **temple** and the royal palace. By extension the word is often used to refer to the whole city of Jerusalem, its inhabitants, or even the whole people of **Israel**. These wider senses seem to be at work in the expression "daughter of Zion" in Matt 21:5 and John 12:15, which are part of quotations from Zech 9:9.

Bibliography

The bibliography that follows lists major scholarly works pertaining to Jesus and history. It is necessarily a selection made from the thousands of books and articles published on the topic in recent years. For many more items in various languages with objective summaries from the mid-1950s to the present, see *New Testament Abstracts*, edited by Daniel J. Harrington and Christopher R. Matthews, and published by the Boston College School of Theology and Ministry.

In quoting biblical texts and in spelling names and places in this volume, I have almost always followed the New Revised Standard Version. It is fairly recent (1989) and widely available. For those in search of a study Bible with the NRSV text and including introductions and comments for each book, I recommend the *HarperCollins Study Bible*, *New Interpreter's Study Bible*, and *Oxford Annotated Study Bible*. For those in search of a Bible dictionary, I recommend the *Anchor Bible Dictionary* (5 vols.), *Eerdmans Bible Dictionary*, and *Harper's Bible Dictionary*.

CONTENTS

HISTORY OF THE QUEST

Allen, Charlotte. *The Human Christ: The Search for the Historical Jesus.* New York: Free Press, 1998.

Baird, William. *History of New Testament Research.* Vol. 1: *From Deism to Tübingen.* Minneapolis: Fortress, 1992.

———. *History of New Testament Research.* Vol. 2: *From Jonathan Edwards to Rudolf Bultmann.* Minneapolis: Fortress, 2003.

Boyer, Chrystian, and Gérard Rochais, eds. *Le Jésus de l'histoire à travers le monde* [The Historical Jesus around the World]. Montreal: Fides, 2009.

Dunn, James D. G., and Scot McKnight, eds. *The Historical Jesus in Recent Research.* Sources for Biblical and Theological Study 10. Winona Lake, IN: Eisenbrauns, 2005.

Evans, Craig A., and Stanley E. Porter, eds. *The Historical Jesus: A Sheffield Reader.* The Biblical Seminar 33. Sheffield: Sheffield Academic Press, 1995.

Fox, Richard. *Jesus in America: Personal Savior, Cultural Hero, National Obsession.* San Francisco: Harper San Francisco, 2004.

Gowler, David B. *What Are They Saying about the Historical Jesus?* New York: Paulist Press, 2007.

Hagner, Donald A. *The Jewish Reclamation of Jesus: An Analysis and Critique of Modern Jewish Study of Jesus.* Grand Rapids, MI: Academie, 1984.

Heschel, Susannah. *The Aryan Jesus: Christian Theologians and the Bible in Nazi Germany.* Princeton, NJ: Princeton University Press, 2008.

Jaffé, Dan. *Jésus sous la plume des historiens juifs du xxe siècle. Approche historique, perspectives historiographiques, analyses méthodologiques.* Patrimoines: Judaïsme. Paris: Cerf, 2009.

Levine, Amy-Jill, Dale C. Allison, and John Dominic Crossan, eds. *The Historical Jesus in Context.* Princeton Readings in Religion. Princeton, NJ: Princeton University Press, 2006.

Pelikan, Jaroslav J. *Jesus through the Centuries: His Place in the History of Culture.* New Haven, CT: Yale University Press, 1985.

Powell, Mark A. *Jesus as a Figure in History: How Modern Historians View the Man from Galilee*. Louisville, KY: Westminster John Knox, 1998.

Prothero, Stephen. *American Jesus: How the Son of God Became a National Hero*. New York: Farrar, Straus & Giroux, 2003.

Schweitzer, Albert. *The Quest of the Historical Jesus*. 1906; 2nd ed., 1913. Ed. John Bowden et al. Minneapolis: Fortress, 2001.

Weaver, Walter P. *The Historical Jesus in the Twentieth Century, 1900–1950*. Harrisburg, PA: Trinity Press International, 1999.

METHODOLOGY

Anderson, Paul N., Felix Just, and Tom Thatcher, eds. *John, Jesus, and History*. Vol. 1: *Critical Appraisals of Critical Views*. Atlanta: Society of Biblical Literature, 2007.

———. *John, Jesus, and History*. Vol. 2: *Aspects of Historicity in the Fourth Gospel*. Atlanta: Society of Biblical Literature, 2009.

Chilton, Bruce, and Craig A. Evans, eds. *Authenticating the Words of Jesus*. New Testament Tools and Studies 28/1. Leiden: Brill, 1999.

———. *Authenticating the Activities of Jesus*. New Testament Tools and Studies 28/2. Leiden: Brill, 1999.

Meier, John P. *A Marginal Jew: Rethinking the Historical Jesus*. Vol. 1: *The Roots of the Problem and the Person*. Anchor Bible Reference Library 21–201. New York: Doubleday, 1991.

Porter, Stanley E. *The Criteria for Authenticity in Historical-Jesus Research: Previous Discussion and New Proposals*. Journal for the Study of the New Testament, Supplement Series 191. Sheffield: Sheffield Academic Press, 2000.

Theissen, Gerd, and Dagmar Winter. *The Quest for the Plausible Jesus: The Question of Criteria*. Louisville, KY: Westminster John Knox, 2002.

GENERAL TREATMENT OF JESUS

Allison, Dale C. *Jesus of Nazareth: Millenarian Prophet*. Minneapolis: Fortress, 1998.

Becker, Jürgen. *Jesus of Nazareth*. Berlin: de Gruyter, 1998.

Borg, Marcus. *Jesus: Uncovering the Life, Teachings, and Relevance of a Religious Revolutionary*. San Francisco: Harper San Francisco, 2006.

Bornkamm, Günther. *Jesus of Nazareth*. 1960. Minneapolis: Fortress, 1995.

Brown. Raymond E. *An Introduction to New Testament Christology*. New York: Paulist Press, 1994.

Bultmann, Rudolf. *Jesus and the Word*. New York: Scribners, 1958.

Chilton, Bruce. *Rabbi Jesus: An Intimate Biography*. New York: Doubleday, 2000.

Crossan, John Dominic. *The Historical Jesus: The Life of a Mediterranean Jewish Peasant*. San Francisco: Harper San Francisco, 1991.

Dunn, James G. D. *Jesus Remembered*. Grand Rapids, MI: Eerdmans, 2003.

Ehrman, Bart D. *Jesus: Apocalyptic Prophet of the New Millennium*. Oxford: Oxford University Press, 1999.

Funk, Robert W. *Honest to Jesus: Jesus for a New Millennium*. San Francisco: Harper San Francisco, 1996.

Gnilka, Joachim. *Jesus of Nazareth: Message and History*. Peabody, MA: Hendrickson, 1997.

Green, Joel B., Scot McKnight, and I. Howard Marshall, eds. *Dictionary of Jesus and the Gospels*. Downers Grove, IL: InterVarsity Press, 1992.

Harrington, Daniel J. *Jesus: A Historical Portrait*. Cincinnati: St. Anthony Messenger, 2007.

Houlden, Leslie L., ed. *Jesus: The Complete Guide*. New York: Continuum, 2006.

Hurtado, Larry W. *Lord Jesus Christ: Devotion to Jesus in Earliest Christianity*. Grand Rapids, MI: Eerdmans, 2003.

Keck, Leander E. *Who Is Jesus? History in the Perfect Tense*. Minneapolis: Fortress, 2000.

Keener, Craig S. *The Historical Jesus of the Gospels*. Grand Rapids, MI: Eerdmans, 2009.

Levine, Amy-Jill. *The Misunderstood Jew: The Church and the Scandal of the Jewish Jesus*. San Francisco: Harper San Francisco, 2006.

Meier, John P. *A Marginal Jew: Rethinking the Historical Jesus*. Vol. 1: *The Roots of the Problem and the Person*. Anchor Bible Reference Library. New York: Doubleday, 1991.

———. *A Marginal Jew: Rethinking the Historical Jesus*. Vol. 2: *Mentor, Message, and Miracles*. New York: Doubleday, 1994.

———. *A Marginal Jew: Rethinking the Historical Jesus*. Vol. 3: *Companions and Competitors*. New York: Doubleday, 2001.

———. *A Marginal Jew: Rethinking the Historical Jesus*. Vol. 4: *Law and Love*. New Haven, CT: Yale University Press, 2009.

Patterson, Stephen J. *The God of Jesus: The Historical Jesus and the Search for Meaning*. Harrisburg, PA: Trinity Press International, 1998.

Ratzinger, Joseph [Pope Benedict XVI]. *Jesus of Nazareth: From the Baptism to the Transfiguration.* New York: Doubleday, 2007.
Sanders, Ed Parish. *The Historical Figure of Jesus.* London: Penguin, 1993.
———. *Jesus and Judaism.* Philadelphia: Fortress, 1985.
Theissen, Gerd, and Annette Merz. *The Historical Jesus: A Comprehensive Guide.* Minneapolis: Fortress, 1998.
Tuckett, Christopher M. *Christology and the New Testament: Jesus and His Earliest Followers.* Louisville, KY: Westminster John Knox, 2001.
Vermes, Geza. *Jesus the Jew: A Historian's Reading of the Gospels.* Philadelphia: Fortress, 1973.
———. *The Religion of Jesus the Jew.* Minneapolis: Fortress, 1993.
Wright, N. T. *Jesus and the Victory of God.* Minneapolis: Fortress, 1996.

SOURCES ABOUT JESUS: CANONICAL GOSPELS

Bovon, François. *Luke 1: A Commentary on the Gospel of Luke.* Hermeneia. Translated by Christine M. Thomas. Edited by Helmut Koester. Minneapolis: Fortress, 2002.
Brown, Raymond E. *The Gospel according to John.* Anchor Bible. 2 vols. New York: Doubleday, 1966, 1970.
———. *An Introduction to the Gospel of John.* Edited by Francis J. Moloney. New York: Doubleday, 2003.
Collins, Adela Yarbro. *Mark: A Commentary.* Hermeneia. Edited by Harold W. Attridge. Minneapolis: Fortress, 2007.
Davies, William D., and Dale C. Allison. *A Critical and Exegetical Commentary on the Gospel according to Matthew.* International Critical Commentary. 3 vols. Edinburgh: T&T Clark, 1988, 1991, 1997.
Donahue, John R., and Daniel J. Harrington. *The Gospel of Mark.* Sacra Pagina 2. Collegeville, MN: Liturgical Press, 2002.
Fitzmyer, Joseph A. *The Gospel according to Luke.* Anchor Bible. 2 vols. New York: Doubleday, 1981, 1985.
Harrington, Daniel J. *The Gospel of Matthew.* Sacra Pagina 1. Collegeville, MN: Liturgical Press, 1991; rev. ed., 2007.
Johnson, Luke Timothy. *The Gospel of Luke.* Sacra Pagina 3. Collegeville, MN: Liturgical Press, 1991.
Luz, Ulrich. *Matthew: A Commentary.* Hermeneia. Minneapolis: Fortress, 1989, 2001, 2005.
Marcus, Joel. *Mark 1–8.* Anchor Bible 27. New York: Doubleday, 2000.
———. *Mark 9–16.* New Haven, CT: Yale Anchor, 2009.

Moloney, Francis J. *The Gospel of John*. Sacra Pagina 4. Collegeville, MN: Liturgical Press, 1998.

——. *The Gospel of Mark: A Commentary*. Peabody, MA: Hendrickson, 2002.

Perkins. Pheme. *Introduction to the Synoptic Gospels*. Grand Rapids, MI: Eerdmans, 2007.

SOURCES ABOUT JESUS: OUTSIDE THE CANON

DeConick, April D. *The Original Gospel of Thomas in Translation: With a Commentary and New English Translation of the Complete Gospel*. Library of New Testament Studies 287. London: T&T Clark, 2006.

——. *Recovering the Original Gospel of Thomas: A History of the Gospel and Its Growth*. Library of New Testament Studies 286. London: T&T Clark, 2005.

Elliott, J. Keith. *The Apocryphal Jesus: Legends of the Early Church*. New York: Oxford University Press, 1996.

——. *The Apocryphal New Testament: A Collection of Apocryphal Christian Literature in an English Translation*. Oxford: Clarendon Press, 1993.

Franzmann, Majella. *Jesus in the Nag Hammadi Writings*. Edinburgh: T&T Clark, 1996.

Kahlidi, Tarif. *The Muslim Jesus: Sayings and Stories in Islamic Literature*. Cambridge, MA: Harvard University Press, 2001.

Kloppenborg, John S. *Excavating Q: The History and Setting of the Sayings Gospel*. Minneapolis: Fortress, 2000.

——. *The Formation of Q: Trajectories in Ancient Wisdom Collections*. Philadelphia: Fortress, 1987.

Mack, Burton L. *The Lost Gospel: The Book of Q and Christian Origins*. San Francisco: Harper San Francisco, 1993.

Patterson, Stephen. J. *The Gospel of Thomas and Jesus*. Sonoma, CA: Polebridge, 1993.

Plisch, Uwe-Karsten. *The Gospel of Thomas: Original Text with Commentary*. Stuttgart: Deutsche Bibelgesellschaft, 2008.

Robinson, James M., Paul Hoffmann, and John S. Kloppenborg. *The Critical Edition of Q: A Synopsis Including the Gospels of Matthew and Luke, Mark and Thomas with English, German and French Translations of Q and Thomas*. Hermeneia. Minneapolis: Fortress, 2000.

Schäfer, Peter. *Jesus in the Talmud*. Princeton, NJ: Princeton University Press, 2007.

Tuckett, Christopher M. *Q and the History of Early Christianity: Studies on Q.* Peabody, MA: Hendrickson, 1996.

Uro, Risto, ed. *Thomas at the Crossroads: Essays on the Gospel of Thomas.* Edinburgh: T&T Clark, 1998.

Valantasis, Richard. *The Gospel of Thomas.* London: Routledge, 1997.

Van Voorst, Robert E. *Jesus Outside the New Testament: An Introduction to the Ancient Evidence.* Grand Rapids, MI: Eerdmans, 2000.

THE WORLD OF JESUS

Chancey, Mark A. *The Myth of a Gentile Galilee.* Cambridge: Cambridge University Press, 2002.

Charlesworth, James H., ed. *Jesus and Archaeology.* Grand Rapids, MI: Eerdmans, 2006.

———. *Jesus and the Dead Sea Scrolls.* New York: Doubleday, 1992.

———. *The Old Testament Pseudepigrapha.* Vol. 1: *Apocalyptic Literature and Testaments.* Garden City, NY: Doubleday, 1983.

———. *The Old Testament Pseudepigrapha.* Vol. 2: *Expansions of the "Old Testament" and Legends, Wisdom and Philosophical Literature, Prayers, Psalms and Odes, Fragments of Lost Judeo-Hellenistic Works.* Garden City, NY: Doubleday, 1985.

Charlesworth, James H., and Loren L. Johns, eds. *Hillel and Jesus: Comparative Studies of Two Major Religious Leaders.* Minneapolis: Fortress, 1997.

Chilton, Bruce, Craig A. Evans, and Jacob Neusner. *The Missing Jesus: Rabbinic Judaism and the New Testament.* Leiden: Brill, 2002.

Collins, John J. *The Apocalyptic Imagination: An Introduction to Jewish Apocalyptic Literature.* Grand Rapids, MI: Eerdmans, 1998.

Crossan, John Dominic, and Jonathan L. Reed. *Excavating Jesus: Beneath the Stones, Behind the Texts.* San Francisco: Harper San Francisco, 2001.

deSilva, David A. *Introducing the Apocrypha: Message, Context, and Significance.* Grand Rapids, MI: Baker Academic, 2002.

Evans, Craig A. *Jesus and His Contemporaries: Comparative Studies.* Leiden: Brill, 1995.

Freyne, Sean. *Jesus, a Galilean Jew: A New Reading of the Jesus-Story.* London: T&T Clark, 2004.

Hanson, K. C., and Douglas E. Oakman. *Palestine in the Time of Jesus: Social Structures and Social Conflicts.* 1998. 2nd ed. Minneapolis: Fortress, 2008.

Harrington, Daniel J. *Invitation to the Apocrypha*. Grand Rapids, MI: Eerdmans, 1999.

Harvey, A. E. *Jesus and the Constraints of History*. Philadelphia: Westminster, 1982.

Horsley, Richard A. *Archaeology, History and Society in Galilee: The Social Context of Jesus and the Rabbis*. Valley Forge, PA: Trinity Press International, 1996.

——. *Jesus and the Spiral of Violence: Popular Jewish Resistance in Roman Palestine*. Minneapolis: Augsburg Fortress, 1992.

——. *Sociology and the Jesus Movement*. 1989. 2nd ed. New York: Continuum, 1994.

Malina, Bruce J. *The New Testament World: Insights from Cultural Anthropology*. 1981. 3rd ed. Louisville, KY: Westminster John Knox, 2001.

——. *The Social Gospel of Jesus: The Kingdom of God in Mediterranean Perspective*. Minneapolis: Fortress, 2001.

Reed, Jonathan L. *Archaeology and the Galilean Jesus: A Re-Examination of the Evidence*. Harrisburg, PA: Trinity Press International, 2000.

Skarsaune, Oskar, and Reidar Hvalvik, eds. *Jewish Believers in Jesus*. Peabody, MA: Hendrickson, 2007.

Stegemann, Ekkehard, and Wolfgang Stegemann. *The Jesus Movement: A Social History of Its First Century*. Minneapolis: Fortress, 1999.

Theissen, Gerd. *Sociology of Early Palestinian Christianity*. Philadelphia: Fortress, 1978.

Vermes. Geza. *The Complete Dead Sea Scrolls in English*. Allen Lane: Penguin, 1997.

——. *Jesus and the World of Judaism*. Philadelphia: Fortress, 1984.

——. *Jesus in His Jewish Context*. Minneapolis: Fortress, 2003.

——. *The Religion of Jesus the Jew*. Minneapolis: Fortress, 1993.

INFANCY NARRATIVES

Borg, Marcus J., and John Dominic Crossan. *The First Christmas: What the Gospels Really Teach about Jesus' Birth*. New York: HarperOne, 2007.

Brooke, George J., ed. *The Birth of Jesus: Biblical and Theological Reflections*. Edinburgh: T&T Clark, 2000.

Brown, Raymond E. *The Birth of the Messiah: A Commentary on the Infancy Narratives in Matthew and Luke*. 1977. 2nd ed. New York: Doubleday, 1999.

Corley, Jeremy, ed. *New Perspectives on the Nativity*. London: T&T Clark, 2009.

Miller, Robert J. *Born Divine: The Births of Jesus and Other Sons of God.* Santa Rosa, CA: Polebridge Press, 2003.

Schaberg, Jane. *The Illegitimacy of Jesus: A Feminist Theological Interpretation of the Infancy Narratives.* San Francisco: Harper & Row, 1995.

Vermes, Geza. *The Nativity: History and Legend.* New York: Doubleday, 2007.

TEACHINGS OF JESUS

Allison, Dale C. *The Sermon on the Mount: Inspiring the Moral Imagination.* New York: Crossroad, 1999.

Bryan, Christopher. *Render to Caesar: Jesus, the Early Church, and the Roman Superpower.* New York: Oxford University Press, 2005.

Chilton, Bruce D., ed. *The Kingdom of God in the Teaching of Jesus.* Philadelphia: Fortress, 1984.

Collins, Raymond F. *Divorce in the New Testament.* Collegeville, MN: Liturgical Press, 1992.

———. *Sexual Ethics and the New Testament: Behavior and Belief.* New York: Crossroad, 2000.

Cullmann, Oscar. *The State in the New Testament.* New York: Scribners, 1966.

Furnish, Victor P. *The Love Command in the New Testament.* New York: Abingdon, 1972.

Harrington, Daniel J. *Jesus and Prayer: What the New Testament Teaches Us.* Ijamsville, MD: Word among Us, 2009.

Harrington, Daniel J., and James F. Keenan. *Jesus and Virtue Ethics: Building Bridges between New Testament Studies and Moral Theology.* Lanham, MD: Sheed & Ward, 2002.

Hoppe, Leslie. *There Shall Be No Poor among You: Poverty in the Bible.* Nashville: Abingdon, 2004.

Jeremias, Joachim. *New Testament Theology.* Vol. 1: *The Proclamation of Jesus.* New York: Scribners, 1971.

Lambrecht, Jan. *The Sermon on the Mount: Proclamation and Exhortation.* Wilmington, DE: Glazier, 1985.

Loader, William R. G. *Jesus' Attitude towards the Law: A Study of the Gospels.* 1997. Grand Rapids, MI: Eerdmans, 2002.

Perkins, Pheme. *Love Commands in the New Testament.* New York: Paulist Press, 1982.

Perrin, Norman. *Rediscovering the Teaching of Jesus.* New York: Harper & Row, 1967.

Viviano, Benedict. *The Kingdom of God in History*. Eugene, OR: Wipf & Stock, 2002.

Wilder, Amos N. *Eschatology and Ethics in the Teaching of Jesus*. New York: Harper, 1939.

Willis, William, ed. *The Kingdom of God in 20th-Century Interpretation*. Peabody, MA: Hendrickson, 1987.

Witherington, Ben. *Jesus the Sage: The Pilgrimage of Wisdom*. Minneapolis: Fortress, 1994.

PARABLES

Crossan, John Dominic. *In Parables: The Challenge of the Historical Jesus*. 1973. Sonoma, CA: Polebridge Press, 1992.

Dodd, Charles Harold. *The Parables of the Kingdom*. New York: Scribners, 1961.

Donahue, John R. *The Gospel in Parable: Metaphor, Narrative, and Theology in the Synoptic Gospels*. Minneapolis: Fortress, 1990.

Gowler, David B. *What Are They Saying about the Parables?* New York: Paulist Press, 2000.

Hultgren, Arland J. *The Parables of Jesus: A Commentary*. Grand Rapids, MI: Eerdmans, 2002.

Jeremias, Joachim. *The Parables of Jesus*. New York: Scribners, 1972.

Scott, Bernard B. *Hear Then the Parable: A Commentary on the Parables of Jesus*. Minneapolis: Fortress, 1989.

Snodgrass, Klyne. *Stories with Intent: A Comprehensive Guide to the Parables of Jesus*. Grand Rapids, MI: Eerdmans, 2008.

MIRACLES

Cotter, Wendy. *Miracles in Greco-Roman Antiquity: A Sourcebook for the Study of New Testament Miracle Stories*. London: Routledge, 1999.

Meier, John P. *A Marginal Jew: Rethinking the Historical Jesus*. Vol 2: *Mentor, Message, and Miracles*, 509–1038. New York: Doubleday, 1994.

Twelftree, Graham H. *Jesus the Exorcist: A Contribution to the Study of the Historical Jesus*. Peabody, MA: Hendrickson, 1993.

———. *Jesus the Miracle Worker: A Historical and Theological Study*. Downers Grove, IL: InterVarsity Press, 1999.

MAJOR FIGURES IN JESUS' LIFE

Brock, Ann G. *Mary Magdalene, the First Apostle: The Struggle for Authority.* Harvard Theological Studies 51. Cambridge, MA: Harvard University Press, 2003.

Brown, Raymond E. et al., eds. *Mary in the New Testament: A Collaborative Assessment by Protestant and Roman Catholic Scholars.* Philadelphia: Fortress, 1978.

———. *Peter in the New Testament: A Collaborative Assessment by Protestant and Roman Catholic Scholars.* Philadelphia: Fortress, 1973.

Chilton, Bruce. *Mary Magdalene: A Biography.* New York: Doubleday, 2005.

Cullmann, Oscar. *Peter: Disciple, Apostle, Martyr. A Historical and Theological Study.* 2nd ed. London: SCM Press, 1962.

DeConick, April D. *Thirteenth Apostle: What the Gospel of Judas Really Says.* New York: Continuum, 2009.

Ehrman, Bart D. *Peter, Paul, and Mary Magdalene: The Followers of Jesus in History and Legend.* Oxford: Oxford University Press, 2006.

Kazmierski, Carl R. *John the Baptist: Prophet and Evangelist.* Collegeville, MN: Liturgical Press, 1996.

Klassen, William. *Judas: Betrayer or Friend of Jesus?* 1996. Minneapolis: Fortress, 2005.

Meier, John P. *A Marginal Jew: Rethinking the Historical Jesus.* Vol. 2: *Mentor, Message, and Miracles*, 19–233. New York: Doubleday, 1994.

Meyer, Marvin. *Judas: The Definitive Collection of Gospels and Legends about the Infamous Apostle of Jesus.* New York: HarperOne, 2007.

Murphy, Catherine M. *John the Baptist: Prophet of Purity for a New Age.* Collegeville, MN: Liturgical Press, 2003.

Paffenroth, Kim. *Judas: Image of the Lost Disciple.* Louisville: Westminster/ John Knox, 2001.

Perkins, Pheme. *Peter: Apostle for the Whole Church.* 1994. Minneapolis: Fortress, 2000.

Schaberg, Jane. *The Resurrection of Mary Magdalene: Legends, Apocrypha, and the Christian Testament.* New York: Continuum. 2002.

Schüssler Fiorenza, Elisabeth. *In Memory of Her: A Feminist Theological Reconstruction of Christian Origins.* 1983. New York: Crossroad, 2004.

Taylor, Joan E. *The Immerser: John the Baptist within Second Temple Judaism.* Grand Rapids, MI: Eerdmans, 1997.

Webb, Robert L. *John the Baptizer and Prophet: A Socio-Historical Study.* Journal for the Study of the New Testament, Supplement Series 62. Sheffield: Sheffield Academic Press, 1991.

Witherington, Ben. *Women in the Ministry of Jesus.* Cambridge: Cambridge University Press, 1984.

PASSION AND DEATH

Borg, Marcus J., and John Dominic Crossan. *The Last Week: The Day-by-Day Account of Jesus' Final Week in Jerusalem.* New York: Harper San Francisco, 2006.

Bovon, François. *The Last Days of Jesus.* Louisville: Westminster John Knox, 2006.

Brown, Raymond E. *The Death of the Messiah, from Gethsemane to the Grave: A Commentary on the Passion Narratives in the Four Gospels.* 2 vols. New York: Doubleday, 1994.

Crossan, John Dominic. *Who Killed Jesus? Exposing the Roots of Anti-Semitism in the Gospel Story of the Death of Jesus.* San Francisco: Harper San Francisco, 1995.

Hengel, Martin. *Crucifixion in the Ancient World and the Folly of the Message of the Cross.* Philadelphia: Fortress, 1977.

McKnight, Scot. *Jesus and His Death: Historiography, the Historical Jesus, and Atonement Theory.* Waco, TX: Baylor University Press, 2005.

Sloyan, Gerard S. *The Crucifixion of Jesus: History, Myth, Faith.* Minneapolis: Fortress 1995.

RESURRECTION

Davis, Stephen T., Daniel Kendall, and Gerald O'Collins, eds. *The Resurrection: An Interdisciplinary Symposium on the Resurrection of Jesus.* Oxford: Oxford University Press, 1997.

Perkins, Pheme. *Resurrection: New Testament Witness and Contemporary Reflection.* New York: Doubleday, 1984.

Segal, Alan. *Life after Death: A History of the Afterlife in Western Religions.* New York: Doubleday, 2004.

Vermes, Geza. *The Resurrection.* New York: Doubleday, 2008.

Wright, N. T. *The Resurrection of the Son of God.* Minneapolis: Augsburg Fortress, 2003.

MAJOR RESEARCH JOURNALS

Biblica (Rome)
Biblical Archaeology Review (Washington, DC)
Biblische Zeitschrift (Paderborn)
Catholic Biblical Quarterly (Washington, DC)
Harvard Theological Review (Cambridge, MA)
Journal for the Study of the Historical Jesus (Leiden)
Journal for the Study of the New Testament (London)
Journal of Biblical Literature (Atlanta)
Journal of Jewish Studies (Oxford)
Journal of Theological Studies (Oxford)
New Testament Abstracts (Chestnut Hill, MA)
New Testament Studies (Cambridge, UK)
Novum Testamentum (Leiden)
Revue Biblique (Jerusalem)
Zeitschrift für die Neutestamentliche Wissenschaft (Berlin/New York)

About the Author

Daniel J. Harrington, S.J. (BA 1964, MA 1965, Boston College; PhD 1970, Harvard University; MDiv 1971, Boston College/Weston Jesuit School of Theology) is a professor of New Testament at the Boston College School of Theology and Ministry and editor of (and a major contributor to) *New Testament Abstracts* since 1972. He entered the Society of Jesus (Jesuits) in 1958 and was ordained a Catholic priest in 1971. His major academic interests have been Second Temple Judaism and the interpretation of the New Testament. He was the editor of the critical Latin text of Pseudo-Philo's *Biblical Antiquities* for the *Sources Chrétiennes* series (Cerf 1976) and prepared *A Manual of Palestinian Aramaic Texts* with Joseph A. Fitzmyer (Pontifical Biblical Institute Press, 1978). He collaborated with John Strugnell in the official edition of *4QInstruction,* an ancient Jewish wisdom text in Hebrew discovered among the Dead Sea Scrolls (Clarendon Press, 1999). He served as the editor of the *Sacra Pagina* series of eighteen major commentaries on the New Testament (Liturgical Press) and contributed to the volumes on Matthew (1991), Mark (2002, with John R. Donahue), and 1-Peter and Jude (2003, with Donald Senior). He is past president of the Catholic Biblical Association of America (1985–1986) and is now chairman of its board of trustees.

Dr. Harrington is the author of more than forty books. His recent publications include *Jesus Ben Sira of Jerusalem* (2005); *How Do Catholics Read the Bible?* (2005); *What Are We Hoping For? New Testament Images* (2006); *Jesus: A Historical Portrait* (2007); *Why Do We Hope? Images in the Psalms* (2008); *Meeting St. Paul Today* (2008); *The Synoptic Gospels Set Free: Preaching without Anti-Judaism* (2009); *Jesus and Prayer: What the New Testament Teaches Us* (2009); and *Meeting St. Luke Today* (2009). He has been a member of the New England Province of the Society of Jesus for over fifty years and serves as a weekend pastoral associate at two parishes in the Boston area. He has received honorary doctoral degrees from the College of the Holy Cross (2005), Boston College (2009), and Fairfield University (2010). He regularly teaches courses on biblical languages, late Old Testament and early Jewish writings, the various books of the New Testament, and biblical theology.

Breinigsville, PA USA
26 July 2010
242395BV00002B/3/P